WORKING MEN'S COLLEGE.

LIBRARY REGULATIONS

The Library is open every week-day evening, from 6.30 to 10 o'clock, except on Saturdays. when it closes at 9.

This book may be kept for three weeks, If not returned within that period, the borrower will be liable to a fine of one penny per week.

If lost or damaged, the borrower will be required to make good such loss or damage.

Only one book may be borrowed at a time.

LIFE IN
MEDIAEVAL
FRANCE

I. The Holy Trinity

French. *c.* 1410

LIFE IN MEDIAEVAL FRANCE

by

JOAN EVANS, B.Litt.

Sometime Librarian of St. Hugh's College, Oxford

OXFORD UNIVERSITY PRESS

Humphrey Milford

1925

PRINTED IN ENGLAND
AT THE OXFORD UNIVERSITY PRESS

TO THE MEMORY OF

ELEANOR FRANCES JOURDAIN

M.A. OXON, DOCTOR OF THE UNIVERSITY OF PARIS

PRINCIPAL OF ST. HUGH'S COLLEGE AND SOMETIME

TAYLORIAN LECTURER IN FRENCH

IN THE UNIVERSITY OF OXFORD

I DEDICATE THIS BOOK

PREFACE

MEDIAEVAL history is like a great tapestry, on which many figures—some splendid, some humble, some sinister, and some beautiful—appear against a shadowy background. A crabbed inscription gives to some a name and a story; many remain nameless and unknown. But all are in artistic relation with the background, and a close study of its shadows reveals a thousand details that help to explain their significance.

It is this background which I have tried to describe; my concern is with neither the political nor the literary history of France, but with the elements of her mediaeval civilization. The background is full of detail; yet much is obscured by shadow or darkened by time, and distance that softens the familiar may add the greater emphasis of mystery to the unusual and the strange. But however misty and remote the Middle Ages may seem to us, however much governed by ways of thought that time has made unfamiliar, it should not be hard to study them with sympathy and comprehension. The men of mediaeval France were men of like passions with ourselves; they knew pleasure and pain, freedom and limitation as we do; like us they were uncertain of the road they trod, yet ever went forward in hope.

For Englishmen they have a peculiar interest. They belong to the time when England held provinces in France; when in the palaces and law courts of England French was the common speech; when English poets wrote in a dialect of French, or, first attempting the rhythms of English verse, found their matter in the romances and *chansons de geste* of France. In literature, in art, in learning, England is the daughter of France; if there had been no such French civilization in the Middle Ages there could have been no such English Renaissance. Indeed, a critic, writing on the life of the French seigneurial class in the thirteenth century, finds that in their passion for sport, in their rural pleasures, in the relations at once free and courteous between men and women, this mediaeval society resembles nothing so closely as that of the England of a generation or two ago. 'Ways of living and acting', he says, 'as well as modes of speech, once very common ... that were originally derived from mediaeval France, have survived until our days only in England. The traces of them that can still be perceived help to give English life its peculiar character. But we must not forget that it is the antiquity of these customs which make them seem, to us, original.' [1]

I therefore venture to beg indulgence for a book, written with a mediaeval want of originality, that aims only at describing some aspects of the civilization of Mediaeval France.

I desire to express my indebtedness to the teaching of Dr. Ernest Barker, to encouragement and help received from the late Miss E. F. Jourdain, Principal of my College, and to the kindness of Professor Studer, who read the book in proof.

---

[1] Langlois, *La Société française au XIIIe siècle*, Introduction.

CONTENTS

BIBLIOGRAPHY

The author has not attempted to compile a complete Bibliography, nor to give a list of original texts, many of which are referred to in the body of the book; the following list includes only a selection of books and monographs in which the student can easily find additional information and a fuller treatment of various aspects of the subject.

Useful general bibliographies will be found in the books marked *, and more special lists in most of the books cited.

FRENCH

Bédier, J.   *Les Légendes épiques.*   Paris, 1914 (2nd edition).
    Les Fabliaux.   Paris, 1911 (3rd edition).
    Les Chansons de Croisade.   Paris, 1909.
Berlière, U.   *L'Ordre monastique.*   Paris, 1921 (2nd edition).
Boissonnade, P.   *Du nouveau sur la Chanson de Roland.*   Paris, 1923.
Borodine, M.   *La femme et l'amour au XIIe siècle d'après les poèmes de Chrétien de Troyes.*   Paris, 1909.
    Le Roman idyllique au moyen âge.   Paris, 1913.
Boutaric, E.   *La France sous Louis le Bel.*   Paris, 1861.
Bréhier, L.   *Les Croisades.*   Paris, 1907.
Calmette, J.   *La Société féodale.*   Paris, 1923.
Clément, P.   *Jacques Cœur et Charles VII.*   Paris, 1866.
Cohen, G.   *Histoire de la Mise en Scène dans le théâtre religieux français du moyen âge.*   Paris, 1906.
Enlart, C.   *Le Costume* (vol. iii of his *Manuel d'Archéologie française*).   Paris, 1916.
Fagniez, G.   *Études sur l'industrie et la classe industrielle à Paris.*   Paris, 1877.
Faral, E.   *Les jongleurs en France au moyen âge.*   Paris, 1910.
*Funck-Brentano, F.   *Le moyen âge.*   Paris, 1923.
Gastoué, A.   *Les Primitifs de la musique française.*   Paris, 1922.
Gautier, L.   *La Chevalerie.*   Paris, n. d. (1883).
Guilhiermoz, P.   *L'Origine de la noblesse en France.*   Paris, 1902.
Kleinclausz, H.   *Histoire de Bourgogne.*   Paris, 1909.
Lacroix, P.   (Bibliophile Jacob) *Mœurs, usages et coutumes au moyen âge.*   Paris, 1877.
    Sciences et lettres au moyen âge.   Paris, 1877.
*Langlois, C. V.   *La société française au XIIIe siècle.*   Paris, 1904.
*   *La vie en France au moyen âge.*   Paris, 1908.
*   *La connaissance de la nature et du monde au moyen âge.*   Paris, 1911.
*Lavisse, E. (ed.).   *Histoire de France,* vols. i–iv.   Paris, 1901–2.
Lecoy de la Marche, A.   *La chaire française au moyen âge.*   Paris, 1886.
    Le Treizième Siècle littéraire et scientifique.   Paris, 1887.
    La France sous Saint Louis et sous Philippe le Hardi.   Paris, 1893.

Longnon, A. *Atlas historique de la France.*
Luce, S. *Histoire de Bertrand du Guesclin et de son temps.* Paris, 1893.
Luchaire, A. *Les communes françaises.* Paris, 1890.
    Manuel des institutions françaises. Paris, 1892.
    La Société française au temps de Philippe Auguste. Paris, 1909.
Male, E. *L'art religieux en France* (3 vols.). Paris, 1908, 1910, 1921.
Michel, A. *Histoire de l'art.* Vols. i and ii. Paris, 1905–6.
Molinier, A. *Les sources de l'histoire de France.* Paris, 1901–6.
Paris, G. *La littérature française au moyen âge.* Paris, 1913 (5th edition, 1909).
Rambaud, A. N. *Histoire de la civilisation française.* Paris, 1887.

ENGLISH

Adams, H. *Mont St. Michel and Chartres.* Cambridge, Mass., 1919.
Barker, E. *The Crusades.* Oxford, 1923.
Coulton, G. G. *A Mediaeval Garner.* London, 1910.
    Five centuries of Religion. Cambridge, 1923.
Haskins, C. H. *Studies in the History of Mediaeval Science.* Cambridge, Mass., 1924.
*Huizinga, J. *The Waning of the Middle Ages.* London, 1924.
Hutton, W. H. *Philip Augustus.* London, 1896.
Ker, W. P. *The Dark Ages.* London, 1904.
King, G. G. *The Way of St. James.* New York, 1920.
Kitchin, G. W. *A History of France.* Oxford, 1881.
Masson, G. *Mediaeval France.* London, 1888.
Morison, J. C. *The Life and Times of St. Bernard.* London, 1863.
Poole, R. L. *Illustrations of Mediaeval Thought.* London (2nd edition), 1920.
Rashdall, H. *Universities of Europe in the Middle Ages.* Oxford, 1895.
Smith, L. M. *The Early History of the Monastery of Cluny.* Oxford, 1920.
Taylor, H. O. *The Mediaeval Mind.* London, 1911.
*Tilley, A. (ed.). *Mediaeval France.* Cambridge, 1922.
    The Dawn of the French Renaissance. Cambridge, 1918.
Vinogradoff, P. *Roman Law in Mediaeval Europe.* New York, 1909.

LIST OF ILLUSTRATIONS

MAPS

I

FRANCE IN THE EARLY MIDDLE AGES.

TOUCHING, or almost touching, Spain, Italy, Switzerland, Germany, the Low Countries, and England, France is for ever rich in that force which arises from the contact and clash of nations. Her own strength has always been great enough to transmute and absorb external impulses into her national being; her own race, unchanging yet never exhausted, has made her for more than seven centuries the focus of civilization for the countries of Europe. Always seeing civilization as social congruity, art as the expression of life, learning as a precious heritage, she has never failed in 'le courage spirituel et l'esprit courageux', and has never ceased to unite a respect for fact to a capacity for philosophic thought.

She is the true heir of Rome in law, in clear thinking, in philosophy; in the urbanity of her civilization, in the relation between social function and position, and in the fitting pageantry that lends splendour to practical things. There is no country more conscious of the continuity of her history, in spite of invasion, resettlement, and revolution; she brings to the Middle Ages the heritage of Roman Gaul. Caesar's *Commentaries* remain the best mirror of the Gallic temperament: 'swiftly and easily inflamed to war or revolution, hating the servile state, unstable, quick-witted, talkative, ingenious'. Yet politically France is neither Roman nor Celtic; she dates from the dark age of barbarism that followed the Roman Empire, when the mediaeval peoples emerged from the chaos of warring races, and the world gradually came to rest on a new balance.

If the history of mediaeval Europe begins with the coronation of Charlemagne, the history of the mediaeval nations begins with the partition of his empire after his death. In thirty years it was divided no less than five times; with the final Treaty

C

of Verdun in 843 the State of France was established. It is a significant fact that the earliest monument of the French language, the Strasburg Oaths, dates from 842. Even the divisions and dissensions of the early Middle Ages did not destroy the sense of the solidarity of France; the bard of the *Chanson de Roland* already sings of 'dulce France', and the name comes again and again as a refrain to point the distance and peril of Roncesvalles.[1] *Cleomadès* tells us that to love France is natural and right,

> Car en anciens escris
> Trueve on que tousjours a esté
> France la flours et la purté
> D'armes, d'onnour, de gentillece,
> De courtoisie et de largece.
> Ce est la touche et l'exemplaire
> De ce c'on doit laissier et faire.

In *Jerusalem* the Count of Flanders goes so far as to say that he wonders that Christ should have chosen to live in the desert of Syria. For his part,

> Miex aim del' borc d'Arras la grant castelerie
> Et d'Aire et de Saint Pol la grant caroierie
> Et de mes biaus viviers la riche pescherie
> Que tote ceste terre, ne la chité antie.

The many political divisions of France after the death of Charlemagne are of considerable importance for its political history, but for considering the growth of its mediaeval civilization they are of secondary interest. Its social, intellectual, and artistic history—and even the history of its legal institutions—naturally group themselves round four centres: Provence in the south, Burgundy in the east, the Île de France in central France, and Normandy in the north-west. Each of these was the centre of a civilization with characteristics of its own, and though interaction between them became more and more frequent a close assimilation was not reached until after the end of the Middle Ages.

Provence is the part of France that has the most ancient and the most continuous recorded history. Marseilles itself was founded as a colony from Hellenic Phocaea about 600 B.C., and Provence

---

[1] The word appears 170 times in the Oxford MS.

owes its name to its foundation as a Roman *Provincia* in 118 B.C. When the rest of Gaul was still under military rule as an occupied territory, Provence was administered directly by the Roman Senate. Pliny calls it ' Italia verius quam provincia ', and whether by sea or by the mountain passes it finds easy access to Italy. Christianity, too, came to Latin- and Greek-speaking Provence in the course of the original dissemination of the faith, to meet with a temporary check only when it encountered a barrier of Celtic speech beyond Lyons. Thus in spite of serious Teutonic inroads classical traditions endured there in laws and institutions, architecture and way of life, in a degree that is only surpassed in Italy. The form of Roman legal institutions survived. In Southern France alone can the mediaeval municipalities be considered direct descendants of the Roman *municipia*. They have the Italian tradition: the noble as well as the merchant lives within the city. They are *municipalités consulaires*; their officers have the title of consul—eight at Avignon, twelve at Marseilles, twenty-four at Toulouse. Roman Law was early studied at Montpellier, Toulouse, and Avignon, and it is remarkable that in the fourteenth century, when Provençal civilization was under an eclipse, the great jurists of Philippe le Bel—Pierre Flotte, Guillaume de Nogaret, Pierre de Belle Perche—were all graduates of Toulouse. Sir Paul Vinogradoff considers the most interesting contribution of France to the revival of Roman Law to be a recently discovered summary of the Code of Justinian written in Provençal in 1149 for the use of the local judges; it is the first treatise on Roman Law to be written in a modern language, and is clearly intended not for academic use, but for that of laymen acting as presiding judges or arbitrators. It is an intelligent and practical work of reference for a region where Roman Law was recognized as the principal legal authority.

But Roman influence in Provence was not confined to law: because there were there many small schools of classical learning rather than a single great one, it is easy to forget that it was a centre of humanistic studies. Guiot de Provins reminds us of the writers studied at Arles:

A Arle oï conter molt gent
Lor vie en l'estoire sanz troffe
Dont furent né li Philosofe—

of whom he cites twenty—Plato, Seneca, Aristotle, Virgil, Socrates, Lucan, Diogenes, Priscian, Aristippus, Cleobulus, Ovid, Statius, Pythagoras, and others. It was in the south that the classical love of beauty and pleasure came most strongly into conflict with the monastic ideal. The Prior of Montaudon leaves his cloister, and keeping his religious habit, wanders about as a troubadour, till in the end he drifts to the Court of his friend Alphonso II of Aragon. His poems express his attitude to life. 'The other day I was in Paradise, because I am merry and joyful, and because I love well the good God whom all things obey—earth, sea, valley, and mountain. And God said to me, " Monk, why comest thou here? And how dost thou fare at Montaudon with all thy brethren?"'

'Lord, I stayed a year or two in the cloister, which was enough to lose me the barons' love; but it is you alone whom I love and would serve.'

'"Monk," replied God, "think not thou gavest me pleasure in shutting thyself up in the abbey; why desist from war and singing? I would rather hear thee laugh and sing. It makes princes more generous, and the priory of Montaudon can only gain by it."'

In the whole of Provençal life there is something of the Italian feeling of the Renaissance: the country surrounds the town, and the citizens go, Italian fashion, to work or to play there in the day, and return singing to the city at nightfall. Life is insecure, and city and country have alike their dangers, but through everything runs a strain of Lorenzo's ' Quant' è bella gioventù '. There is the same Italian note in Provençal architecture, but this is directly attributable to the influence of the splendid classical buildings of Roman times in Arles, Nîmes, Orange, and the other Roman cities. The monastic carvers of the cloister of St. Trophime at Arles decorated their work with the figures of Jupiter, Juno, Hercules, Silvanus (with oak leaves for hair), Faunus, Diana, Neptune, Ceres, Bacchus, Pan, Venus, Paris, and Helen. As late as the beginning of the twelfth century the characteristic Provençal church is constructed like a classical temple with a single nave, walls unpierced by windows, fluted columns crowned with the Corinthian acanthus, and pediments, entablatures, and mouldings that in their form as in their propor-

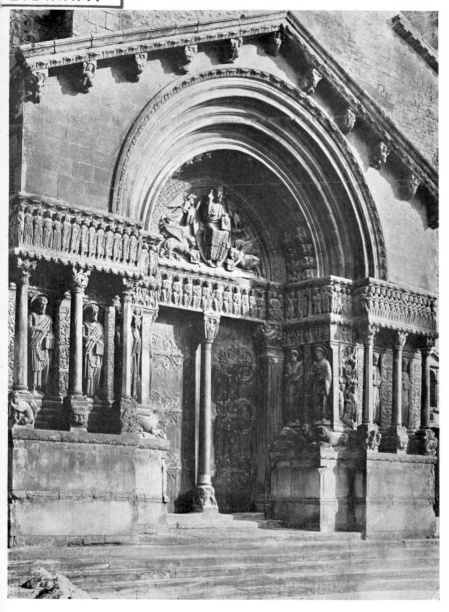

II.   The Church of St. Trophime, Arles

Last quarter of the 12th Century

tion are classical and Roman. The poet Fortunatus, on seeing the church of St. Sernin at Toulouse, thus expressed his astonishment:

> Quod nullus veniens Romana gente fabrivit
> Hoc vir barbarica prole peregit opus.

In all the territory once belonging to *Provincia Narbonensis*, including Toulouse and a part of Guyenne, Roman influence is strong, but there is also a second influence, the influence of the East. The Mediterranean brought the whole coast from Nice to Perpignan and the country behind it into close connexion with half-Eastern Spain and even with Africa and the commercial cities of Asia Minor; the sea might be stormy, but it was safer than the highways of France. As early as the time of Charlemagne the coast towns had relations with the Baghdad of Haroun-el-Raschid, with Byzantium, Egypt, and Syria, and imported purple stuffs, spices, Indian pearls, Egyptian papyrus, and even monkeys and elephants. Benjamin of Tudela, writing in 1160, describes Montpellier as a very good city for commerce to which Christians and Mohammedans come from all quarters to trade, so that its streets are thronged with Arabs of North Africa, merchants of Syria, Lombardy, Rome, Genoa, Pisa, and England.

Even when Southern France found herself in conflict with an Eastern people, as she did in 1018 when a Crusade was undertaken against the Moors, conquest only preceded assimilation. The leaders of the army gained great riches, and stayed to lead an Oriental life in Moorish palaces. A Jewish merchant has left a story of waiting upon one of these French leaders in his palace at Barbastro, and finding him in Eastern garments seated upon a divan, surrounded by evidences of his riches, while a tearful Arab girl played the lute and sang songs in a language that he could not understand.

Thus the Eastern element was important in the development of the life of the south-western cities in particular. Indeed, the foundation of Montpellier itself is traditionally ascribed to fugitives from the Saracen city of Maguelone, destroyed by Charles Martel in 737. From its considerable Arabic and Jewish population may be derived the tradition of medical knowledge, which in the twelfth century made Montpellier second only to Salerno as a University of Medicine. Another sign of Eastern influence is the Oriental character of the architecture of Périgord, as Eastern as that of St. Mark's at Venice. St. Front de Périgueux, built after 1120, shows the classical single nave, without divisions or side chapels, surmounted by a characteristically Eastern series of cupolas. Even so far north as Poitou we find the East in the fantastic and imaginative decoration of the dark churches, allied no longer to Rome but to Celtic Gaul. Perhaps the finest architectural development is to be found in the Auvergne, where all three influences unite, and the problem of the equilibrium of the vault is solved by a crown of chapels clustering round the choir, which is surmounted by a cupola. ' C'est sans doute le plus beau crescendo architectural qui existe,' says M. Mâle, 'théorème au dedans, l'église auvergnate s'achève en ode au dehors.'

It is in Provence that the first efforts were made to bring the perpetual warfare of feudalism within the control of the Church. The *Pax Dei* and the *Pactum Pacis* are characteristic of Southern France. They were the first expressions of that almost Hellenic feeling for the gentler side of life, that wish, not for strength alone, but for strength allied with grace, which Provence shared with Greece, ' that made gracious the life of the world'. They were its contribution to the early military chivalry of the Middle Ages; and Provence remained the home of *courtoisie.*

This is not the place to consider the history of Provençal literature, which, like that of Greece, rose, blossomed, and died in a short three hundred years, between the end of the tenth and the end of the thirteenth century. It is possible that Provençal lyric art may have owed something to the great tenth-century Arab school of lyric poetry, and that the Provençal troubadours may have gained some of the complexity of their versification from this source.

Another influence of the East helped to bring Provençal civilization to a violent and an untimely end. The Eastern conception of a dualistic religion, of a Spirit of Good and a Spirit of Evil inherent in all things and ever at war, had influenced the Manichaeans of Early Christian times. In the

III.   Périgueux.   Cathedral of St. Front

early Middle Ages the belief flourished in the Balkan peninsula, and during the eleventh century it reached Provence. The sect of Cathari, later called Albigensians from their head-quarters at Albi, maintained that all physical and material things pertained to the Spirit of Evil, and that all who wished for salvation must utterly renounce them. Their dualism denied the Christian doctrine of Redemption, and by 1163 the Council of Tours denounced them as heretics. In 1199 Innocent III seriously took up the work of suppressing the heresy, and with it the Provençal free spirit which had found a more orthodox expression in such sects as the Vaudois. His Albigensian Crusade hastened the end of Provençal chivalry and Provençal civilization, already menaced by the centralizing influence of Paris. The Crusade, indeed, was not only the expression of hostility between the established order and heresy, but also of the instinctive and resentful envy that always lies between north and south. Over seven thousand helpless women and children were killed in the church of St. Mary Magdalene at Béziers alone, and the chivalry and peasantry of the Midi, Catholics and Cathari alike, were killed by the Crusaders 'avec un extrême allégresse'. The *Chanson de la Croisade* tells us that the grass of the fields was dyed red as roses, since no prisoners were taken.

Provence and the surrounding country is then an entity of which the lines of demarcation from the rest of France can be established. It finds a pendant in the north, but one of which every characteristic is different. Provence has a history going back to Rome and even to Greece: Normandy enters history, to all intents and purposes, when it is granted to Rollo and his followers in 911. The Norman expansion from the ninth to the twelfth century may be thought of as the last wave of the Great Migrations. But whereas Goth and Vandal, Hun and Frank, had been nomads on the land, the Northmen were driven by the configuration of their land to become nomads upon the waters, 'nageans par l'Océan en manière de pyrates'. Three sea routes lead from Scandinavia, apart from any in the Baltic itself: the first leads direct to Iceland, the second to the eastern shores of Britain, and the third, skirting the Frisian coasts, reaches the northern coast of France. Therefore it is natural that the migrations of the Northmen should have led to the establishment of a Scandinavian principality in Iceland, the Danelaw in England, and Normandy in France.

Their tendency was naturally enough to settle at the mouths of great rivers: the Humber, Elbe, Weser, Rhine, Meuse, Scheldt, Seine, Loire, Garonne, and Guadalquivir. Theirs was a genius for colonization. Their contemporary Geoffrey Malaterra has described them, balancing light and shadow in the portrait: they are a cunning and revengeful race, he says, despising their own inheritance in the hope of winning a greater elsewhere, eager for gain and eager for power, quick to imitate whatever they see, at once lavish and greedy; given to hunting and hawking, delighting in horses and accoutrements and fine clothing, yet ready if needs be to bear labour and hunger and cold; skilful in flattery and the use of fine words, but unbridled unless held down by the yoke of justice. This quickness and eagerness, this gift for imitation without loss of their own personality, made it possible for them to assimilate much that was French while retaining many northern characteristics. In spite of continued migration from the north, by the eleventh century Normandy had become French in law and language, recognizing federation if not feudation to the King at Paris. The second Duke, William Longsword, had to send his son to learn Norse at Bayeux, for it was no longer spoken at Rouen.[1]

But Normandy was not French in outlook; rather was it the centre of an Atlantic Empire that stretched from Scotland to the Pyrenees. It sent its knights to fight the Moors in Spain, its crusaders to Jerusalem, and its younger sons to Sicily. There a handful of Normans so dealt with the problem of a mixed population of Mohammedans, Greek and Roman Christians and Jews in a country which had never been the home of a single nation or a single speech that they gave Sicily the most brilliant epoch in her history since classical Syracuse. Such a feat shows great administrative ability and a gift for dealing with the forms of law: a code of Lombard and Roman law and Norman custom had to be administered to a mixed population so that Greek, Saracen, Lombard, Norman, and Jew should be

[1] Scandinavian survivals remained chiefly in the language of the sea, whence they crept into the naval vocabulary of modern French.

alike protected; and an Arab, Latin, and Greek Chancery had to invent and administer a system of exchequer and administrative writs. The love of legal action is a Norse characteristic, and is early shown in such sagas as that of Burnt Njal. The *Coutume de Normandie* was the connecting link between the Frankish law of the Continent and English Common Law. Trial by jury, for instance, is of Frankish origin, but was developed and disseminated by the Normans.

It is characteristic of the Norman habit of order and organization that the military service of nobles was there exactly and systematically defined earlier than in the neighbouring counties of Northern France. The military service owing to the Duke was assessed in units of five or ten knights, representing so much land, and the amounts of service were fixed by custom and regularly enforced. The unit of life was thus the knight's fee and the castle. These castles could not be built without the Duke's licence; they were all built for defence, and the life of their inhabitants was narrowed by defensive necessities. Further, the Duke had the power of limiting private wars and blood-feuds, and a large monopoly of jurisdiction was reserved for him.

The Norman gift for administration is notably shown in the financial system. Taxes and dues were collected more in money and less in kind than in Capetian France; their collection, checking, and administration were in the hands of skilled officers. The English Chancery under Henry II—then the most advanced in Europe—was typically Norman.

The Normans, then, were a practical people, immediately concerned with concrete things. Ways and means and not ideas were their pre-occupation; their literature deals in fact and not in speculation. History in the vernacular, which developed earlier in France than elsewhere, developed earliest in Normandy and in the English lands which share Norman speech. Its first production, the *Histoire des Engles* of Gaimar, was written between 1147 and 1151 at the Court of Henry II and Eleanor of Aquitaine, to whom are also dedicated the histories of Wace and Benoit de St. More.

The same tendencies achieve greatness in Norman architecture; breadth, space, a certain grand manner from which no unessential ornament detracts; solid reasoning and powerful will lie behind it, and give an effect curiously reminiscent of the Dorian architecture of the Spartan Peloponnese. As conditions became more settled in the eleventh century there was an immense amount of church building done by the bishops. The chronicler shows Geoffrey de Mowbray, for instance, labouring night and day for the enlargement and beautification of his church at Coutances, which was dedicated in 1056. He bought the better half of the city from the Duke to get a clear space for his cathedral and palace, he travelled as far as Apulia to secure for it gold and gems and vestments from Robert Guiscard and his fellow Normans, and he maintained from his rents a force of sculptors, masons, goldsmiths, and workers in glass. Nearly forty years later, when the church had been damaged by earthquake and tempest, he brought a plumber from England to restore the leaden roof and the fallen stones of the towers and to replace the gilded cock which crowned the whole; and when he saw the cock once more shining at the summit, he gave thanks to God and died, pronouncing eternal maledictions upon those who should injure his church.

In 1204 the Duchy of Normandy became a part of the Kingdom of France. Powicke's *Loss of Normandy* concludes: 'When the Normans became French they did a great deal more than bring their national epic to a close. They permitted the English once more to become a nation, and they established the French nation for all time'. They kept their own spirit of enterprise: it was Norman seamen who visited Senegal and Guinea and established the Gold and Ivory Coasts in 1365; and it was a Norman gentleman who was Lord of the Canary Islands in 1402. They added something to the national heritage of enlightened common sense, they aided the development of an adequate financial system and of the Parlement of Paris, and thus did their share in the gradual centralization of authority and power in the monarchy and the capital.

If the vitality of Normandy flows through the channels of the seas, the life of Burgundy runs through the ways of the land. Michelet has said, ' La France n'a pas d'élément plus liant que la Bourgogne, plus capable de réconcilier le nord et le midi '.

IV. Paris : the Sainte Chapelle

1242–1247

It lies at the centre of the river-system of France, and so has been from time immemorial a centre of trade. The fairs of Châlon, Autun, Dijon, Auxonne, Beaune, Châtillon, and Tonnerre carried on a commercial tradition dating from Carolingian and even from Roman times. But besides being the home of commerce, it is the home of religion; its abbeys—Cluny, Cîteaux, Clairvaux, Vézelay, Flavigni, Tournus, St. Pierre de Bèze, Pothières, St. Benigne de Dijon, and the rest—were not only important in themselves but did much to bring religion into feudal life. Cluny made Burgundy the land of crusaders and pilgrims. The first Capetian Duke, Hugh I (1076-9), fought the Saracens in Spain; Odo I besieged Tudela for two years; Hugh II died in 1143 after making the pilgrimage to Compostella; Hugh III was at the taking of St. Jean d'Acre and died at Tyre; Odo III took a prominent part in the Albigensian Crusade; Hugh IV fought the infidels in Palestine and Egypt, and then in 1258 made the pilgrimage to Compostella; his successor, Hugh V, is King of Thessalonica; and Odo IV, Prince of Achaea. Even in 1436 Philippe le Bon still has the idea of crusade, and the Byzantine ambassadors have faith 'after God in him only'; and only the Pope's death brings the last Burgundian Crusade of 1465 to nothing.

The story of the core of France—the Île de France that has its centre at Paris—is bound up with the story of the Capetian monarchy. Intellectual argument has flourished in the atmosphere of Paris at least since the time of Julian the Apostate, and intellectual argument kept the idea of sovereignty alive. Here Law and Theology flourished, and the lawyers and the clergy were the two sections of society least dependent upon feudalism and most addicted to theory. The clergy held that the King through an eighth sacrament of coronation received a divine commission, different in kind from the power of any feudatory [1]; that he alone was Defender of the Church, and that to him pertained the execution of justice throughout the kingdom. The lawyers, fresh from the study of Roman Law, not only exalted the principle of his

[1] The King wore the dalmatic beneath the royal mantle, as the kings of England still do, at their coronation.

prerogative but also found legal methods and formulas to extend his power. Because the tradition of the Roman idea of sovereignty survived, monarchical feeling remained strong enough to give that centralized force to feudalism without which disintegration would have been inevitable.

The coronation oath of Hugh Capet and his successors concludes : ' I promise to grant to the people who are entrusted to my care Justice according to their rights'; and down to the end of the monarchy the King of France is the only sovereign in Europe who holds, besides the sceptre, not à sword but the ' main de justice '. As early as the tenth century Abbo could describe the monarchy as ' the incarnation of justice '.

So it is as Justiciar that the King consolidates his power, and by ecclesiastical and legal help that he attains and keeps it. The elevation of the Capetian dynasty had been due neither to a national movement nor a feudal movement, but to the ecclesiastical support given to the King by the French clergy, led by the Archbishop of Rheims. The Capetian monarch justly held the title of ' Eldest son of the Church and most Christian King ', and, though in friendly relation with the Papacy, remained a strong supporter of Gallicanism. The history of the French Church in the late eleventh century is the history of its bishoprics, and thus the King found in the bishoprics a counterbalance to the power of lay feudalism. But a third power arose, that of the people, and it was in allying itself with this power that the French monarchy attained a really national position.

The strength of this monarchy lay not only in its relations with Church and people—that made it less dependent upon the support of its feudatories—but also in its possession of a compact royal domain, with Paris as its centre. Every other monarchy in Europe owned scattered tracts of land, which afforded no strong *point d'appui* for the royal struggle against the barons. But the Île de France formed a core, round which, by purchase, marriage, and conquest an ever-increasing royal domain was built up, and it is owing to this possession that the centralization of power in Paris and in the monarchy was possible. In the administration of the first Capetians the provosts and the mayors combined all functions, giving the

V.   The Louvre in the time of Charles V

King a fixed yield and retaining the rest of the dues and taxes. Not until Norman methods of administration were introduced were the royal revenues increased. Further, the justice of the King became sovereign in a gradually widening area, while its seat at Paris made the city a true metropolis.

With the accession of Louis VI in 1108, a certain balance of power appears to restrain the unbridled forces of early feudalism. It is royal justice that modifies the feudal order and makes France a nation. From the royal domain, compacted into a central demesne round Paris, the monarchy made itself the centre of a modification of feudalism : one in which the Church, while becoming national, was to a great extent de-feudalized ; in which the bourgeoisie of the towns was given a place in society, and became the King's allies at the expense of the nobles ; in which the rural population was gradually permitted to escape from the servitude of the glebe. By the time of St. Louis the monarchy was already the fundamental institution of the realm. Its divine origin was recognized ; ' le roi ne tient que de Dieu et de son épée ' ; the dynastic succession was established. But its true consecration lay in the justice it administered ; the friar, Hugues de Digne, could preach to St. Louis: 'I have never seen in the Scriptures or any other book that a kingdom or a lordship of any kind has ever passed from one House to another, except for default of justice.' The best title-deeds of the monarchy are such edicts as the *Grande Ordonnance* of 1254 :

' The seneschals and other royal officers shall swear and observe the oath, under pain of punishment by the King himself, to give justice without distinction of persons, according to the approved customs and uses ; to protect the rights of the King without encroaching on those of private persons; to receive no gift, neither they, nor their wives, nor their children, and to give back any they may have taken ; never to borrow from those under their jurisdiction a sum over twenty livres, and to repay within two months ; not to take any share in the proceeds of sale or appointment to subordinate posts, of rents due to the King, &c. ; not to protect their subordinates who may be guilty of peculations or abuse of power . . . but on the contrary to punish them. . . . They shall not buy any house within the area of their jurisdiction without the King's consent, under pain of confiscation. . . . They shall not make the monasteries admit their relations or their servants, or procure for them ecclesiastical benefices. . . . They shall take neither bed nor board in monastic houses without the King's authorization. . . . They shall only have a small number of bedels and sergeants to execute their judgements. . . . The seneschals and bailiffs and their servants shall cause no man to be arrested for debt, unless the money be due to the King. They shall not be able to detain a man accused of crime who may be in a position to clear himself. . . . Persons of good reputation, however poor, shall not be put to the question on the evidence of a single witness. . . . They shall not collect any imposition. . . . They shall not forbid the exportation of corn, wine, and other provisions except after the Council has debated the question. . . . The royal officers, after their term of office has expired, shall remain for fifty days on the spot to answer any complaints which may be laid against them.'

St. Louis endowed the monarchy with an added dignity, a dignity of moral greatness which survived even the lower standards of his successors. When he was ill he said to his son, ' Fair son, I pray you that you make yourself beloved of your people; for truly I would rather that a Scot should come from Scotland and govern the Kingdom loyally and well than that you should govern it ill '. This good government he defines in the testament addressed to the same son, the future Philippe III: not to take away the goods or the rights of another, to do everything to enable his subjects to live in peace and righteousness, not to make war against Christians unless forced to do so, to appease quarrels, ' comme faisait St. Martin ', and to do his best to stamp out sin and heresy. This policy was not invariably followed by his successors, but the tradition of it made such a dictum as Beaumanoir's ' Ce qui plaît à faire au roi doit être tenu pour loi' the subject of less controversy than it would have been if St. Louis had not invested the monarchical power with the dignity of saintliness. In Joinville's words, ' Et ainsi comme l'escrivain qui a fait son livre, qui l'enlumine d'or et d'azur, enlumina ledit roy son royaume '.[1]

Under this policy the prosperity of the royal demesne increased. Private war was there more strictly limited, and the *droit coutumier* more carefully codified and corrected.[2] But it was definitely *royal* France; the right of ennobling, taxing, and

[1] ' Like the scribe who, having made his book, illuminates it with gold and blue, did this King illuminate his kingdom.'

[2] The *royal* rights were not codified, and therefore they could grow gradually.

VI.   The Knight standing between the Priest and the Roman Warrior

Rheims Cathedral.   End of 13th Cent.

striking money was insisted on as a royal prerogative, and there were no sovereign republics, no elected magistrates, no town belfries, no town seals, no independent militia, no justice but royal justice. But the *corvées* due to the King were carefully determined by *chartes octroyées*, and privileges thus granted were precious, since they were directly guaranteed by the monarchy. *Les Libertés de Lorris*, quite a small town, served as a model;[1] under such a charter it was more advantageous to be a *bourgeois du roi* than to be the member of a commune with rights of making war and peace: to be the citizen of a kingdom rather than of a single township.[2] At first residence in the royal city was necessary, but as the jurists of Philippe le Bel accustomed men's minds to accept legal theory as well as fact, by 1288 it was decided that it sufficed to make a formal disavowal of the old lord and to avow the King as master. Thus an important bourgeois class was created directly dependent on the King, who recruited from them his civil service. Further, they played a part in political life; the first exclusively bourgeois assemblage was summoned by Philip Augustus in 1185, and a century later began the political development of the États Généraux.

The reign of Philippe le Bel is an era of change. The Parlement of Paris was given a regular constitution and made a real court of justice, with political, judicial, and financial functions, and met twice a year for a session of two months in the Palais de la Cité, afterwards called the Palais de Justice. An additional Chambre des Enquêtes was formed for extra-feudal jurisdiction. As Boutaric remarks, 'Il y eut désormais en France une noblesse; il n'y eut pas d'aristocratie'.

Philippe le Bel not only added considerably to the privileges of the *bourgeois du roi*, but also did much to encourage trade. The great fair *du Lendit* (indictum), held on land belonging to St. Denis and dating back to Frankish times, was regulated by him in 1295; already every town and craft in France was represented at it each year, but it was now opened to foreigners also on the payment of certain dues. Further, merchants going

[1] It even influenced town charters in the west of England.
[2] Private war was forbidden : every dangerous conflict was an attempt against public security, and as such punishable by the King.

to the *foires franches* of Champagne—at Troyes, Provins, Bar-sur-Aube, and Lagny—at the junction of the trade routes of the north and south, were declared exempt from local tolls on their way. Thus companies of Italian merchants came to frequent the fairs, and occasionally to found fixed establishments. It was through them that Villani, Boccaccio, Brunetto Latino, Francesco da Barberino, and the rest came to visit France; and it was through the position of the great Lombard merchants as financiers to the King that the financial basis of the monarchy made it more independent of its feudal vassals.

Further, the monarchy took political advantage of a growing feeling against arbitrary servitude. There was a preference to engage men into definite contracted service; it was more consistent with Christian principles and on the whole it yielded better work : an *œuvre de piété* was justified by its economic results. Such freedom, however, was usually bought, and when Louis X, in 1315, freed all the serfs of the royal domain, since according to natural law every man should be born free, such freedom had compulsorily to be bought at a fairly high price.

From the time of Philip Augustus the power of the monarchy was supported by legal opinion. This study of law—customary, Canon, and especially Roman—is one of the characteristic developments of Capetian France, though its elements are not in the first instance Parisian. Roman Law was the heritage of the south, and Canon Law, in so far as it had a local source, sprang from Lorraine and the eleventh-century jurists of Lorraine such as Bruno of Toul, Cardinal Humbert, and Wazo of Liège. But under St. Louis juristic study was encouraged in the royal demesne, the Digest was translated into French, and schools of Roman Law were established at Orléans and Angers. Legal power appears unchecked by piety or any moral consideration under Philippe le Bel. Guillaume de Nogaret and his colleagues were Roman in their juristic education and feudal in their violence : they had no consideration for the rights of any one but their master. By legal process they wrested Guyenne from Edward I, more territory from the Count of Flanders, more power from Pope Boniface VIII, and more

VII. The Donjon of Loches

11th and 12th Centuries

PARIS
c. 1350

For the sake of clearness the width of road
is considerably exaggerated

N

Sᵗ Lazare

TO Sᵗ DENIS

Bastille

Porte
St. Martin

Porte du Temple

Porte St. Denis

RUE Sᵗ DENIS

Palace
of King
Robert

The
Temple

RUE Sᵗ MARTIN

Hôpital
de Sᵗ
Julien

Porte
Montmartre

Hotel de
Bourgogne

RUE DU TEMPLE

MONT MARTRE

Halles

Cimetière
des
Innocents

Hotel
d'Armagnac

Porte St.
Honoré

RUE Sᵗ HONORÉ

VILLE

LOMBARDS
CURRIERS

BUTCHERS

WEAVERS

Hotel de Ville

Palais des
Tournelles

Porte
Sᵗ Antoine

The
Louvre

Grand
Châtelet

CUTLERS

Bastille
Sᵗ Antoine

Tour
de Bois

PLACE DE GRÈVE

River Seine

CITÉ

PONT AU CHANGE

PETIT PONT

Law
Courts
(Palace of Sᵗ Louis)

Notre
Dame

Parvis
Notre Dame

R. Seine

Tour de Nesle

Les Augustins

PRÉ AUX CLERCS

Petit
Châtelet

Châtelet

Clos du
Chardonnet

FAUBOURG
Sᵗ GERMAIN

UNIVERSITÉ

Sᵗ Julien le
Pauvre

Sᵗ Séverin

BERNARDINS

Coll. de Sorbonne

Coll de Navarre

Benedictines

RUE Sᵗ JACQUES

College of
Navarre

College de Montaigu

ABBAYE
Sᵗ VICTOR

Porte
St. Germain

FRANCISCANS

Jacobins

Les Écoles

Sᵗ Geneviève

Porte Sᵗ VICTOR

Foire
Sᵗ Germain

Porte St. Jacques

Porte
Sᵗ Victor

ABBEY OF
Sᵗ GERMAIN DES PRÉS

Sᵗ Sulpice

Sᵗ Jacques du Haut Pas

Notre Dame
des Champs

● Moulins des Gobelins

□ Chartreuse

W. T. Wright   del.

money from the Order of the Temple. The jurist du Bois, in his 'Inquiry touching the power of the Pope', says that the Pope is evidently the temporal lord of the Emperor, for the latter needs to be confirmed and crowned by him; but no such authorization is needed in France, and no such authority should be recognized. He decides that it would be the best thing for society that the whole world should be subject to French rule, for 'it is a peculiar merit of the French to have a surer judgement than other nations, not to act without consideration, nor to place themselves in opposition to right reason'.

Philippe le Bel was the last King of France to be excommunicated, and he had his revenge. The captivity of the Popes at Avignon from 1308 to 1378 put even the papal power in the hands of the monarchy.

Paris and the Île de France, through the King's relations with Church and people, thus became the seat of a monarchy, backed by a system of burgess administration and supported by a system of legal theory. Thus Paris and the privileged provinces came to be the seat of order and authority. Though the west and the south might be plunged in anarchy, and the country in general a prey to superstition, vagabondage, robbery, and feudal guerilla warfare, none the less in Paris and the royal demesne life was civilized, urbane, and comparatively speaking secure. The Dominican André de Châlis, preaching in 1272, said that while everywhere the wife called her husband 'Monseigneur', at Paris he in his turn called her 'Madame'. The centre of the Île de France was Paris, the seat of monarchy and university: a city thus described by Gui de Bazoches between 1175 and 1190, at the time when it had first reached political importance under Philip Augustus:

'I am in Paris,' he writes, 'in that royal city where abundance of natural wealth not only holds those who live there, but also attracts those from afar. Just as the moon outshines the stars in brilliance, so does this city, the seat of the monarchy, lift her proud head above the rest. She lies in the embrace of an enchanting valley, surrounded by a crown of hills which Ceres and Bacchus make fruitful. The Seine, proud river of the East, runs there a brimming stream, and holds in its arms an island which is the head, the heart, the marrow of the whole city. Two suburbs extend to right and left, of which the lesser alone rivals many cities. Each of these suburbs communicates with the island by two bridges of stone; the Grand Pont towards the north, on the side of the English Channel, and the Petit Pont towards the Loire. The first—great, rich, trading—is the scene of seething activity; innumerable ships surround it, filled with merchandise and riches. The Petit Pont belongs to the dialecticians, who walk there deep in argument. In the island, by the side of the King's palace that dominates the whole city, is seen the palace of philosophy, where study reigns as sole sovereign in a citadel of light and immortality.'

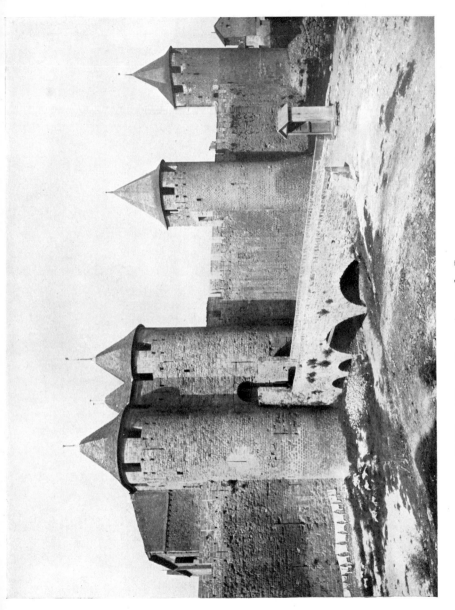

VIII. The Castle of Carcassonne

II

FEUDAL SOCIETY

The theorists of the Middle Ages divided men into three classes: *bellatores*, those who fought; *oratores*, those who prayed; and *laboratores*, those who worked with their hands; and in fact in France from the ninth to the twelfth century there were three such classes living side by side on the same soil under three different laws: the nobles, living under the feudal government in right of their tenure of land; the clerics, living under ecclesiastical government and under the rule or canons to which they had voluntarily subjugated themselves; and the people, living under the arbitrary law of the lord of the domain in which they lived. The strength of feudalism lay in the fact that it recognized and established the peculiar function of each of these classes and of its individual members in the State, and thus both justified their existence and assured their livelihood. When Robert of Courçon in the time of Philip Augustus announced that reform could only come when each member of the State should be forced under pain of excommunication and of civil condemnation to work either spiritually or manually, 'so that none may eat bread not gained by his labour', instead of bringing forward a doctrine of revolution, he was emphasizing the doctrine, obscured by time, that is as much the spiritual basis of feudal society as a system of land tenure is its material basis.

The early thirteenth-century poem *Miserere* expresses the truth :

Labours de clerc est Dieu prïer
Et justice de chevalier.
Pain lor truevent li laborier.
Chil paist, chil prie, et chil deffent.
Au camp, a le vile, au moustier
S'entreaïdent de lor mestier
Chil troi par bel ordenement.[1]

[1] 'The labour of the clerk is to pray to God, of the knight to do justice, and the labourer finds their bread. One provides food, one prays, and one defends. In the field, the town, and the church these three help each other with their services in a well-ordered scheme.'

Feudal society, indeed, ultimately rests on the necessity for mutual help between men whose powers and needs are different. During the centuries when there was no strong central government the poor and the weak had to seek the protection of those who could give it, and protection meant dependence. As the *Chanson de Guillaume* says, 'Gent senz seignur sunt malement bailli'.[1] So feudalism arose in some sense as a defence against the dangers of the Dark Ages, invasions by Huns, Arabs, and Northmen; internecine strife and unjust oppression. *Sidrach* tells us that if there were not authority and lordship, men would live 'en guise de poissons; le fort manjeroit le foible et le grand le petit. Et toute justice doit estre fort'. The mediaeval view of the feudal pact recognized its historic basis; the *Coutume de Bayonne*, of about 1273, states:

'The people come before lords; it is the lesser folk, more numerous than the others, who, wishing to live in peace, create lords to restrain and defeat the strong and to maintain each man in his rights, so that each may live according to his condition, the poor with their poverty and the rich with their wealth. And to assure this in perpetuity, the populace has submitted itself to a lord, has given him what he holds, and has kept what the people hold for themselves. It is in witness of this that the lord should take the oath to his people before the people take it to their lord; and this oath taken by the people to their lord is only binding as long as the lord keeps his oath.'

By the time of the death of Charles the Bald in 887 the State was definitely feudal,[2] but its feudalism was of a different spirit from that which was to develop round the increasing power of the French monarchy. At this early date the vassal limited his freedom by a free contract, and recognized no authority that he had not in the first instance voluntarily imposed upon himself. He still had the rights of waging war and concluding peace, that in a more developed society fall to the King alone; his 'bonne épée' was still the best guardian of his privileges, and he could be judged in law only by his equals.

The social conditions of the age forced men to live by the land and not by commerce or industry, and since this involved

---

[1] 'Men without a lord are ill provided for.'

[2] In 853 he ordered that the old manors should be rebuilt and fortified, and that others should be erected, in order to check the invasions of Normans, Danes, and Saracens.

IX. The Tournament

Late 13th Century ivory

a 'natural' economy and the absence of a money economy,[1] this land was held by individuals conditionally on their rendering service for it. Such service fell into two classes, depending on the size of the fief and the relations of the tenant and his lord. The first, and most important, was political service; the land was held conditionally on the tenant doing government work, both military and civil. He owed *auxilium* in war, and thus supplied the army ; and *concilium* in peace,[2] and thus supplied the deliberative assembly. Incidentally, since tenants did justice on their own holdings, feudalism supplied executive officers for the law.

The second class of service was economic; a manor was divided into small agricultural tenements held by peasants, rendering service not with the sword but with the plough, not in political service but in produce. Thus the edifice of the whole commonwealth rested upon the land, and since public duties were incidents of land tenure the constitution was part of the land laws. Gradually the feudal relationship between lord and vassal, which had at first been for life only, became hereditary, and with the right to be a lord's vassal descended the right to hold the fief from him. Such descent was generally recognized by the tenth century, and in token of it family names were lost in the territorial appellations that descended from father to son.

In this system, as in all the political theory of the Middle Ages, two elements can be distinguished: a Teutonic and a Roman. These elements had been acting one upon the other long before the Middle or even the Dark Ages. The Gallo-Roman kept his language and his property, and continued to live under the Roman law; the Frank lived under his own Salic or Ripuarian system of tribal custom. A gradual assimilation of the two elements eventually made it impossible to distinguish between the two, and a territorial law superseded the law of race. Clovis was a Teutonic king, yet he accepted the title of Consul and put the effigy of the Eastern Emperor on his coins. It is this double power welded by custom into one that made it possible for Hugh Capet, elected monarch in

[1] Money became increasingly scarce from the later days of the Roman Empire. Even as early as Diocletian (300) taxes were paid in kind, as they continued to be for eight centuries more.

[2] By custom the vassal went three times a year to the King's court, at Christmas, Easter, and Whitsun.

987, to establish an hereditary dynasty. Similarly, both Roman and Teutonic institutions had prepared men's minds for the establishment of a feudal State. On the one hand the old Germanic levy of freemen serving the King is the precursor of his successor's bodyguard of knights; and on the other the Roman system of land tenure on the frontiers by men who owed military service for their land,[1] and were attached to the administrative service of the Empire, is a precedent for the conditions of mediaeval feudalism. So the Middle Ages were able to invest feudalism with the glamour of antiquity, and the *Image du Monde* of 1247 can explain that the three 'Manières de gens' were established by the philosophers at Athens, that they taught it to Rome, and Rome to France.

Caesar states[2] that 'In all Gaul there are but two classes of men who are of honour and account; for the common folk are reckoned as but little better than slaves, dare nothing of themselves, and have no voice in council. . . . The two classes left are the nobles and the knights.' They keep their precedence in the Middle Ages; not only do they hold the land, but they also fight for it. In the early Middle Ages, indeed, it is as *bellator* pure and simple that the knight takes his place. His two virtues are courage and wisdom,

> Rollant est proz e Oliver est sage,

and their balance makes the 'prud'homme'. It is by his courage and wisdom that the structure of society is maintained:

> Itel valor deit aveir chevaler
> Ki armes portet e en bon cheval set;
> En bataille deit estre forz et fiers,
> U altrement ne valt ·iiij· deners,
> Einz deit monie estre en un de ces mustiers,
> Se prierat tuz jurz por noz peccez.[3]

Further, it is through battle that he has a strong link with his dependents; there they fight as one united household, and

---

[1] When Probus re-colonized the two Germanies he let the German colonists (Laeti) into Flanders in this way, and the Ripuarian Franks held the Rhineland on a similar tenure.

[2] *de Bell. Gall.* vi, 13.

[3] 'Such valour should the knight have, who bears arms and bestrides a good horse ; in battle he must be strong and brave, or else he is not worth a groat. Otherwise let him rather be a monk in a monastery and pray every day for our sins.' (*Chanson de Roland.*)

X.   The Death of the Boar

there the lord loves his men as he does his family. *Raoul de Cambrai* describes the Count of Artois' grief when he sees the men of his 'mesnie' lying dead on the field of battle : 'His household is there, dead and covered with blood; with his right hand he blesses them ; over them he mourns and weeps, and the tears roll down to his girdle.' Even at Mansourah the old spirit was not dead, and Joinville tells us that Guy Mauvoisin covered himself and his men with glory, 'nor is this to be marvelled at, that he and his people should approve themselves well on that day; for it was told to me, by those who had knowledge of his affairs, that all his company, save but few, were knights of his own lineage or knights who were his liegemen '.

  If Roland is the perfect *bellator* of epic, William the Marshal is of history. Fighting was the dominant interest of his life. When not engaged in war, he found occupation in fighting in tournaments;[1] at one time he tourneyed every fortnight. These tournaments were very different from the chivalric contests of the fourteenth and fifteenth centuries ; there was no *courtoisie* to inspire them and no elaborate rules and conditions to regulate their risks. They were fought like battles in the open, with all the arms and weapons of war and all its manœuvres and ferocity of attack; they differed from it mainly in being voluntary, in lasting for a single day, and in doing comparatively little damage to the country in which they were waged. Even in scale they resembled real warfare ; at the tournament of Lagny over three thousand knights were engaged at once. Nor were the blows given and received less hard ; when William the Marshal was sought after one tourney to be acclaimed victor he was eventually found in a smithy, with his head on the anvil and the smith working with hammer and pincers to remove his battered helmet.

  This purely military knighthood was modified in two directions. Firstly, the actual ceremony of bestowing knighthood was brought into the province of the Church. The ancient Germanic usage had been, as Tacitus tells us, for no man to bear arms until he had reached the age of citizenship. 'Tum, in ipso concilio, vel principum aliquis, vel pater, vel

  [1] Tournaments were a French invention; Matthew Paris calls them 'Conflictus Gallici '.

propinquus scuto frameaque juvenem ornant. Hoc apud illos toga; hoc primus juventae honos.' In early feudal days the boy was dubbed knight by the accolade; so, when in *Ogier le Danois* Charles dubs his son Louis knight,

> Haucha le palme, ens el col li assist:
> 'Chevaliers soies', dist li peres, 'biaus fix,
> Et corageus envers tes anemis.'[1]

By the end of the eleventh century this ceremony was greatly changed; the initiate received a ritual bath, spent a night in solitary prayer in the church, made his Confession and received Communion, heard a sermon on the duties of knighthood—to be pure, honest, and faithful; to protect the Church, widows and orphans, and all that are desolate and oppressed. Finally he received the honour of knighthood in the name of the Trinity.

The French *Pontifical* of Guillaume Durand describes the ceremony. At the pontifical mass, as the last Alleluias of the Gradual die away, the bishop, laying the naked sword upon the altar, says: ' Bless this sword, that Thy servant may henceforth defend churches, widows, orphans, and all those who serve God, against the cruelty of heretics and infidels. Bless this sword, Holy Lord, Almighty Father, Eternal God; Bless it in the name of the coming of Christ and by the gift of the Holy Ghost the Comforter. And may Thy servant, armed with Thy love, tread all his visible enemies underfoot, and, master of victory, rest for ever protected from all attack.' Then the bishop reads from the Old Testament: ' Blessed be the Lord God who forms my hands for battle and my fingers for war. He is my salvation, he is my refuge, he sets me free.' After further prayer, the bishop puts the sword in the knight's right hand, saying, ' Take it in the name of the Father, and of the Son, and of the Holy Ghost.' Then he girds it on him as he kneels before him. The knight brandishes it three times, and sets it back in the scabbard. Then the bishop gives him the kiss of peace, and bids him ' Be a soldier peaceful, courageous, faithful, and devoted to God'. Then he solemnly blesses the knightly banner; 'his dictis, novus miles vadit in pace'. This religious consecration added not only to the moral force of

[1] ' He raised his palm, and brought it down upon his neck. " Be a knight," said the father, " fair son, and show courage in the face of thine enemies." '

XI.   The Chess Players

15th Century

chivalry but also to that of feudalism, for knight and vassal were almost synonymous terms, and the knight often received the accolade from the lord whose vassal he was. So strong was this force, indeed, that it modified even the virtues of feudalism. Not only did it increase that respect for the sanctity of the oath on which the fabric of society rested, but it also modified the idea of feudal duty. *Legalitas* was originally the feudatory's discharge of the legal duties of his position as defined by custom; but *legalitas*, under the influence of Christian chivalry, became *loyalty*: a fine idea of generous obligation owed by one man to another. Further, under the influence of this moral force, the feudal duty developed into the knightly *devoir*.

The second force that modified the purely military form of chivalry was the second class of duties that the vassal owed his lord: that of *concilium* in peace, and of administration of the lands held. Justice and mercy came to be added to the tale of feudal virtues; the thirteenth-century poem ' Carité ' tells the lord:

> Tu ki des lois tiens le droiture,
> Quant avient si gries aventure
> Ke damner t'estuet par besoigne
> Un hom por se forfaiture,
> Et destruire le Dieu faiture,
> Soiés discrés en tel essoigne
> Que pietés au cuer te poigne! . . .
> Toi le convient amer et pendre;
> Amer por chou qu'il est tes frere,
> Pendre por chou ke il est lere.[1]

In the twelfth century a great system of ducal castles was created in Normandy; new strongholds were built on the frontiers, and those of Rouen, Caen, Falaise, and Argentan were enlarged. They did not remain merely a system of frontier defence, but under Henry II became the chief administrative centres of his domain. Their *châtelains* were royal officers rather than feudal vassals; the baronial system has in it the

---

[1] ' Do thou, who upholdest the rights of the law, when the hard hap befalls that it is thy work to condemn a man for his crime and to destroy the handiwork of God, do thou have care for thy justification that pity move thy heart! It behoves thee to love him and hang him : to love him because he is thy brother, and to hang him because he is a thief.'

germ of a royal bureaucracy. It is they who develop the communications of their region :

> Bons pons fist faire, chemins haus,
> De piere, de sablon, de caus,

and it is they who, for certain dues, protect the traveller. Thus with a more developed society the fighting knight gradually became the administrator; and the rough-and-tumble of the *mêlée* was superseded by the political and tactical strategy involved in the taking of an enemy's stronghold without loss of control over the assailant's own castle and domain. The King in this respect is the archetype of baron; the *Livre des Manières*, written by Etienne de Fougères in 1178, shows him :

> Ça et la veit, sovent se torne,
> Ne repose ne ne sejorne.
> Chasteaus abat, chasteaus aorne,
> Sovent haitié, plus sovent morne.
> Ça et la veit, pas ne repose
> Que sa marche ne seit desclose.[1]

The same author again shows what importance was attributed to the judicial functions of the lord when he upbraids Henry II (Plantagenet) for spending too much time in hunting. Such a pursuit, he says, is not worthy of one who has been anointed with the holy oil. It is better to be at all times at the disposition of those who need justice, and to be ready to punish those who seek after war or discord.

The castle, then, is the crystallization of developed feudalism. It emphasizes the fact that the suzerainty of the lord is a local fact, based on the possession of land; it is the symbol of his force, which if it sometimes serves as a weapon of oppression yet also serves as a weapon of defence for the neighbouring villages. Its great hall, where lord and vassal, servant and peasant, dine together according to their degree, is an expression of the fact that they form a community within the State bound together by mutual obligations. Moreover, practically every man belonged to such a community; the story of *Les Quatre Fils*

---

[1] 'He goes here and there, often turning his path, neither resting nor staying in one place. He destroys castles and he adorns them, and is often merry and more often sad. He goes here and there, and rests not until his borderlands be freed.'

XII. From Notre-Dame de Paris
13th Century

Aymon tells that from Senlis to Orleans, from Orleans to Paris, and from Laon to Rheims, in fact in the real core of France :

> N'i trovissiés nul homme qui de mere fust nés
> Qui ne soit en chastel ou en tor enserés.[1]

The development of feudalism is reflected in the development of the castle. In the tenth century it is a wooden tower[2] with a moat ; a fortified farm, in which the lord's family leads a life like that described by Lambert d'Ardres, where the first son of the lord is a fighter, the second a hunter, the third a farmer, and the fourth a stock-raiser. In the next century wood gives place to stone, and the house becomes the fortified donjon. Jean de Colmieu, Archdeacon of Térouanne, who died in 1130, describes such a castle :

'They throw up a little hill of earth as high as they can ; they surround it by a fosse of considerable width and awful depth. On the inside edge of the fosse they set a palisade of squared logs of wood, closely bound together, which is as strong as a wall. If it is possible they strengthen this palisade by towers built at various points. On the top of the little hill they build a house, or rather a citadel, whence a man can see on all sides. No one can reach its door except by a bridge, which, thrown across the fosse and resting on coupled pillars, starts from the lowest part of the fosse and gradually rises until it reaches the top of the little hill and the door of the house, from which the master can control the whole of it.'

In the twelfth century the donjon is retained for purely defensive purposes (as at Coucy), and within the same fortified enclosure a second building—the *palais*—becomes the home of the lord and his family. Later in the century there is often a second enclosure, which affords shelter for the lord's lesser dependents and for the ' retrahants ' who seek a refuge at the castle in time of danger. Even a fortress that was not the home of its lord offered a similar plan ; Guillaume le Breton describes Cœur-de-Lion's Château Gaillard: 'He had the summit of the hill made round and walled with strong fortifications ; he cleared it of stones, and then, having flattened the interior of the enclosure, he caused a number of small habitations to be built there, to hold many people, and only kept the centre for the construction of the donjon.'

[1] 'You will find no man born of a woman who is not shut up in a castle or a tower.'

[2] The first datable stone donjon is that of Langeais, built by Foulques Nerra, Count of Anjou, in 992.

The creation of the *palais* shows more clearly than anything else how the late twelfth and the thirteenth centuries were years in which men were not entirely absorbed in the struggle to obtain a working scheme of life, but had time to seek grace as well as strength. In and for its hall were created not only courtesy and the refinements of honour, but also much that is of material beauty—tapestry, painting, and the decorative arts of everyday life:

> And beauty making beautiful old rhyme
> In praise of ladies dead and lovely knights.

This mediaeval feeling for the graces of life appeared first in France; Brunetto Latino tells us in his *Livre dou Trésor* of 1265:

'Les Ytaliens, qui souvent guerroyent entre eux, se délitent à faire hautes tours et maisons de pierres; et, si c'est hors de ville, ils font fossés et palis, et murs, et tourelles, et ponts, et portes coulisses, et sont garnis de mangoniaux et de saiettes, et de toutes choses qui appartienent à la guerre. . . . Mais les français font maisons grandes et planières, et paintes, et chambres lées, pour avoir joie et délit sans noise et sans guerre. Et pour ce savent mieux faire préaux et vergers et pommiers autour de leur habitacle que autre gent.'[1]

This new spirit made as great a modification in thirteenth-century chivalry as religion had made in the military knighthood of the early Middle Ages. The boy of noble birth comes to the castle to serve as a page; the *Ordene de Chevalerie* tells us that it befits him to serve before others serve him, for otherwise he will not understand the nobility of lordship. So, in the romance, Galeran goes to the Court of Lorraine and 'serves' there as squire, at table, in the chase, in the tourney, for two years. Then the time comes for him and his companions to be dubbed knights, and there is a great feast. Galeran puts on hauberk, shoes, and helmet; a cloak of Indian samite, embroidered like his banner with his double eagle before and behind. The Duke does him the honour of putting on his right spur, and gives him a splendid Eastern sword, 'claire et lettrée, à pommeau d'or'. Then he asks a knight who is present 'lui

[1] 'The Italians, who often make war among themselves, delight in making high towers and houses of stone; and if they are outside the city, they make fosses and palisades and walls, turrets and bridges and portcullises, and furnish them with mangonels and arrows and all things that belong to war. . . . But the French build houses that are large and open and painted, with spacious rooms, to have joy and delight without injury and war. Wherefore they know better than other folk how to plant gardens and orchards and apple trees round their habitations.'

faire honneur de l'épée', and the knight girds him with the
sword, and then with his right hand gives him

> La collée qui signifie
> L'Ordre de chevalerie;
> Et si li a dit au donner:
> 'Chevalier, Dieux te puit tourner
> A si grand honneur en la somme
> Qu'il face de ton corps proudomme
> En penser, en dit et en fait.'[1]

Then the Duchess hangs the shield with the golden eagle round
his neck, and all the company go to mass, which the newly
dubbed knights hear in helmet and armour. After the service
they receive the sacrament, and then, taking off their armour
and donning robes of silk, 'qui sont faites en la terre aux
Maures', sit down to feast. The next day they tourney for the
first time. Afterwards Galeran goes with a train of thirty
white pack-horses and ten Spanish chargers to Metz. The streets,
strewn with herbs, are full of knights on horseback, of squires
carrying presents to ladies, of young men airing their hawks.
Coloured banners and shields hang out of the windows, and the
walls are gay with festival draperies. The market is full:
venison, game, fish in the cool corner, wax, pepper, and spice
are being sold. The shouting money-changers, with their
wares of jewels and plate; the wandering mountebanks, with
their lions and leopards and bears, the fiddlers and singers, and
over all the church bells ringing through the town, fill the air
with gay and cheerful sounds, and give the new knights spirit
for the morrow's jousting.

But if we have to turn to the romances for the life of youth,
more sober sources describe the life of the *châtelain* who has
settled down. The *Quatre Ages de l'homme* advises him how
he is to spend the day. He is to begin with a triple sign of the
Cross and prayer; then, before getting up, he is to think of what
is to be done in the course of the day for himself, for others, or
for 'un commun profit de païs', and to repeat it to himself
three times that he may not forget. Then he is to hear mass;
to give alms, if only a little; to dress very carefully, and to see

---

[1] 'The accolade which signifies the order of knighthood; and as he gives
it he says, "Knight, may God so dispose you to high honour in all things that
He may make you a *prud'homme* in thought, in word, and in deed".'

his nails are clean; and then to proceed with his business diligently. At midday it should be finished, so that he may eat and drink in peace. The sort of meal he had we may guess from Fra Salimbene's account of St. Louis' dinner on a *maigre* day in 1248: 'primo cerasas, postea panem, vinum . . . postea . . . fabas recentes cum lacte decoctas; pisces et cancros; pastillos anguillarum; risum cum lacte amigdularum et pulvere cynamomi; anguillas assatas cum optimo salsamento; turtas et juncatas; fructus. . . .' Then, having eaten, he is to rest an hour, and afterwards is the time to amuse himself, 'por avoir remede et repos in son cuer'. The *Roman de Joufroi* describes Madame Agnès de Tonnerre, shut up in a tower by a jealous husband, consoling herself by looking from her window into the square below. There, under the shade of a splendid pear tree,

> joent li chevalier
> As dez et autres jous divers.
> Enqui est tot an li josters
> Et les dances et les caroeles.
> Enqui vienent et fous et foles
> Et menestreil et jugleor.[1]

There the story-tellers tell of Priam and Pyramus; of fair Helen, of Ulysses, Hector, Achilles, Aeneas and weeping Dido; of Lavinia, Tydeus and Eteocles, Alexander, Cadmus, Jason, Narcissus, Pluto and Orpheus, Hero and Leander, Daedalus and Icarus, Goliath and David, Samson and Delilah; of Julius Caesar, who was so brave that he crossed the sea without invoking the name of Christ; of the Round Table and of Charlemagne; of the squire of Nanteuil and of Olivier de Verdun.[2] One plays the 'lai de chèvrefeuille', another the song of Tintagel; one plays the harp, another the lute; one the flute, another the fife; one makes his marionettes dance, another juggles with knives.

The development of château life had no less effect on women, since their lives were bound up with those of the fighting nobles. In the early days of chivalry their life was almost incredibly hard; they lived exposed to every discomfort and danger. They shared in the victories and defeats of their lords and masters,

---

[1] 'The knights play at dice and other games. There, all the year round, is jousting and dancing and carolling. There come fools and jesters and minstrels and jongleurs.'

[2] The list is taken from *Flamenca* (1234).

XIV.   Jeanne d'Armagnac
Wife of Jean, duc de Berry
Palais de Justice, Poitiers
14th Century

and helped them with advice. In the *Chanson de Guillaume* the hero comes back, beaten and despairing, to his wife:

> 'Or m'en fuirai en estrange regné
> A saint Michiel al Peril de la mer
> U a Saint Piere, le bon apostre Deu,
> U en un guast ou ne soie trovez:
> La devendrai hermites ordenez
> Et tu nonein, si fai tun chief veler.
> 'Sire', dist ele, 'Ço ferum nus assez,
> Quant nos avrom nostre siecle mené.'[1]

But gradually, as life grew more settled and more civilized, the castle became the woman's sphere. Over their wheels and frames they sang the *Chansons de Toile*, with the rhythm of the clashing loom:

> Bele Yolanz en chambre coie
> Sur ses genouz pailes desploie,
> Cost un fil d'or, l'autre de soie.
> Sa male mere la chastoie
> > 'Chastoi vos en
> > Bele Yolanz . . .'
>
> 'Mere de coi me chastoiez?
> Est ceu de coudre ou de taillier
> Ou de filer ou de broissier?
> Ou se c'est de trop sommillier?' —
> > 'Chastoi vos en
> > Bele Yolanz.
>
> Ne de coudre, ne de taillier,
> Ne de filer, ne de broissier
> Ne ce n'est de trop sommillier . . .
> Mais trop parlez au chevalier.
> > Chastoi vos en
> > Bele Yolanz.'

By the thirteenth century the *Chansons de Toile* had fallen out of use, and the life of the *jeune fille comme il faut* could be thus described in *Galeran*:

> Que je ne face aultre mestier
> Le jour fors lire mon saultier

[1] 'So will I flee into a strange land, to St. Michael by the peril of the sea, or to St Peter the good apostle of God, or to some desert where I shall not be found: there will I become an ordained hermit, and thou shalt be a nun and shalt veil thy head.' 'Sire,' said she, 'we shall do those things soon enough when we have finished our life in the world.'

Et faire oeuvre d'or ou de soie,
Oÿr de Thebes ou de Troye
Et en ma herpe lays noter
Et aux echez autruy mater
Ou mon oisel sur mon poign pestre.
Souvent ouÿ dire a mon maistre
Que tel us vient de gentilesse.[1]

The women of the house helped to receive and entertain distinguished guests. The romance of *Guillaume de Dôle*, written about 1200, describes the Emperor's messenger paying a polite visit after dinner to Guillaume's mother. She tells him:

‘ Biaus filz, ce fu ça en arriers
Que les dames et les roïnes
Soloient fere lor cortines,
Et chanter les chançons d'istoire.’
‘ Ha! ma très douce dame, voire,
Dites nous en, se vos volez . . .’
Quant ele ot sa chanson chantée,
‘ Certes, mout s'est bien aquitée’,
Fet cil, ‘ madame votre mere.’ [2]

Already a century earlier Guibert de Nogent had been lamenting the advent of new manners:

‘ Alas, how miserably . . . maidenly modesty and honour have fallen off, and the mothers' guardianship hath decayed both in appearance and in fact, so that in all their behaviour nothing can be noted but unseemly mirth, wherein are no sounds but of jest, with winking eyes, and babbling tongues, and wanton gait, and most ridiculous manners. The quality of their garments is so unlike to that frugality of the past that in the widening of their sleeves, the tightening of their bodices, their shoes of cordovan morocco with twisted beaks—nay, in their whole person, we may see how shame is cast aside. Each thinketh to have touched the lowest step of misery if she lack the regard of lovers and measureth her glory of nobility or courtliness by the ampler number of such suitors. . . . Thus and in such-like ways is our modern age corrupted.’

His laments are echoed with equal force and futility by

---

[1] ‘ I should do no other work in the day but read my psalter, work in gold or silk, hear the story of Thebes or Troy, play tunes on my harp, checkmate some one at chess, or feed the hawk on my wrist. I have often heard my master say that such a way of life was gentle.’
[2] ‘ Fair son, it was in past times that ladies and queens used to make their hangings and sing songs spinning.’ ‘ Indeed, sweet lady, sing us some, if you will.’ When she had sung her song, ‘ In truth your lady mother has acquitted herself well,’ said he.

XV.   St. Martin, St. Jerome and St. Gregory

Chartres Cathedral.   First half of 13th Century

Bernard, but occasionally the Church took a more practical view. Etienne de Bourbon tells us that he knew a holy man who had the gift of working miracles, who lived in the monastery of St. Antoine at Paris. One day some ladies came to him to ask him to pray for a lady of the Countess of Montfort's household who suffered from dreadful headaches. He consented, but asked to see her. When she came, he said, 'Promise me first, madam, to take off all those vain adornments, all that proud scaffolding which surmounts your head, and then I will pray Our Lord for you in full confidence'. The lady refused; the sacrifice was too great. But her headaches grew worse and worse, until she resigned herself and laid before the servant of God her false hair, her golden circlet, and all the rest, promising that she would never wear anything of the kind again. The holy man at once began to pray; but the miracle had already been effected, and the pain was gone.

The preachers must not be allowed to make us forget the part played by the feudal noblewoman in mediaeval history; and, indeed, the preachers who hurl the most violent diatribes against women in general are loudest in praise of the saintliness of their own mothers. In all the historic dramas of the Middle Ages women play leading and often noble parts:

> Où est la tres sage Helloïs
> Pour qui fut chastré et puis moyne
> Pierre Esbaillart à Saint Denis?
> Pour son amour ot cest essoyne.
> Semblablement, où est la royne
> Qui commanda que Buridan
> Fust gecté en ung sac en Saine?
> Mais où sont le neiges d'antan!

> La royne Blanche comme lis,
> Qui chantoit à voix de seraine;
> Berte au grant pié, Bietris, Allis;
> Haremburgis qui tint le Maine,
> Et Jehanne, la bonne Lorraine,
> Qu'Englois brulerent à Rouan;
> Où sont elles, Vierge souvraine?
> Mais où sont les neiges d'antan!

The *oratores*, those whose life is devoted to prayer, may seem at first to be outside the sphere of feudalism. But the Church

grew up sufficiently under the shadow of the Roman
Empire to rest upon a land basis; the lords of the ecclesiastical
provinces—in other words the bishops—stood side by side,
feudally speaking, with the seigneurs of the King. The
'Twelve Peers of France' at the coronation of Philip Augustus
were six laymen: the Dukes of Normandy, Burgundy, and
Guienne, and the Counts of Champagne, Flanders, and Toulouse;
and six ecclesiastics: the Archbishop of Rheims, and the
Bishops of Laon, Noyon, Châlons, Beauvais, and Langres.
Even the theory of the organization of the Church became influenced by feudalism, and we find the bishop holding certain
offices to be 'fiefs incorporeal' and demanding liege-homage
from his dean, chancellor, precentor, and other officers. So
Bishop Robert of Coutances, who died in 1048, gave the prebends
of his cathedral to his relations and made them do homage for
them. Moreover, in much disturbed times there was a tendency
for royal lands to be added, as it were for safe custody, to the
bishop's domain, which generally lay compactly, in comparative
security, round his cathedral city. Therefore he held land not
only as bishop, exercising ecclesiastical rights, but also as lord,
exercising seigneurial rights. The Bishop of Puy, as Count of
Velay, holds on his seal not only the pastoral crozier, but also
the naked sword of secular jurisdiction; the Chapter of Roye
in Picardy has on its seal an armed and mounted knight. Up
to 1788 the Count-Bishop of Cahors had the right, when he
said mass in state, to have upon the altar his helmet, cuirass,
and sword.

The Church, indeed, took its place in the feudal system, and
though its functions were extra-feudal, its activities were sometimes those of feudalism. Turpin, the fighting archbishop of
the *Chanson de Roland*, is the type of many :

> Par le camp vait Turpin, li arcesvesque,
> Tel coronet ne chantat unches messe
> Ki de sun cors feïst tantes proecces.
> Dist al paien : 'Deus tut mal te tramette
> Tel as ocis dunt al coer me regrette.'
> Sun bon ceval i ad fait esdemetre
> Si l'ad ferut sur l'escut de Tulette
> Qui mort l'abat desur l'herbe verte.[1]

[1] 'Over the field went Turpin the archbishop. Never did a clerk sing mass
who in his own person had done such gallant deeds. He said to the infidel :

XVI.   Two Labourers

Relief from Notre-Dame de Paris

13th Century

Hugh de Noyers, Bishop of Auxerre in the late twelfth century, took up arms against the nobles and resisted even the King. His palace was 'surrounded by wide fosses, to which water is brought from afar at great expense, bounded by huge palisades, dominated by a donjon with ramparts and turrets and a drawbridge.' When Richard Cœur-de-Lion was asked by one of the papal legates to free Philippe de Dreux, Bishop of Beauvais, whom he held prisoner, he indignantly replied that Philip had not been captured as a bishop but as a knight in full armour, a knight, moreover, who was 'a robber, tyrant, and incendiary, who did nothing but devastate Richard's lands day and night'. So in 1356 the Bishops of Châlons, Sens, and Melun cover themselves with glory at Poitiers, and the Archbishop of Sens dies sword in hand on the field of Agincourt. It is because they formed part of feudal society, because they shouldered their share of feudal duties and responsibilities, that the bishops of France were able to christianize feudalism.

There remain the people : *laboratores*, men who worked with their hands. We have seen how far the feudal obligations of the lord to the King affected his life, and we shall find the obligations of the villein to his lord moulding his life even more straitly. The serf was not even free in person, and his dues were arbitrary and fixed by his master. The relation between serf and master is indeed in a sense unfeudal, since it rests upon no contract; its origin is to be sought in the Roman institution of slavery. So even the serf's children were not his own, as is shown by many deeds for the division of families of servile birth.

'We, the monks of Marmoutier and Gautier Renaud, held in common men and women serfs, who were to be divided between us. Therefore, in the year of the Incarnation of Our Lord 1087, on the sixth day of June, in the time of Abbot Bernard, we proceeded to the division of the male and female children of several families. We have received for our share, among the children of Renaud de Villana, a boy, Barthélemi, and three girls, Hersende, Milesende, and Letgarde ; and among the children of Guascelin, a girl, Aremburge, and a boy, Gautier. There was excepted from the division one very young girl-

"God send you all ill. You have killed one whom my heart mourns." He drives his good horse forward and strikes the infidel on his shield of Toledo with such a blow that he lays him dead on the green grass.'

child, who remained in her cradle.   If she lives, she is to be our common property until the conclusion of an agreement that shall assign her to one or other lordship.'

Even in the time of Robert the Pious Adalberon of Laon was preaching: 'This unhappy class owns nothing which is not bought by hard toil.   Who can estimate, in counting on the beads of an abacus, the sorrows, the toil, the weariness which the poor serfs have to endure?'   Sometimes the lord took the view that they came of a class from which nothing could be expected.   Robert of Blois, like many another thirteenth-century moralist, warns the knight to have no confidence in his serfs: 'Serf sont por que servir doivent', and they have no sense of fidelity:

> A lor gré voudroient chascun jor
> Tel genz avoir noveaul seignor,
> Qu'il ne sevent de cuer amer.[1]

This point of view led to the diminution of serfdom by enfranchisement, whether individual, collective, or regional;[2] the lord gained considerable sums of money from those he freed, and the better feeling and more defined relation of the villein made for better administration on his estate.   By the end of the Middle Ages serfdom was dead.   The free villein was free in person, but was bound—*adscriptus*—to cultivate a particular piece of land belonging to some one else, and owed fixed dues and service at fixed seasons.   The *Conte des Vilains de Verson* gives an account of such service.

'In June the peasants must cut and pile the hay and carry it to the manor house.   In August they must reap and carry in the convent's grain; their own grain lies exposed to wind and rain while they hunt out the assessor of the *champart* and carry his share to the barn.   On the Nativity of the Virgin the villein owes the pork-due, one pig in eight; at St. Denis's Day the *cens*; at Christmas the fowl, fine and good, and thereafter the grain-due of two *sétiers* of barley and three quarters of wheat; on Palm Sunday the sheep-due; at Easter he must plough, sow, and harrow.   When there is building the tenant must

---

[1] 'Such men would like each day to have a new lord, for they know not how to love sincerely.'

[2] Philip Augustus freed those of Chambly, Beaumont-sur-Oise, Orléans, and other fiefs.   St. Louis many more.   His brother the Count of Poitiers freed all upon his domain.   Many more were freed by the great abbeys, St. Germain and the rest

XVII. The Acorn Harvest

bring stone and serve the masons; he must also haul the convent's wood for two deniers a day. If he sells his land, he owes the lord a thirteenth of its value: if he marries his daughter outside the seigniory, he pays a fine. He must grind his grain at the seigneurial mill and bake his bread at the seigneurial oven, where the customary charges do not satisfy the attendants, who grumble and threaten to leave his bread unbaked.' [1]

Garin le Lorrain describes the typical villein, Rigaut [2]: with enormous arms and massive limbs, his eyes separated from each other by a hand's breadth, his shoulders large, his chest deep, his hair bristling, and his face black as coal. He goes for six months without washing, and no water but rain ever touches his face. The sculptured and illuminated calendars show the brighter side of his life. January is a month of rest and feast days; he drinks in peace. February is a dull month; he sits by the fire at home to dry himself after his work. In March he tends the vines. April is for him, as for the noble, the best month in the year.

> Biau fut li tans, resplandissent li jor;
> Ces eues doces reperent en vigor,
> Foillissent bois et traient a verdor;
> Cil oiselet chantent par grant doçor,
> Chevalerie quierent tornoieor,
> Dame qui aime a plus fresche color
> E mielz se vest et de plus bel ator . . . [3]

and the villein sees the corn sprout and prunes the vines. In May, while the gentleman walks, and hunts and hawks, the villein rests in the shade. In June he is busy with the hay-making, in July and August with the harvest, and in September with the vintage. In October the wine is made and the sowing is done; in November he takes the pigs to gather acorns in the forest, and gets in his own store of wood for the winter; and then at Christmas there is once more feasting. The villeins live in a *villete* or hamlet of scattered *mesnils* or cottages, such as is described in *Galeran*: each house alone in its little field, shut in with an old thorn hedge and a ditch bridged by a plank. The *manse* or cottage has three separate buildings; one for grain, one for fodder, and one for the family.

[1] Cf. the *corvée* of the Egyptian fellaheen under Turkish rule.
[2] A similar description is to be found in *Aucassin et Nicolette*.
[3] *Les Narbonnais.*

There a fire of peat and faggots crackles in an immense chimney. There is a pothook for the kettle, a trivet, a shovel, and heavy fire-dogs; a saucepan and a ladle, by the side an oven, and next to it a huge bed that can shelter all the family at once. On the other side are a cupboard, a table, a bench, a cheese-press, a crock and some baskets. Besides such furniture the villein owns a mortar, a ladder, fishing tackle, hedging gloves, a plough, a billhook, spade, knife, shears and harrow, and a little cart. He has a small garden with a dog for watchman, and at least one cow.[1] The thirteenth-century *Dit des vingt-trois manières de vilains* describes types that we all know. Some say to the wayfarer who asks his way, 'You know it better than I do'; some sit at their cottage doors on Sunday to mock at passers-by, and some are against everybody—God, the saints, the Church, and the gentry. There is the poacher; the man who is always bringing his case before the bailiff, saying that his grandfather had rights of pasturage over such and such fields; the miser, and the wastrel.

The villeins were by no means crushed by knightly oppression. In 987 those of Normandy rose against their lords to demand rights of chase, of fishery, and of administration of their own affairs, legal and judicial; and this was the first of many such revolts. The *Roman de Rou* describes

> Li paisan et li vilain,
> Cil del boscage et cil del plain

saying of their lords

> Nus somes homes cum il sunt,
> Tex membres avum cum ils unt;
> Et altresi grans cors avum;
> Et altretant sofrir povum.

The *Besant de Dieu*, written about 1230, describes the sins of clerk and noble, but does not consider the peasant blameless:

> Car il ne prenent mie a gré
> Lor sofreite e lor povreté
> Et sont felons et envios
> Et mesdisant et orguillos
> Et plains d'envie et de luxure.

---

[1] The description is taken from the thirteenth-century *fabliau* ' *De l'oustille-ment au vilain* '. The resemblance between the villein's *manse* and a cottage in the remoter parts of modern Finland is striking.

XVIII.   Peasants cutting wood.   Tapestry

Late 15th Century

[Tosjors] li est avis por veir
Que se il puet del riche aveir,
Coment que seit, n'est pas pecché.[1]

None the less, many men held a high ideal of what the relations between lord and man should be. Etienne de Fougères in 1178 said :

Grainour foi deit sire a son home
Que non a seignor et a dome;
Molt devon chiers aveir nos homes,
Quar li vilein portent les somes
Dont nos vivon, quant que nos summes,
Et chevaliers et cleres et domes.[2]

Though he admits that the poor peasant grumbles too much against God and man, and cheats the Church and his lord of their dues when it is possible, he pities his lot :

Terres arer, norrir aumaille,
Sor le vilain est la bataile.
Quar chevalier et clerc sanz faille
Vivent de ce que il travaille.[3]

In the time of Philip Augustus Jacques de Vitry preached :

'All the peasant amasses in a year by stubborn work, the knight, the noble, devours in an hour. Not content with his pay as soldier, not content with his revenues and with the annual tax levied upon his subjects, he furthers despoils them by illicit taxes and heavy exactions. The poor are exhausted, the fruit of their years of pain and sorrow is extorted from them. . . . The great must make themselves loved by the small. They must be careful not to inspire hate. The humble must not be scorned: if they can aid us, they can also do us harm. You know that many serfs have killed their masters or have burnt their houses.'

But the great movements in which both lord and peasant played their parts side by side helped to heal the breach

---

[1] 'For they do not take cheerfully their need and poverty, and are dishonest and envious, and backbiting, and proud and full of envy and vice. Indeed, he [the peasant] thinks that if he can get anything from the rich man, by whatever means, it is no sin.'

[2] 'A lord owes greater loyalty to a tenant than to a lord or a lady ; very dear should we hold our men, for the villeins bear the burdens by which we live whether we be knights, clerks, or ladies.'

[3] 'To plough the fields and feed the beasts is the struggle for the peasant, for the knight and the priest live on his work.'

between them, and we find the Lord of Bourlemont saying to
Joinville : ' You are going oversea ; now take heed how you
come back ; for no knight, be he poor or be he rich, can come
back without dishonour if he leaves in the hands of the
Saracens the meaner folk of Our Lord, in whose company he
went forth.'

The feudal order was established to meet a national need ;
like knighthood, it became ennobled by the feudal virtues,
' souffrance, service, valeur, honneur '; and like all social
systems it had its good and bad points. Its chief source of
weakness was that while definite relations were assured
vertically between lord and vassal, and between vassals and
their dependents, the horizontal relations *inter pares* were not
regulated at all. As a consequence twelfth-century France
was divided into provinces, whose inhabitants formed so many
small nations living in a state of mutual hatred ; these provinces
were divided into a multitude of seigneuries and fiefs, whose
owners lived in a perpetual state of private war, and further
rivalries were prolonged between city and city, village and
village, valley and valley, until war seemed to spring spon-
taneously from the soil itself. It was in an attempt to mitigate
this evil that the Church for the first time played an important
part in the feudal world. It did not attempt the impossible
task of bringing war to an end, but strove to impose on feudalism the Augustinian view, ' Pacem habere debet voluntas, bellum
necessitas '. The Archbishop of Bordeaux in 969 at the
Council of Charroux initiated the *Pax Dei* by anathematizing
all those who in the course of a private war broke into
churches, stole goods from the poor, or struck a clerk. The
movement came from the Church, and first concerned those
who served her or were her dependents. But in the next year
the ordinance was repeated, and infringed on the temporal
sphere, for merchants and their goods were included under its
protection. Gradually it grew into a *pactum pacis*, a league
not of nations but of seigneurs, bound together to keep its rules.
The oath administered at Beauvais in 1023 is typical :

' I will not invade in any way churches, or the crypts of churches,
unless it be to seize malefactors who have broken the peace or committed homicide; I will not assault clerks or monks not bearing
secular arms. I will carry off neither ox, nor cow, nor any other

XIX. Cottage at La Béraudie, Cahors

beast of burden. I will do nothing to cause men to lose their possessions on account of their lord's war, and I will not beat them to make them give up their property. From the first day of May until All Saints' Day I will seize neither horse, nor mare, nor foal from the pastures. I will neither destroy nor burn houses, nor root up nor cut down the vines under pretext of war.'

The great development of the *pactum pacis* was in Berri; by 1038 every man at the age of fifteen, whether clerk or layman, was sworn into the diocesan forces for keeping the peace. For the first time the whole population of a district was enrolled as a *garde nationale*. A fresh development was the *Truga Dei*, or Truce of God, which ordained a close time in which private war might not be waged. At the Council of Elne in 1027 this truce was proclaimed from the ninth hour of Saturday to the first of Monday, to leave Sunday free. By 1041 it was extended from Wednesday night to Monday morning: Thursday, the Council of Nice declared, was sacred as the day of the Ascension; Friday as that of the Passion; Saturday as that of the Adoration at the Tomb; and Sunday as the day of the Resurrection. In the same year private war was interdicted from Advent to Epiphany and from Septuagesima till Easter. Thirteen years later this was extended to Pentecost, and the feasts of the Virgin, St. John Baptist, St. Peter in Vinculis, St. Lawrence, St. Michael, St. Martin, and the Ember days were also included. Further, a new sanction for its keeping was devised in addition to excommunication. When once a *forma pacis* had been legislated by a Council, *Judices pacis*, Justices of the Peace, were appointed to decide when it had been broken. Thus the Church appointed a new legislature, judicature, and executive to do the work which the temporal power was as yet too weak to undertake.

> Gaudet lancea falx, gaudet spatha
> Devenire vomer:
> Pax ditat imos, pauperat superbos.
> Salve, summe Pater, fer et omnibus
> Integram salutem,
> Quicumque pacis diligunt quietem.[1]

[1] 'The lance is happy to become a scythe, the sword to be a ploughshare. Peace enriches the poor, impoverishes the proud. Hail, Almighty Father, give thy perfect well-being to all men who long for the rest of peace.' (Fulbert of Rheims, d. 1029.)

III

TOWN LIFE

THE second half of the eleventh century witnessed a general revolution in Europe as widespread and as far reaching as that which began three generations ago with the French Revolution. In things spiritual the Gregorian movement sought to make the clergy dependent on the Papacy and independent of the local state, substituting for a territorial and proprietary Church one that should be universal and free ; in things intellectual Anselm and Berengar of Tours, each the head of a flourishing school, were precursors of later scholastic thought ; the Crusades enlarged the horizon of feudalism ; and in temporal things the establishment of the Latin kingdom of Jerusalem and of the Norman kingdoms of England and Sicily led to a great awakening of communication and trade. All these combined to stimulate the growth of towns ; the Gregorian movement helped to weaken the hold of bishops of the old type over the cities of their diocese ; the growth of men's intellectual interests added scholars and students to the urban population ; the Crusading Truce of God with its protection of merchants and its associations for keeping the peace improved economic conditions ; and the Crusades themselves, and the Norman Conquest, opened up new routes ; Western Europe began to communicate through its length and breadth along great highways of trade. It is along the line of these great trade routes that the towns develop ; in Northern France, south of a line from Cologne to Bruges, and along the line of the Rhine into Northern Italy, from Cologne to Venice. The chief centres of development in France are the Oise, Aisne, Somme, Lys, and Scheldt. The age was one of danger and instability ; even the balance between production and population was precarious, and forty-eight years of the eleventh century were years of famine. Because of this there was movement ; whatever the law, starvation will drive labourers to seek new fields of toil, artisans to found new centres of industry; troubled times when justice is rare will compel men from all parts to seek it where it can be found, whether in the cathedral city, the lord's castle, or the King's court.

Pilgrimage brought yet other cohorts upon the road, and helped to make the Church the protector of travellers against feudal oppression. How necessary was such protection in the eleventh century is shown by such documents as this:

'I, Landru the Fat, seduced and tempted by the greed that often creeps into the hearts of worldly men, admit that I have stopped the merchants of Langres who passed through my domain. I took their merchandise from them and kept it until the day when the Bishop of Langres and the Abbot of Cluny came to me to demand reparation. I had kept for myself a part of what I had taken and restored the rest. The merchants to obtain this remainder, and to be able in the future to cross my land without fear, consented to pay me a certain sum for tribute. This first sin suggested to me the idea of a second, and I undertook to impose and to cause to be imposed by my officers, an exaction called a toll on all those who crossed my territory for business or for pilgrimage. The monks of Cluny, knowing that my predecessors had never levied a tax of this kind, complained strongly and asked me, through my brother Bernard, *Chambrier* of their abbey, to give up this unjust exaction, hateful in the eyes of God. To buy it off and assure safety to travellers, they have given me the sum of three hundred sous.'

By the end of the twelfth century the town enters literature. The *Philippide* of Guillaume le Breton describes Ghent, proud of its turreted houses, of its treasures and its large population; Ypres, famous for its wool dyeing; Arras, an ancient city filled with riches and eager for prosperity; Lille with its wealthy merchants and the brilliant textiles it exports to foreign lands; Angers with its vineyards, Tours with its grain, and Nantes, carrying on a trade in salmon and lampreys with distant countries. Towns even invade the feudal *Chansons de geste*; in *Aubri le Bourguignon* are descriptions of Arras, Courtrai, and Lille, in *Aiol* of Poitiers and Orléans.

The eleventh century was an age of lordship and vassalage; the twelfth of brotherhood and equality. In every rank men lived in close and corporate association with their compeers; in the Church, in the Orders of monks and canons; in the battle-field, in the Orders of Templars and Hospitallers; in centres of learning, in the new guilds of masters; in town and village, in political and religious confraternities; and in street and workshop, in guilds of craftsmen and traders.

In the eleventh century a man had his proper place in a society that was either feudal, ecclesiastical, or agricultural. But while the feudal structure regulated the relation between men and their lords, it left the relation between man and man undefined and unsanctified by an oath. Yet men were bound together on an equal footing by their very sufferings at the hands of their lord, and their sense of comradeship was soon expressed in formal brotherhood. The Church, before whom all men were equal, by the institution of the *pactum pacis* enlisted men into a quasi-religious confraternity with the political aim of restraining the feudal abuse of war, and other such societies of men sworn together against feudal excesses soon came into being. Indeed such were the needs of the time that any confraternity of men sworn to give mutual aid was apt to become hostile to the feudal order. In 1182, for instance, the Virgin of Puy appeared to a carpenter of that town,[1] bearing the Child and a scroll with the legend 'Agnus Dei, qui tollis peccata mundi, dona nobis pacem'. She bade him go to the bishop and ask him to found a confraternity of all those who wished to keep the peace. The brotherhood was founded, each member wearing on his hood or *capuchon* the leaden pilgrim's sign of the Virgin of Puy. But this devout brotherhood of peace-lovers sought peace actively by exterminating the brigands of the Auvergne, Berri, Aquitaine, and Gascony. Then, when the brigands had been dealt with, they turned against the nobles who oppressed the countryside. The chronicler of Laon, who had at first been much impressed by their piety and usefulness, by 1184 has changed his note. The nobles, he tells us, trembled on every side; they no longer dared levy from their men any but the legal dues. 'This mad and undisciplined body had reached the crowning point of its insanity. Its members dared to inform the counts, viscounts, and princes that they must treat all those subject to them with greater kindness, under pain of feeling the effects of their anger.' But feudalism was

[1] A contemporary chronicler states that the vision was stage-managed by the canons of Puy because brigands were diminishing the influx of pilgrims to the shrine.

too strong for the Capuchonnés, and suppressed them as they had suppressed the brigands.

None the less other confraternities were instituted, all avowedly religious in intention, and many working for political ends. For the most part they have left no written documents and have passed out of history ;[1] but the traces of their work are clear enough to indicate their importance in securing collective rights. The merchant confraternity of the Assumption, for instance, founded about 1110, created the commune of Mantes ; the brotherhood of the Saint Esprit acted as the governing body of the city of Marseilles, and similar corporations ruled Avignon, Arles, Digne, and many other cities of the south before they were formally enfranchised. At Poitiers in the time of St. Louis the 'confrérie de St. Hilaire' included the hundred men who formed the corporation ; it was in fact the municipal body, though its statutes were pious ones dealing only with such matters as the burial rites of its members. In many places the name given to the commune in the eventual charter shows what its origin has been ; that given by the Count of Flanders to the town of St. Omer in 1127 simply confirms the privileges of the guild without changing its name ; the charter of Arras confirms its *Charité* and that of Lille its *Amitié*. Similarly the characteristic French institution of a rural commune which includes the villages and hamlets of the countryside, sometimes, as in Ponthieu and Laonnais, as many as fifteen in number, arises from a religious confraternity covering the same area. Pious brotherhoods, indeed, were so far identified with political activities that in some districts they came under the ban both of the Law and the Church. Philippe le Bel tried in vain to abolish all the confraternities of Paris and the other towns of his domain, and they were forbidden by the Councils of Toulouse (1229), Montpellier and Arles (1234), Valence (1248), and Avignon (1281 and 1326). The Council of 1326 stated : 'They meet under pretext of brotherhood once a year in a fortified place, and, taking a mutual oath, swear to defend each other against all comers, and to give each other aid in all circumstances. It often happens that they dress alike, with particular badges, and that they elect a head or mayor, whom they swear to obey in

[1] Exceptions are the Charité of Valenciennes, before 1070, and the guild of St. Martin de Canigou, c. 1195.

all things. Such misdeeds offend justice, entail murder and pillage, destroy peace and security, and end in the oppression of the poor and innocent.'

The communal movement started in 1076 at Cambrai and continued for two centuries until it died out with the death of Louis IX in 1270. It was a rising of commerce and industry against feudal exploitation, with the object of constituting a sworn association of townsmen as a collective feudatory.

The movement was in fact less destructive than constructive. The people were not anti-feudal in theory, however often in practice they might find themselves in conflict with their overlord. Indeed the lord, civil or ecclesiastical, alone made town life possible; the body of artisans who collected round the monastery, the cathedral, or the castle were as dependent upon its protection as any other vassals; they too were *laboratores*, but their only holdings were their cottages and gardens, and their labour lay not in the fields but in the workshops. In virtue of these differences they sought relief from the burdens of the agriculturists, forced labour, frequent payments, and restrictions upon freedom of movement and freedom of buying and selling. Their economic needs drew them together into industrial and commercial centres of population, and these demanded to be treated as communities. They did not ask for the overthrow of the feudal system, but for a place within it that should recognize their peculiar economic and political interests; and their efforts, when fully successful, established what has been called a *collective seigneury*,[1] standing as a community in the relation of vassal to lord or king, and owing the obligations of homage, fealty, and communal military service. Even this was often limited to the actual defence of the town; at Cambrai it was decreed that 'neither the bishop nor the emperor can impose tax or tribute, or can order out the militia, except for the good keeping and defence of the city, and that only between cockcrow and night'.

A full-grown commune aimed at more than obtaining fixed feudal payments. A civil code might enable the poorest class to escape servile dues, it might satisfy the merchants and the artisans

[1] So the Hôtel de Ville is made like a noble house, with a machicolated tower, surmounted by a weathercock with the town arms, a great hall, chapel, and prison.

XX.   Town Hall of St. Antonin, Tarn-et-Garonne

12th Century

who got fixed fines and tolls, but the leading townsmen, holders
of burgage tenements and possibly even knights, realized that
unless they got their own magistrates little was really gained.
Something more was needed than their lord's plighted word, or
even than guilds of merchants and artisans, which might form
the basis of a successful rising, but could not maintain what had
been thus secured. Thus by the explicit grant of the lord, with
his tacit consent, or in opposition to his will, the townsmen
endeavoured to secure by a constitution such a measure of self-
government as was exemplified in the *établissements* of Rouen
—by a mayor, by *jurats*, who formed an administrative council,
and often also by *échevins*, judges in the town court of common
law. Their real functions are those of the officers of the confraternity, for the commune is still a brotherhood. The charters
of Senlis, Compiègne, and Soissons state : ' Within the limits of
the commune, all men shall give mutual help according to their
power, and shall in no wise suffer that any man whatsoever shall
take any thing or impose payment of *tailles* on any one of them.'
In France the mediaeval commune was the home of but one
estate of commons, merchants, and artisans, and they had to
struggle for freedom from the feudal nobles and their courts.
Fra Salimbene of Parma notices with surprise, ' In France only
the townspeople live in the towns; the knights and noble
ladies stay in their castles and on their own domains '. The
townsmen developed a borough custom for which they desired
free working, adjusted to the mercantile and industrial character
of their community ; they did not aspire to be city states, but
were franchises within the greater state. Sometimes—as at
Laon—a sworn union might employ force, and the confraternity
had usually a militant and military side. Thus the commune
had its belfry to summon its citizens to resist attack ; it maintained militia and fortified its walls, and had usually an armed
horseman upon its seal.

After the eleventh century two types of towns must be distinguished : the *old* towns, which had survived as centres of
partly urban activity from antiquity (such as Paris, *Lutetia
Parisiorum*), or had grown up round an abbey, cathedral, castle,
fair, or market; and the new towns—*villes neuves*—of the
twelfth century. In that century the old towns themselves
developed, and in the last half of it are found to fall into three

classes—towns which are free in that their inhabitants are freemen and not villeins, such as Paris; towns enjoying certain privileges but under the authority of a lord, such as Rouen; and outside France itself towns with complete self-government, such as Bruges and Ghent.

The beginnings of the political life of the city of Paris are obscure, but under Louis VII the privileges of the Hanse or Guild of Paris merchants, which under the name of *marchands de l'eau de Paris* had the monopoly of carrying goods from St. Germain-en-Laye up the river, and of levying toll on all goods entering the city by river, were confirmed. Once more the continuity of tradition is manifested; the guild is as old as Roman times—its members dedicated an altar to Jupiter in the time of Tiberius—and it is their badge, a ship, with the motto, *Fluctuat nec mergitur*, which still appears as the arms of the city of Paris.[1]

Twelfth-century Paris, like eighteenth-century Moscow, was an assemblage of castles, each fortified and each with its gardens and dependencies, and of churches and monasteries all lying within the walls.[2] The lord or abbot held feudal rights over his own land, and there was no corporate city life. But Philip Augustus not only added to the defences and amenities of the city, but made its citizens *francs bourgeois*[3] with a provost and a council of six burghers. Men flocked to the city; numbers and prosperity alike increased. 'To be a free burgess', says *Renart le Contrefait*, 'is to be in the best estate of all; they live in a noble manner, wearing lordly garments, having falcons and sparrow-hawks, fine palfreys and fine chargers. When the vassals are obliged to join the host, the burgesses rest in their beds; when the vassals go to be massacred in battle, the burgesses go to picnic by the river.' Crafts, trades, and commerce flourished and continued to flourish, 'en l'an 1400, et quant la ville estoit en sa fleur, passoient tant de gens tout jour sur ce Grand Pont, que on y rencontroit adéz ung blanc moine, ou ung blanc cheval'.[4]

Rouen was an 'old town' of a different kind, with a con-

---

[1] The cries of the modern boatmen working up or down stream go back to a Latin prototype.

[2] Even down to the time of Louis XIV thirty-four seigneurs owned half Paris, and each had the rights of justice on his land.

[3] The word 'bourgeois' first appears in an ordinance of 1134.

[4] Guillebert de Metz, *Description de Paris*, ch. xxii.

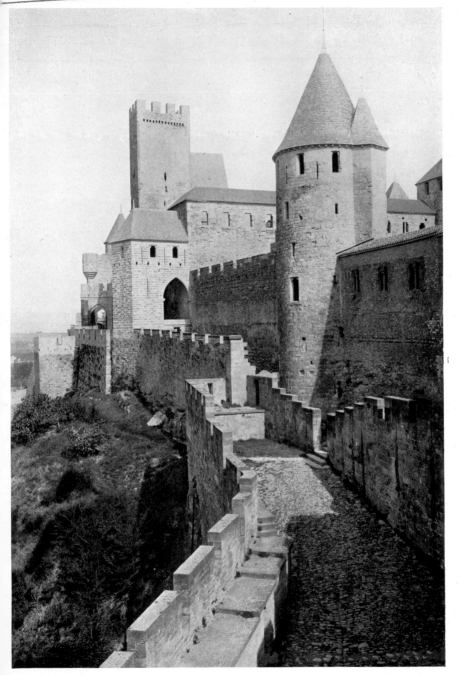

XXI. Carcassonne : Tour de Justice

stitution dating from 1171. One hundred of its citizens met once a fortnight for judicial and other business, and chose each year from among themselves twelve *échevins* or magistrates and twelve councillors to assist them. They also chose three candidates for the mayoralty, from whom the King appointed one. Their administration, indeed, was felt to exercise its powers only by delegation of the royal authority; the King's presence, or a session of his assize, automatically suspended the communal powers of justice.

But if Rouen had fewer rights, its connexion with the King of England gave it many privileges. Except for one ship yearly from Cherbourg, it had the monopoly of the trade with Ireland. In England its merchandise was free of all the markets in the land. In London its merchants were quit of all payments except for wine and great fish, and had exclusive rights in their special wharf of Dowgate. In its own territory only a citizen might take a shipload of merchandise past Rouen or bring wine to a cellar in the town. These privileges led to a growing trade in leather, cloth, grain, and salt fish, and in the end recouped their royal donor, for under Henry II the ducal rights over the town were worth more than 3,000 livres annually.

The *établissements* of Rouen, that provided for government by a hundred of its citizens under the King's suzerainty, were copied by the chief towns of Western France—Tours, Poitiers, Angoulême, and La Rochelle, and even by Bayonne on the Spanish frontier.

Both Paris and Rouen, however many elements were represented among their citizens, achieved unity under their sovereign lords. Many cities were an agglomeration of townships each under a different jurisdiction. At Arles, for instance, there were four towns: the *cité*, under the archbishop; the *vieux bourg*, divided into three fiefs held by the archbishop, the Count of Provence, and the family of Porcellet; the *marché*, depending upon the archbishop but held by two vassals; and the *bourg neuf*, belonging to the Seigneur des Baux.

The new towns, or *villes neuves*, were in their beginnings a result of the Truce of God, by which abbeys or churches, being sacrosanct, were enabled to offer asylum and thus to attract settlers.[1] But in time the lay lords, attracted by the

---

[1] The first *ville neuve* is Vaucresson, founded by Abbot Suger in 1125.

prospect of revenue, founded towns also, sometimes in alliance with the local bishop. Four crosses were set up at the four points of the compass to mark the town boundary, and within this the future town was traced upon the ground: the church, the market, the town hall, and the regular and symmetrical streets.[1] A typical *ville-neuve* charter, by the privileges it enumerates, explains the causes that brought citizens to the new towns:

'Know all men by these presents that I, Henry Count of Troyes, have established the customs defined below for the inhabitants of my Ville Neuve near Pont-sur-Seine between the highways of the bridges of Pugny: every man dwelling in the said town shall pay each year twelve deniers and a measure of barley for the price of his domicile; and if he wishes to have an allotment of land or meadow, he shall pay four deniers an acre as rent. The houses, vines, and fields can be sold or disposed of at the will of the buyer. Men dwelling in the said town shall neither go with the army in the field nor on any expedition if I do not myself lead them. I further accord them the right to have six échevins, who shall administer the common business of the town and shall assist my provost in hearing his pleas. I have decreed that no lord, knight or other, shall take away from the town any of its new citizens, for any reason whatsoever, unless the citizen be his 'homme de corps', or unless he be in arrears with his *taille*. Signed at Provins, 1175.'

Breteuil, founded by a Norman lord in 1060, came to be a model followed as far away as Ireland and the Welsh marches. The privileges conferred by the *leges Britoliae* were three: a town-peace, protecting the settlers; a town market, with a court of *lex mercatoria*; and fixed and moderate tolls.

Since communes were most apt to arise in towns of a certain size, they were more often directed against the power of a bishop or an abbot than that of a lay lord, as the cathedral or monastery had usually proved a more secure focus for industry than the lord's castle. Consequently, however much the sworn unions that demanded the charter might approximate to religious confraternities, the Church condemned them out of hand. Jacques de Vitry laments:

'Not only do they crush and ruin the knights and the country side, taking away the lords' jurisdiction over their men; but they even usurp the rights of the Church; they demolish the independence of the

---

[1] Montferrand is a good surviving example of such planning, which was also followed by Stephen of Penchester at Winchelsea.

XXII. Pont Valentré, Cahors

13th Century

clergy by their iniquitous statutes, contrary to all canonical law. This is not all; nearly all breed brotherly enmity, desire the destruction of neighbouring towns, or even attack them. They rejoice in the death of a neighbour, and women share these evil feelings with men. Strangers and travellers, defenceless against the communes, are made to pay new and illegal tolls; every one is envious, every one deceitful, every one selfish, every one destructive; without the walls there is battle, and within unceasing alarms.'

The dominant fact in the history of the communes of north-central France is their relation to the King, and the complement to this is their importance in the development of the monarchical power. Up to 1180 the policy of the monarchy towards the communes appears to be opportunist, but is really subordinated to the royal dependence on the bishops against the feudatories. If a commune arose in opposition to the bishop, his appeal to the King usually resulted in the suppression of the commune, but if it arose in opposition to a dangerous lay lord the King usually supported it, particularly if it had the favour of the Church. Thus it came about that in the next period, from 1180 to 1220, the natural policy of the monarchy was alliance with the communes against the feudatories.[1]

St. Louis on his deathbed exhorted his son: 'Especially maintain the good cities and commons of thy realm in the same estates and with the same franchises as they enjoyed under thy predecessors; and if there be aught to amend, amend and set it right, and keep them in thy favour and love. For because of the power and wealth of the great cities, thine own subjects, and especially thy peers and thy barons, and foreigners also, will fear to undertake aught against thee.'

The French communes had greatly developed under Philip Augustus, who granted seventy-eight communal charters in the course of his reign. One of the earliest, that granted to Corbie in 1180, reserves the lord's rights over the members of the commune: 'The inhabitants who hold fiefs shall acquit their ordinary services to their immediate lords, without prejudice to that which is due to the King and to the commune.' The

---

[1] Here France resembled England, where the towns supported the Angevins, and differed from Germany, where Frederick II sacrificed the towns to gain the support of the bishops and princes; and from Italy, where the feudal nobles took their share in town life and thus in the struggle against the monarchy under Frederick I and II.

charters of Voisines, St. Quentin, and Athies have a clause forbidding serfs of the district to join the commune. But the royalty of Philip Augustus ended by being antagonistic to feudalism, and by 1223 the charter of Beaumont-sur-Oise contains the clause, 'There shall be included in this franchise all men, belonging to whatever seigneury, who shall wish to settle at Beaumont'; the only exception being the bondmen and bond-women of the King and his sons.

The administration of Philip Augustus introduced two new elements: jurists experienced in Roman Law, and burgesses from the free towns. It was by legal sentence that he deprived John of England of his French provinces, but it was by the towns who acted as fortified posts on the frontier that he held them, as it was by the help of their militia that he defeated John at Bouvines.[1] It was by the aid of his jurists that he declared that all communes were the King's, and by this elision of the feudatories gained a new source of power and revenue in granting and confirming charters to the communes throughout the kingdom. Beaumanoir in the *Coutumes de Beauvoisis* says that the King's intervention in communal affairs is necessary because he is the natural guardian of all civil and religious associations established within his realm; because he only can create communes, and all 'nouvelletés' must be forbidden. The conduct of the mayors must be under his control in order that 'the poor inhabitants may earn their bread in peace'.

The King's most striking innovation appeared to be a temporary measure, but its results were lasting. Immediately before his departure on Crusade in 1190, he deputed authority to deal with city affairs in every city of the royal domain to a provost and four burgesses. In Paris there were six, and these were appointed guardians of the royal treasure and the royal seal. On his return he continued to use burgesses as officials, and ordered the officers of his demesne to act in co-operation with the townsmen where the towns had not communal rights. Thus with him the urban class reached political importance, and hence arose dynasties of *grands bourgeois* who dominated Paris and the great towns. But with this development of a bourgeois aristocracy communal democracy suffered, and after 1220 a period of decline begins. An oligarchical element

[1] Cf. the defeat of Frederick I by communal militia at Legnano.

appears in their government; the *parlement* or mass meeting of the burgesses disappears or becomes unimportant, and the whole power passes into the hands of a patriciate of wealthy townsmen, owners of land, merchants, or both, who by co-optation and influence gain a monopoly of the offices of mayor and jurats, which tend to become hereditary. This introduces two elements of weakness: internal strife within the oligarchy, and the disaffection of the excluded artisans. It was partly a question of economics; unorganized commerce had been succeeded by organized industry, and as a social institution the commune was out of date. The mercantile oligarchy tried to put the burden of the taxes on the artisan masses, and ran into debt rather than shift the burden when changing conditions made it intolerable.

Already by the end of the twelfth century, Lambert of Waterloo is lamenting the decline of the commune of Cambrai:

'At the beginning it was greeted with favour, because it had been instituted by men held in high esteem, men whose lives were just, simple, honourable, and not avaricious. Each was content with what he had; justice and concord reigned among them; avarice was rare. Citizen respected citizen; the rich did not despise the poor; all shunned strife, discord, and lawsuits. Their only rivalry was in honour and justice. What a change has come over the commune! It has suddenly become dishonourable, such fair beginnings have led to such a state of shame and perversity for reasons that are only too clear. The citizens have become numbed by prosperity; they have risen one against the other; they have left sin and crime unpunished, each thinks of nothing but his own enrichment by dishonest means. Little by little the great have set themselves to oppress the poor by lies, perjury, and open force; right, equity, and honour have disappeared; the very strength of the commune has vanished.'

Thus the communes of thirteenth-century France were centres of struggle and bankruptcy, and the King was forced to interfere in the name of order and of reputable finance and to destroy municipal liberty in favour of government by royal officials. The commune came with revolt against the financial oppression of the feudal lord, and it went in the bankruptcy of an oligarchical government. The artisan and merchant had exchanged the rule of a seigneur first for democracy and then for oligarchy, and hence passed to direct control by a strong monarchy.

The importance of the charter of the *Hanse des marchands*

de l'eau in the political development of the city of Paris has been mentioned. With the twelfth century town life everywhere led to the organization of such corporations within the corporation of the city—guilds of traders, or merchants' guilds, since mutual association facilitated both transport and exchange, especially when such exchange was more apt to be in kind than in money ; and secondly, manufacturing corporations, craft guilds, for the protection and regulation both of trades carried on in every city—baking, meat selling, and so on—and of skilled crafts more or less special to the locality, such as enamelling at Limoges. But industry remained to a certain extent under seigneurial control, since certain necessities —ovens, wine presses, flour mills, cloth mills, and so on—were seigneurial monopolies, and the members of the guilds owed seigneurial dues. When they had obtained a collective seigneury, whether as members of a commune or as *bourgeois du roi* under a charter, this seigneurial power over industry passed into municipal hands. Here, since the municipal potentates were usually of commercial origin, it tended to be more intelligently employed than under a feudal seigneur. In these cities, statutes such as those codified by Étienne Boileau remained for a very long time the basis of French industry. The root principle of apprenticeship and examination before admittance is usually thus expressed : ' Whosoever wishes to practise the craft as master, must know how to do it in all points, by himself, without advice or aid from another, and he must therefore be examined by the wardens of the craft.' Further, the members supervised the quality of material used in the trade, and saw that its secrets were kept. Similarly, partnerships and multiple shops were forbidden except with the consent of the guild. Some crafts were even more strictly limited ; no one, for example, could be a weaver in Paris who was not a weaver's son. In few instances was it permissible to have more than one apprentice outside the master's own family.

Up to the time of Philippe le Bel the number of masters in each *métier* was unlimited, and some industries—*métiers libres*— were not corporate. But by the end of the thirteenth century these also became guilds, and the existing *métiers* were further subdivided. The French guilds were not divided according to the thing produced, but according to the material of which it

XXIII.   Fifteenth-Century Houses

L'Isle, Tarn

was made. The cutlers, for instance, were in two corporations, 'couteliers fabricants de lames' and 'couteliers faiseurs de manches', since blades and handles were of different material. On the other hand the lantern-makers and comb-makers were in one guild, since both worked in horn. In the thirteenth century the 'tailleurs de robes fourrées' were separated from the 'tailleurs de robes', and new corporations were formed for *métiers* —for example, embroidery—that had hitherto been free. The rosary-makers, again, were divided into those who made in bone and horn, those working in ivory and shell, and those working in amber and jet. A single object not only passed through several hands in the course of its manufacture, but through hands belonging to members of different corporations. This brought about difficulties similar to those in a modern industry of a complex kind—such as shipbuilding—through the overlapping of trade unions. Even thieves, assassins, beggars, and vagabonds were organized in corporations like honest men, and had their 'masterpieces' and *épreuves de maîtrise*.[1]

Many of the guild regulations are of the sort that the cycle of the world has just brought back upon the statute book; the number of hours a week are limited, and certain crafts—such as the weaving of tapestry on the *haute lisse*—are forbidden to women as being too fatiguing. Some *métiers*, on the other hand, were reserved for women; for instance the 'feserresses de chapeaux d'orfrois', or makers of embroidered head-dresses, had to be women; six years' apprenticeship was needed, and since the work to be well done must be done in a good light, 'nulle mestresse ne aprantice de ce mestier ne peuvent ouvrer en yver ne en esté au soir, ne au matin si ce n'est par la clarté du jour'. The guilds are religious confraternities, and therefore owe a duty of almsgiving; each Sunday one goldsmith is to keep his shop open, and the proceeds of the day's sale are to go to provide a fine feast on Easter Sunday for the poor of the Hôtel Dieu. If a journeyman tailor spoils a piece of stuff, he is to give a day's work to mending the clothes of the poor. Strikes were not unknown; the jurist Beaumanoir defines the 'alliance which is made against the common good, when any sort of people swear or engage or covenant that they will not

---

[1] Cf. the thieves' guilds of Russia. During the war they walked in unemployment processions.

work any more at as low a wage as before . . . and so if they
are permitted are they against the common good, for then will
there never be cheap merchandise, since those of each trade
will struggle to get higher wages than is reasonable and the
public interest will not permit all work to stop.'

It is further admitted that the artisan works as little as he
can, and has the time-worker's aptitude for knocking off work
too punctually :

> A tierce dit que il est none
> Et a none que il est nuit,
> Et si tost com il puet s'enfuit.[1]

A sermon of the time of St. Louis suggests that even guild
regulations did not do much to improve the moral standards of
trade.   'The innkeepers and wine merchants secretly mix
water with their wine, or bad wine with good.   The innkeeper
charges for a bad candle at six times its value, and demands
extra payment if you use his dice.   Wretched old women water
the milk . . . and try to make their cheeses look richer
by soaking them in broth.   Flax which is to be sold by
weight is left out all night on the damp grass, so that it may
be heavier.   Butchers blow out their meat.   Before delivering
a pig they drain away its blood and use it to redden the gills of
stale and discoloured fish.   The drapers make up on the *bure*
what they lose on the scarlet cloth; they have one yard
measure for selling and another for buying.   They only display
their goods in dark streets, so as to deceive the buyers as to its
quality.'   The butchers also sold cooked meat.   The preacher
tells the story of the old customer who asked to have his
sausages cheaper as he had dealt only with the one butcher for
seven years.   'Seven years!' cried the charcutier, 'and you're
still alive!'

Paris soon outgrew the walls built by Philip Augustus, and
on the side of the *ville* they eventually became an inner defence within the *enceinte* of Étienne Marcel.   The *taille* rolls
of 1292 enumerate 352 streets, 10 squares, 11 cross roads, and
over 15,000 taxpayers.   The narrow and unpaved streets were
thronged and noisy ; the shopkeepers cried their wares, and the

---

[1] 'At tierce (nine o'clock) he says it is three o'clock, and at three o'clock
that it is night, and gets off as soon as he can.'

XXIV.   The Carpenter's Shop

15th Century

street hawkers vied with them. The thirteenth-century *Dit des Crieries de Paris* gives all their cries; the apple woman

> Primes ai pommes de ronviau
> Et d'Auvergne blanc duriau,

the chestnut seller from Lombardy; the fruit-seller with

> Figue de Melités sans fin.
> J'ai roisin d'outre mer, roisin . . .

and the cheese hawker,

> J'ai bon fromage de Champaigne;
> Or i a fromage de Brie!

Each trade had its quarter: the apothecaries in the Cité; the literary trades—parchment sellers, scribes, illuminators, book-sellers—in the Latin Quarter; money changers and goldsmiths on the Grand Pont; butchers near the Grand Châtelet; Lombards near the Rue St. Martin, and mercers near the Rue St. Denis. Paris still has its Rues des Parcheminiers, des Écrivains, des Enlumineurs, de l'Écorcherie, de la Buffleterie, de la Verrerie, de la Tannerie, des Lavandières-Sainte-Opportune. There were recognized hiring-places for every trade; men seeking work as fullers, for instance, congregated near the apse of St. Gervais, in front of the house with the sign of the Eagle. Each shop had its gaily-painted sign; a few still survive in the names of the streets or alleys, du Chat qui pêche, du Coq-Héron, des Marmousets, des Trois Poissons, des Trois Canettes, des Trois Visages, du Pied de Boeuf. There were numerous markets, each with special wares and special privileges; one in the Place Maubert for bread, one near the Grand Châtelet for meat, one near St. Germain l'Auxerrois for sausages, one on the Petit Pont for flowers and eggs; the herb market—the *grant orberie*—was on the quayside of the Île de la Cité, near where the flower market is now. Saturday, when many of the shops were closed, was the great day for shopping in the Halles.[1] There each trade had its quarter, and the provincial towns—Beauvais, Cambrai, Amiens, Douai, Pontoise, Lagny, Gonesse—each had its section.

Everywhere was movement, activity, and gaiety. A fourteenth-century manual of polite conversation tells us the proper

---

[1] The modern Halles are on the site of the famous Marché aux Innocents, which dates from the time of Philippe le Hardi.

salutations: to an equal you say, 'Mon Signour, Dieus vous donne bone matin et bonne aventure', or 'Mon amy, Dieus vous doint bon jour et bonne encontre'. To a priest or a monk the proper greeting is 'Dieus vous gart', while a workman or a labourer is saluted with 'Dieus vous ait, mon amy', or 'Dieus vous avance, mon compaignon'.

The class of the wealthy bourgeois became more and more important, and developed a society and standards of its own. An old bourgeois wrote the *Ménagier de Paris* between 1392 and 1394 for the instruction of his young wife, and his good counsels incidentally give an admirable picture of bourgeois life. He begins by telling her 'sachiez que je ne pren pas desplaisir, mais plaisir, en ce que vous aurez a labourer rosiers, a garder violettes, faire chappeaulx, et aussi en vostre dancer et en vostre chanter et vueil bien que le continuez entre nos amis et nos pareilz et n'est que bien et onnesteté de ainsi passer l'aage de vostre adolescence feminine, toutes voiez sans desirer ne vous offrir a repairier en festes ne dances de trop grans seigneurs, car ce ne vous est mie convenable, ne afferant a vostre estat, ne au mien'. She is to rise early, but not so early as the bell for matins, and to say her prayers. 'Gardez que vous soiez honnestement vestue, sans induire nouvelles devises et sans trop ou pou de bouban'; she is to be particularly careful that her chemise and underdress do not ride up at the back of her neck and appear above her collar. She is to go into town or to church properly accompanied by her duenna, 'en alant ayant la teste droite, les paupieres basses et arrestées et la veue droit devant vous quatre toises et bas a terre, sans regarder ou espandre vostre regard a homme ne a femme . . . ne arester a parler à aucun sur les rues'. Arrived at the church she is to choose a quiet corner before a fine altar or image and to pray there with 'la teste droite et les bolièvres tousjours mouvans en disant oraisons ou prières'. Her chief, and indeed her only occupation is to be the supervision of her establishment. She must know how to garden and how to manage servants. Her *dispensier* or steward will help her to choose day labourers and people of special trades, such as bakers, furriers, and shoemakers; her *béguine* or duenna will advise her about the domestics. The work of the household must begin early in the morning; 'les entrées de vostre hostel, c'est assavoir la salle et les autres lieux

XXV.   Paris : the Grand Pont in 1317 (I)

par ou les gens entrent et s'arrestent en l'ostel pour parler, soient au bien matin balleyés, et tenus nettement, et les marchepiés, banquiers et fourmiers qui illecques sont sur les fourmes, despoudrés et escoués ; et subsequemment les autres chambres pareillement nettoiées et ordonnées pour ce jour, et de jour en jour, ainsi comme il appartient a nostre etat'. The duenna is to remind her mistress to look after the ' bestes de chambre comme petis chiennés, oiselets de chambres . . . et . . . autres oiseaulx domeschés, car il ne peuvent parler et pour ce vous devez parler et penser pour eulx '. She must look after her own linen-chest and wardrobe, and ' en temps convenable, par vos femmes essorer, esventer, et revisiter les draps, couvertures, robes et fourreures, pennes et autres telles choses '.

Most important of all, she must see that the kitchen is kept clean, and that proper dinners are ordered. The anxious husband gives a systematic cookery book and many specimen menus for her guidance. She must see that the men and maids are set to work in different places, ' l'un a mont, l'autre a val, l'un aux champs, l'autre en la ville, l'un en chambre, l'autre en solier ou en cuisine . . . chascun selon son endroit et science '. The servants' meals must be regular, but at each they should have only one sort of meat and one of drink. ' Et si tost qu'ils commenceront a compter des comptes ou des raisons, ou a eulx reposer sur leurs coustes, commandez a la beguine qu'on les face lever et oster la table.' At night the steward is to lock up and to see that no tramp or robber is hidden in the cellars; and then all go off to bed, each armed with a flat candlestick.

In the streets of Paris, far more than in the provincial cities, every class in the nation was represented ; the beggars who sat at the church doors and by the bridges, the peasants who came in from the country to buy and sell, the artisans and craftsmen in their open shops, the hawkers and merchants ; jongleurs and mountebanks, monks and friars, canons of the cathedral and professors of the university, students and schoolboys; couriers with their white wands, heralds in tabards, knights in armour ; nobles riding out to hawk or hunt outside the city, ladies taking the air in litters, judges in their scarlet riding to the Law Courts, pilgrims going to Ste. Geneviève, prisoners, gyved and bound, being driven to the Grand Châtelet ; and secure within his turreted fortifications, the King in the Louvre. Paris was then, as now, an epitome of the life of France.

IV

MONASTIC LIFE

THE early ages of Christianity were haunted by the sense that the life of the world and the life of the spirit were antagonistic; and, impelled by this instinct, many renounced the world and retired to a desert place to lead a hermit life. Ascetic mortification was their only employment; mystic ecstasy their only joy.

But in France religion is always the concern not only of the individual but also of the community, and the mystic sense is usually accompanied by a power of organization in practical affairs. Long before Benedict had imposed monasticism on Europe, those who renounced the world were there living in communities under a Rule. About 360 St. Martin founded a monastery at Ligugé,[1] near Poitiers. The Rule was one of life in common, but the activities of the monastery were self-contained: it was not a centre of religious life for any but its own monks. However its ascetic severities may compare with those of the ordered monasticism of later times, they were not blind imitations of Eastern austerities. When a visitor from the East spoke of the cooked herbs and barley bread which formed the diet of the African hermits, the brethren replied: 'Let a Cyrenean endure it if he will, necessity and nature have accustomed him to eating nothing; but we Gauls cannot live after the manner of angels.' None the less, all early monasticism in France received its inspiration from the East; by 410 St. Cassian, a Provençal who had visited Egypt, had established his Rule at Marseilles, and it is after a pilgrimage in the East that St. Honorat founds the famous monastery in the Île de Lérins. By 530 Caesarius of Arles, a monk of Lérins, had compiled a Rule for his monks and another for his nuns. The tale of monasteries rapidly increased; in the fifth century those of Marmoutier, La Morinie, St. Martin near Tours, and St. Victor of Marseilles

---

[1] The first monasteries in Rome are little earlier.

XXVI. Paris : the Grand Pont in 1317 (II)

were established.   They were followed by monasteries of royal
foundation; Childebert I founded the abbey of St. Vincent—
afterwards St. Germain des Prés—outside the gates of Paris;
Chlotor I endowed St. Médard at Soissons, Radegund Ste. Croix
at Poitiers.   But as yet the monastic rule was subject to considerable variation, from the excesses of Oriental asceticism
to the disorders of relaxation; and monastic life was hardly
developed enough to influence the nation as a whole.

The first attempt to strengthen its force came with the
reform of the monastery of Luxeuil by Colombanus at the end
of the sixth century.   In his attempt to introduce a more homo-
geneous and severe organization he borrowed something from
the contemporary system of law; his penitential code, with its
classification of sin and crime, gives clear evidence of this.
Indeed, the evolution of Christian discipline throughout the
Middle Ages runs parallel with that of national discipline—
witness the gradual substitution in both of the money payment
for any expiatory act.

But French monasticism only really became national when
the centre of its spiritual life shifted from Provence to Burgundy.
From the ninth century until the end of the Middle Ages,
Burgundy was the source of the monastic inspiration of France.
It is there, after the reforms of Colombanus had been effected,
that the Rule of Benedict of Nursia was first practised in France;
and it is thence that the French form of Benedictinism spread
through the land.   Benedict of Aniane, who took the monastic
vow and remained for some time in the monastery of St. Sequanus
at Dijon, was the instrument of the reform.   As 'rector et
doctor' of the Church of Christ, Charlemagne, on the advice of
Alcuin, gave him the task of reforming the monasteries of
Aquitaine.   In 817 he presided over a reforming synod at Aix,
and by royal authority all Frankish monasteries were ordered
to accept his reformed Benedictine Rule.   It is characteristic of
the age that this Rule lays great emphasis on the saying of the
Office and on devotion, and shows great contempt for profane
learning.   But, like the earlier Benedictinism, it involved three
main principles.   First, obedience to the abbot, as to a father.
The Benedictine monastery is thus always a family under its
abbot, and the Benedictine is always a member of it.   Thus,
too, the Benedictine monastery was and is an autonomous body:

all abbeys followed the same Rule, but each was self-governing and not subject to any central authority within the Order.[1] Second, *conversio morum*; every member of the Order took vows of poverty and celibacy. Third, *stabilitas loci*; the Benedictine was as definitely attached to a community and a place as the serf to the manor and the glebe. Marbode, Bishop of Rennes in the eleventh century, describes the typical monastic building:

> Quadratam speciem structura domestica praefert
> Atria bis binis inclyta porticibus.
> Quae tribus inclusae domibus, quas corporis usus
> Postulat, et quarta quae domus est Domini,
> Discursum monachis, vitam dant, et stationem,
> Qua velut in caulis contineantur oves.
> Quarum prima domus servat potumque cibumque,
> Ex quibus hos reficit juncta secunda domus.
> Tertia membra fovet lassata labore diurno;
> Quarta Dei laudes assidue resonat.[2]

The clergy were divided into two classes: *clerici saeculares*, living in the world, administering the sacraments, and concerned with the cure of souls; and *clerici regulares* or *religiosi*, following a monastic Rule (*regula*) and belonging to an Order (*religio*) that they might better follow the counsels of perfection of the Christian faith.[3] They had abandoned the world, not in the sense that they had ceased to work in it or for it, but that they had put aside its passions and vowed themselves to poverty and celibacy. Their life differed fundamentally from that of the hermits, for it was as a community—an Order—that they existed, and not as individuals; they lived as a cohort of the Church militant. The prologue to the Order of St. Benedict

---

[1] It was, however, subject, unless the abbot was a mitred abbot, to episcopal visitation and control; and of course to the Papacy.

[2] The house presents a four-square shape; the cloister-court is adorned with four open walks, which, enclosed by three buildings required for bodily needs and a fourth which is the church, provide the monks with exercise, food and repose, so that here the sheep are kept as in a fold. The first of these buildings stores their bread and meat, and the second, counting next, feeds them therewith. The third provides rest for their limbs wearied by the day's labour, and the fourth for ever rings with the praises of God.

[3] There was always some rivalry between seculars and regulars. Theobald of Étampes, speaking in Oxford in the early twelfth century, described convents as prisons of the damned. The monks retaliated by calling him a wandering chaplain in effeminate dress.

expresses this: 'To thee are my words directed, whosoever thou mayest be, who, renouncing thine own self-will, and assuming the strong and splendid arms of submission, art ready to fight for the Lord Christ, the true King.' Further, monasticism differed from anchoretism in the part played in it by mysticism and asceticism; true to the spirit of the Latin Church it did not renounce practical activity, but endeavoured to keep the balance between the *vita activa* and the *vita contemplativa*.

After the reform of Benedict of Aniane the Order was devoted primarily to prayer and the faithful saying of the Office, and secondarily to labour. Benedictine labour was largely physical; their agriculture brought waste land under cultivation and their industries did as much for the development of material civilization as did their intellectual efforts in the propagation of learning. The Benedictine worked for the world and in the world.

'If the monk said his Office regularly, it was not for his own sake only or primarily, but for the sake of all Christ's Church of which he was himself one member among many, but one whose especial function it was to pray. If he sought perfection and followed its counsels it was not in order to get a certain salvation for himself in which others did not share; it was in order to show the world that the perfect law of Christ could be followed, and to stimulate others to follow it by showing a way. This was one reason why the monks were the apostles of England in the seventh century, and of Germany in the eighth, for they preached no more than they obviously practised.'[1]

Further, they worked in the world; the duty was laid upon them when Gregory the Great instituted a monastic apostolate and sent monks to convert the heathen. This function may be said to have ended when England and Germany became christianized, but the work went on in other forms. In the Dark Ages it was Benedictinism that kept the flame of learning tended; it is to its scriptoria that we owe our manuscripts as well of classical authors as of the Fathers of the Church. The styles of French Carolingian illumination all have their centres in the monasteries—the Palace style, at Paris and Soissons; the style of the Loire valley, at Tours and Fleury; and the styles of Rheims and Corbie. By the ninth century Saint Wandrille, Saint Germer de Fly, Saint Riquier, Saint Armand, Corbie,

[1] E. Barker, 'Oxford Lectures on Principles of Mediaeval History'. (Unpublished.)

Charroux, and Aniane all have fine collections of books. Abbot Loup of Ferrières gets books from Fulda, Tours, Rome, and York to be copied by his schools of scribes at Ferrières and at St. Josse-sur-Mer, and the scriptorium of the Abbot of St. Bénigne at Dijon is equally active.

Benedict might decree ' Artifices si sint in monasterio cum omni humilitate faciant ipsas artes ', but Benedictinism cherished and developed the arts in an age when the outside world was distraught with warfare and struggle—music for its services, architecture, sculpture and glass for its buildings, frescoes and work in gold, bronze, and ivory for their adornment. The mediaeval technical handbook, the *Diversarum artium schedula* of Theophilus, was written in a Benedictine monastery, and its preface shows how even the crafts had become sanctified.

' Let him who shall have knowledge of the technical arts glorify not himself, since it is not a conquest but a gift; rather let him be joyful in the Lord from Whom and through Whom all things come, without Whom there is nothing. Let him not wrap this gift in jealous silence, but rather setting aside all boastfulness let him share it in gracious simplicity with all who seek it. . . . So I, a man, puny, unworthy, and almost nameless, offer freely to all who desire with humility to learn, the gift which divine mercy has freely bestowed upon me.'

The social work—road building, road repair, and poor relief —which the Carolingian Capitularies specifically assign to the monasteries, shows their importance in the economic system. Indeed it may be said that until the development of the towns in the eleventh century it is the monasteries who are the pioneers of industry and commerce. The best French vine-yards are all of monastic planting, and many monasteries, like the abbey of La Chaise Dieu in the Auvergne, became important agricultural trading centres.

But the most fruitful of their fields of labour, and that which they made most peculiarly their own, was that of education. Every monastery had its school, primarily for its own novices, secondarily and more rarely for external pupils. To monks such as Gerbert of Aurillac and Fulbert of Chartres the foundation of learned education in France is due. Such schools as these were the universities of their age: and the life of a university is not one of complete seclusion and selfish isolation from the world.

On the side of politics and administration such seclusion soon became equally impossible. A monk as an individual held no property, but the existence of his community involved at least the existence of monastic buildings held by the community, and the lands attached to these buildings tended to increase. Kings in particular gave land cheerfully to churchmen, for they were exempt from the feudal vice of heredity and the appointment of worthy and loyal successors might be secured. One of the functions of the monk was to pray, and much land was given to the monasteries from the motive of assuring the good of the souls of the donor's family through their prayers. A typical deed of gift is one made in favour of the abbey of Gomerfontaine in 1207: 'I, Hugh of Chaumont, with the consent of my wife Petronilla, of my sons John and James, and of my other sons, for the salvation of my soul, of the soul of my wife, the soul of my father Galon, and of my mother Matilda, for the salvation of the souls of all my predecessors and of all my heirs, I make and concede in pure and perpetual alms the following donation. . . .' When lands were not ceded by gift, they were often bequeathed as a legacy. The poem *Hervis de Metz* (written in the time of Philip Augustus) begins, ' To-day when a man falls ill, and lies down to die, he does not think of his sons or his nephews or his cousins; he summons the Black Monks of St. Benedict, and gives them all his lands, his revenues, his ovens, and his mills. The men of this age are impoverished and the clerks are daily becoming richer.' Further, many a man, whether knight or secular priest, joined the monastic Orders towards the end of life, ' ad succurrendum ', as a last hope of salvation, and endowed the monastery with ' all his inheritance, whether of lands or of bondmen and bond-women or of woods and meadows '. These lands, revenues, ovens, and mills involved the exercise of seigneurial rights, and by their acquisition the monasteries strengthened their link with the world by their relation with feudalism. Moreover they acquired not only land but men: a serf flying from his master could take refuge in a monastery, and ask either to live there as a monk or to work there as a labourer. When once the abbot had declared him the monastery's man and had put the monastery bell rope round his neck to signalize his new servitude, his old master could not regain him. Such relations with the world greatly modified the plan of the monastery itself. As early as the end of the ninth century the abbey of Corbie in Picardy was in the middle of a considerable space of ground, enclosed and fortified by a wall. Within the enclosure were three basilicas and four oratories; a monastery to hold between three and four hundred monks and a hundred and fifty lay brethren, with refectories, kitchens, cellars, dormitories, and chapter house; a guest house with quarters for bishops, lords, monks, clerks, and beggars, each with its separate oratory; a school; outbuildings to shelter the abbey's vassals in troubled times; and homes and workshops for forty workmen—cobblers, smiths, coopers, parchment-makers, founders, masons, carpenters, wood-carvers, brewers, and gardeners. Even the troubled years of the ' dark centuries ' made little change to monastic life, and the remains of such an abbey as Fontenay in Burgundy are much like what Corbie must have been. Feudal lands and feudal dependents made the abbot's life very different from that originally contemplated by the founder of the Order. A record exists, for example,[1] of the activities of the Abbot of Mont St. Michel, Robert de Torigni, in relation to the abbey's property from 1155 to 1159. In these five years he goes to England and the Channel Islands, to the King's Assizes at Gavrai, Domfront, Caen, and Carentan, to the courts of the Bishops of Avranches, Coutances, and Bayeux, and to that of the Archbishop of Rouen; proving his rights, exchanging, purchasing, receiving by gift or royal charter; acquiring here a piece of land, there a mill, a vineyard, a tithe, a church to add to the lands and rents, mills and forests, markets and churches, and feudal rights which the abbey already possessed. There are in these five years several instances of loans on mortgage, for the monasteries were the chief source of rural credit in this period, and as the land with its revenues passed at once into the possession of the mortgagee, the security was absolute, the annual return sure, and the chances of ultimate acquisition of the property considerable. With the resources of the monastery during his administration of thirty-two years this abbot was able to increase the number of monks from forty to sixty, to enlarge the conventual buildings, and to add a great façade to the abbey church. He also restored the library and added some 120 volumes to it, besides himself composing a variety of

[1] See Haskins, *Normans in European History*, p. 172.

XXVII.   Monks from the Tombs of the Dukes of Burgundy

Early 15th Century

historical works which make him the chief authority for half a century of Norman history. Abelard laments that

'we, who ought to live by the labour of our own hands (which alone, as St. Benedict saith, maketh us truly monks) do now follow after idleness, that enemy of the soul, and seek our livelihood from the labours of other men. . . . So that, entangling ourselves in worldly business, and striving, under the sway of earthly covetousness, to be richer in the cloister than we had been in the world, we have subjected ourselves to earthly lords rather than to God. We take from the great men of this world in the guise of alms, manors and tenants and bondmen and bondwomen . . . and to defend these possessions we are compelled to appear in outside courts and before worldly judges, before whom we contend so shamelessly that we compel our own men not only to swear for us, but even to fight for us in single combat, to the extreme peril of their lives. . . . Who doth not know that we exercise heavier exactions upon those subject unto us, and oppress them with more grievous tyranny, than worldly potentates?'

So even monasticism, the first mediaeval counterbalance to feudalism, had become tainted by it. But if the monastic ideal suffered, the country gained, since the abbot was the head of a corporation that like a lay foundation owed both *auxilium* and *concilium*. An able churchman, though a monk, might, like Anselm and Lanfranc, rise high in the civil service of the country. The effect of all this was not only to secularize the monastic vocation, but also to make the monastery a local institution rather than a part of a Universal Church. Further, under its influence the observance of the Rule decayed, and monasteries tended to become comfortable residential communities.

The need for reform was felt as early as the tenth century, and resulted in the institution of a new Order, following the Benedictine Rule but with *Consuetudines* of its own—the Order of Cluny. It was endowed and founded by William Duke of Aquitaine in that Burgundian country where the monastic impulse was still strongest. Its first abbot, Berno, of noble Burgundian birth, had already founded a model monastery on his own land at Gigny, and had reformed the community of Baume, also in Burgundy, before he came to Cluny. The Burgundian tradition remained strong in the abbey; Odo, its second abbot, belonged to Semur, as did its greatest abbot, Hugh. The foundation deed of the Order begins thus: 'For those who consider things sanely it is evident that Divine Providence counsels the rich to use well those goods which they possess

in transitory fashion, if they wish for eternal recompense.'
Therefore the founder endows the new abbey; but first asserts
its rights of independence: 'The congregation of the monks
shall be absolutely freed from the jurisdiction of royal greatness
and shall never submit to the yoke of any earthly power.'
The Cluniac interpretation of the Benedictine Rule followed
that of Benedict of Aniane, but there was less of *labor* and
more of *oratio*. Cluny remained the home of liturgical prayer,
and the singing of the psalter took up much of the time that
Benedict had allotted to manual labour. Indeed, Cluniac attach-
ment to work in the fields was always half-hearted; even
when, about 1140, Peter the Venerable contemplated reform,
he only decreed, 'We have ordained that the holy and ancient
custom of manual work should be restored, at least in some
degree, either within the monastic buildings, or wheresoever
it may be carried on decently, far from the gaze of secular
folk'. In other respects the Rule was strict enough; the
Consuetudines Cluniacenses of 930 insist on black robes, silence,
and downcast eyes. But the most important Cluniac idea is the
abandonment of the old policy of monastic autonomy in favour
of a policy of centralization that is typically French. When
new houses were founded, or old ones reformed on the model
of Cluny, they were attached to and subjected to the mother-
house. With papal confirmation of this practice, which was
granted in 931, Cluny became a congregation of monasteries
under the control of its abbot. This central organization had
important effects on the Cluniac policy, which was anti-epis-
copal and pro-papal. The control of the Abbot of Cluny over
his congregation could not co-exist with the control of the
bishop; and Cluny, thus interested in evading the episcopate,
turned to the Papacy, claiming to be subject to it and to it alone.
The founder put it under the jurisdiction and protection of
St. Peter, and Cluny was thus impelled to preach the universal
power of Rome as the cover and shield of all its houses in
Western Europe. On the other hand the Cluniacs were ready
to buttress their Order with the aid of the secular power, and
Odilo, the fourth abbot, and Abbo of Fleury are closely connected
with the early Capets. Moreover, the Cluniac communities
played an important part in bringing certain aspects of monastic
learning, experience, and enthusiasm into relation with the life
of the laity. Every Cluniac monk, whatever his monastery,

had to come to the mother-abbey to make his profession, so that Cluny became as it were a centre of monastic pilgrimage. Thus it is fitting that to Cluny should be due not only the impulse to Crusade and pilgrimage, but also the revivification of the historical traditions that lay behind the pilgrimage. To Cluny, too, was due the first French missionary impulse; it was with a missionary purpose that Peter of Cluny had the Koran translated in 1141. To Cluny is due the admission of the symbolic figures of Honorius of Autun's *Imago Mundi* into twelfth-century Church sculpture. The abbey of Cluny is almost destroyed, yet still on the great portal of Vézelay we can study symbolic sculpture of Cluniac inspiration. Christ stands in the centre, a tall and splendid figure from whom the Holy Spirit issues as beams of light to fall upon the apostles. Round them stand the pagan nations receiving the Gospel, the cynocephali, the great-eared Scythians, and the pigmies, whom mediaeval learning inherited from Herodotus; and beyond them all the Zodiac marks their place in space, and points for the pilgrim to the way he is to follow. It is thanks to Cluny that the monastic saints—Benedict, Anthony, and the rest—appear in the sculpture of the Burgundian churches at a time when the other provinces of France only so celebrated the saints of the district.

Cluniac reforms, moreover, had a favourable influence on learning in establishing a firmer discipline and a better moral order in the monasteries. In the strange picture of monastic life in the early thirteenth century afforded by the *Bible Guiot* the strictness of the Rule is insisted on. Guiot does not wish to join the Order, for

> Trop tiennent bien leur convenanz
> Que il prometent la dedenz.
> Il me promistrent, sans mentir,
> Que quant je voldroie dormir
> Que il me convenroit veillier,
> Et quant je voldroie mengier
> Qu'il me feroient geüner.[1]

Yet even the Cluniac Rule implied an insufficient degree of renunciation for some spirits, and Burgundy witnessed yet

[1] 'They keep too closely the vows which they make in there. They would insist, in truth, that when I wished to sleep I should have to keep awake, and when I wished to eat they would make me fast.'

another attempt to return to the strictness of the Benedictine
Rule. St. Robert, Abbot of Molesme, after seeking monastic
perfection in several monasteries of Champagne and Burgundy,
instituted the monastery of Cîteaux on the Feast of St. Benedict
in the year 1098. Raymond Vicomte de Beaune gave the
land; Eudes Duke of Burgundy, the endowment. Under the
English abbot Stephen Harding of Sherborne the abbey reached
a standard of almost puritanical simplicity; but its real force
came when in 1112 Bernard, himself descended on the mother's
side from the ducal house of Burgundy, retired there with his
brothers to renounce the world. He came of that mixed
Burgundian race that has produced so many men of spiritual
and intellectual eminence; and he brought greatness to Cîteaux.
The letter and spirit of Benedict's Rule continued to be rigor-
ously kept. They had but one meal a day, and had done
twelve hours' work to earn it; they never tasted meat, fish,
fat, or eggs, and had milk but rarely. Their day began with
matins at two in the morning, lasting till four. Next came
the service of lauds at dawn. The interval between the two
must have been the most precious time of the day, for the
monk was free to spend it as he chose, whether in study in
the cloister or in meditation. After lauds the celebration of
Mass kept him in the chapel till nine, when he worked in the
fields till two, and vespers and compline ended the day.

> Omnem horam occupabis
> Hymnis, psalmis, et amabis
> Tenere silentium.
> Super hoc orationem
> Diliges et lectionem,
> Nutricem claustralium.

The constitution of the Order was not monarchical like that
of Cluny, for the daughter-houses, as they arose—and sixty-five
of them were founded in the lifetime of Bernard—were subordinated on the feudal plan of subinfeudation, the right of
visitation being vested in the immediate mother-abbey and not
in Cîteaux herself. The Order was in fact a federation, governed
by an aristocracy of abbots assembled in council. All were to
follow the same Rule, the same customs, the same forms of chant,
prayer, and service, ' ut una caritate, una regula, similibusque
vivamus moribus '.

In interests, as in constitution, Cîteaux was opposed to Cluny.

XXVIII.   Monk from the Tomb of Phillippe le Hardi, Dijon
15th Century

One of the clauses of the *Carta Caritatis* decrees that no Cistercian should compose verse; in none of the abbey churches of the Cistercian Order do we find the representation of a human head or figure carved in stone. It is against Cluny that Bernard's strictures on the beautification of churches are directed:

' " What do you suppose is the object of all this ? " he asks. " Is it the repentance of the contrite, or the admiration of the beholders? Oh! vanity of vanities! but not more vain than foolish. The church's walls are resplendent, but the poor are not there . . . the curious find wherewith to amuse themselves, the wretched find in them no stay for their misery. What has all this imagery to do with monks, with professors of poverty, with men of spiritual minds? I will not speak of the immense height of the churches, of their immoderate length, of their superfluous breadth, costly polishing, and strange designs, which while they attract the eyes of the worshipper hinder the soul's devotion, and somehow remind me of the ancient Jewish ritual. Let all this pass. We will suppose that it is done, as we are told, for the glory of God. But, as a monk myself, I ask other monks: 'Tell me, O ye Professors of Poverty, what does gold in a holy place?'... Again, in the cloisters, what is the meaning of those ridiculous monsters, of that deformed beauty, that beautiful deformity, before the very eyes of the brethren reading there? . . . In fact, such an endless variety of forms appears everywhere that it is more pleasant to read in the stonework than in books, and to spend the day in admiring these oddities than in meditating on the Law of God. Proh Deo! Si non pudet ineptiarum, cur vel non piget expensarum? " '

Cîteaux, on the other hand, laboured in a field which Cluny hardly touched. Stephen Harding devoted profound study to producing a better edition of the Biblical text, and established standard versions of the missal, epistolary, collects, gradual, antiphonal, hymnal, psalter, lectionary, and calendar which had to be used in all Cistercian houses. Bernard's own great learning made him not only the opponent of Abelard, but also the arbiter in many disputes and the director of such work as the institution of the Rule of the Templars. He followed dialectic less than rhetoric; coming from the ' pays des orateurs ', it is by the natural bent of his mind that he fights against the application of strict logical methods to revealed religion, even in its support.

Bernard kept Cîteaux from pursuing the arts of decoration, but he led them to the study of the art of music. He encourages his disciple Guy de Cherlieu to write a treatise *de Cantu* for the use of his Order ; he tells his monks to sing ' Pure et strenue ... non parcentes vocibus . . . sed virili, ut dignum est, et sonitu et affectu', and, with the help of his brethren, he reforms the music of the antiphonal.

Cistercian foundations were always made in solitary places; close touch with the world was avoided. Manual and not intellectual labour was to be the monk's portion, and teaching was forbidden to him. He might only read Gratian's *Decretals* at need; and in 1198 the chapter took action against a brother convicted of learning Hebrew. The only literary activities of the Order were in the field of ascetic oratory and allegorical comment.[1]

It is in the Cistercian convent of Clairvaux that the thirteenth-century story of the *Tombeur Notre Dame* is laid. The ignorant acrobat became a monk, but acquired no monkish learning in the cloister :

> Car n'ot vescu fors de tumer
> Et d'espringier et de baler.
> Treper, saillir, ice savoit;
> Ne d'autre rien il ne savoit.

So he secretly performed his best somersaults before the altar of the Virgin, since that was the only service he could render.

> Hé! fait il, très douce roine
> Par vo pitié, par vo francise,
> Ne despisiés pas mon servise!

And the monks who came to spy upon him saw the Virgin descend from her altar to fan his brow with the corner of her mantle.

Bernard himself had some of the simplicity of St. Francis. Jaques de Vitry tells us that ' when he rode abroad in the morning and saw boys keeping their flocks in the fields, he would say to his monks : ' Let us salute these boys, that they may answer to bless us; and thus, armed with the prayers of the innocent, we shall be able to ride on with an easy mind.' As a true follower of Stephen Harding, he found real literary force in his knowledge of the text of the Bible. In spite of his mystic and ascetic piety, he kept the saving common sense of

[1] The most far-fetched interpretations of the Song of Solomon are Cistercian in origin.

the Frenchman,[1] and defined a wise man as 'one to whom all things taste even as they really are'. He had a true sense of the social side of religion, and a corresponding love of the word 'ordo', and so his passionate *vita contemplativa* seems only to have added new power to his active life. For a quarter of a century he dominated the religious life of France, giving new life to monasticism; reforming the secular clergy, warring against heresy, dogmatic, intellectual, and superstitious, ending the papal schism, and preaching the Crusade. Even the great Suger did not escape his criticism : 'At St. Denis', he said, 'they certainly render justly unto Caesar those things which are Caesar's; but do they render unto God those things which are God's?' Bernard was the greatest monk of the Middle Ages, but there was no monk who lived oftener and for longer periods outside his abbey. He found it grievous and monstrous; but circumstances were too strong for him, and he could not fail to answer the call of a world which needed him.

Perhaps because the Cistercian Order depended too personally and directly upon him, perhaps because their inspiration to follow the austerities of his life was derived too immediately from his personal example, after his death the Order fell upon evil days. It was primarily a Burgundian Order, and Burgundy was commercially rich because of the traffic on the Brenner route to Italy. Trade gradually crept within the cloister, brought by the concourse of 'frères convers' who lived there without taking monastic vows. A hundred years after its institution the corruption was admitted by the Order itself; the Chapter General of 1191 says, 'the congregation does not cease from acquisition, and the love of property has become a scourge'. Similarly the *Bible Guiot* states:

> Provendes, Eglises achatent,
> En maintes manieres baratent;
> Acheter savent et revendre
> Et le terme molt bien atendre
> Et la bone vente dou blé.
> Et s'ai bien oï et taasté
> Qu'as Juis prestent lor deniers.[2]

[1] In spite of his devotion to the Virgin, he firmly withstood the attempt to popularize the idea of the Immaculate Conception; and in spite of his views on crusading he took a stand against the persecution of the Jews.

[2] 'They buy livings and churches, and cheat in many ways. They know

But any attempt at internal reform proved ineffectual; the Cistercians continued in commerce, selling their corn, retailing their wine, and even owning their own mercantile marine for sea and river traffic.

The development of monasticism gradually influenced the anchoretic life of the hermit. In 1086 the Italian Peter Damian first founded the Carthusian Order, in which the hermit leads a solitary life as a member of a community,[1] working, praying, cooking, eating, and sleeping alone, and only seeing his brethren at the morning mass and at meals in the refectory on the great feast days of the Church. The Order made some headway in France, and in sympathy with it the Limousin Étienne de Muret founded the contemplative Order of Grandmont, and another Frenchman, Aimeric Malefaye, Patriarch of Antioch, reformed the hermits of Mount Carmel; but it never became really naturalized in France. Guiot de Provins condemned the Carthusians out of hand: they live in solitude and are no better than murderers, for they do not give their monks better food when they are ill.

These, then, are the chief Orders of the regular clergy. Between the regular and the secular clergy come the canons or *canonici*, following not *regula* but *canones*. Like a monk, the canon lived a corporate life attached to a cathedral or a collegiate church in a cloister or close. The monk was a member of an Order, but he was not necessarily 'in orders', though a certain number of monks in every monastery were ordained so that they might perform the sacraments for the community. The canon, on the other hand, was ordained, and, like a secular priest, might have a cure of souls and take the services of a church. As a member of a cathedral chapter or of a collegiate church he had two functions to perform. First, he and his colleagues were the officers of public prayer, and were responsible for the proper celebration of the Christian feasts. An ordinary week-day had five offices or 'canonical hours': matins, lauds, mass, vespers, and compline. On Sundays there were nine; and others were added for the greater feasts.

how to buy and re-sell, how to wait for settling day and the best sale of their corn, and I have certainly heard and proved that they lend their money to the Jews.'

[1] Peter Damian was however kept in the world by Hildebrand to lead an extremely active political life.

Second, he and his colleagues formed the council of the bishop and were with him the administrators of the diocese. They therefore were monks, in so far as they led a corporate life, and secular priests, in so far as they had cure of souls. Their position was consequently anomalous, and about 750 St. Chrodegang of Metz attempted to bring them under a Rule—to make them *regular* clergy. Thus in time a distinction came to be drawn between canons secular—that is a community of secular priests—and canons regular, primarily monastic but also able to take charge of parishes. The common element in their rule of life was based on the writings of St. Augustine, and the first canons regular were black Austin Canons, who devoted themselves among other works of piety to the maintenance of hospitals. Such service, however, did not compare in hardness with the rigours of the Benedictine Rule. Their intercourse with the world was necessarily not limited, since they were also parish priests, and as such they received considerable dues. Peter, Precentor of Notre Dame de Paris about 1190, is bitterly eloquent on the part money played in their lives. Where the chapter deducts a certain sum for the canon's non-attendance at service, you may see them running up at the last moment 'like old women after a greased pig; some bent forward, others leaping over the bar to enter, others pressing in disorderly fashion through the open door'. It is to the Austin Canons that Guiot de Provins would belong:

> Benoeiz soit sainz Augustins!
> Des bons morsiaux et des bons vins
> Ont li chanoine a grant plenté.
> Molt sont gentilment atorné.
> Ici pourroie-je bien souffrir,
> Que j'aim miex vivre que morir.[1]

However, a stricter rule was followed by the white canons, the Premonstratensians, founded by St. Norbert at Prémontré in Burgundy in 1119.

Benedictinism was the source of the monasticism of the early Middle Ages, and its activities justify their description as the

---

[1] 'Blessed be the holy Augustines! The canons have great plenty of fat morsels and good wine, and are very well provided for. Here I could very well endure, for I had rather live than die.'

Benedictine Age. In the course of the twelfth century the leadership passed from the Order: the monastic schools declined before such cathedral schools as those of Laon, Tours, Chartres, Orléans, and Paris, and the source of new developments in the history of the Religious Orders is to be found in the communities of canons who served the cathedrals. It is in a sense the reflection of the growing importance of the cities: the cathedral city is the capital of a province, but the monastery is apt to be hidden in some remote rural solitude—Clara Vallis, Fountains, or Vallombrosa. So it is in connexion with the cathedrals that learned and didactic literature comes into close touch with vernacular literature through the *Miracles* and *Mystères*; that Latin hymns remain in relation with lay lyrics; and that the classical cycle—*Romans de Thèbes, de Troie, d'Enée, d'Alexandre*—passes from the scriptoria into French narrative verse, and that the foundations of the lay culture of the later Middle Ages are laid.

When monasticism was established idealism was impracticable in the world outside, and the cloister was the only place where a holy life could be led. But as the Church gradually influenced the national life the need of the nation for the wisdom and knowledge of the monks increased, and the division between the cloister and the world grew less marked. The greatest monks, such as Bernard, were driven by force of circumstance to spend much of their lives outside the cloister; and if for them this relaxation of the vow of *stabilitas loci* was a penance, for many it was a pleasure. By the time of Philip Augustus we find Philippe d'Harvengt, Abbot of Bonne Éspérance, asking, 'Where is the street, the square, the cross-roads where one does not see monks on horseback? Is there a feast, a fair, or a market where they do not appear? They are seen at every tournament and every battle.' Clearly *stabilitas loci* was not congenial to the age; and the accounts of the corruption of the monasteries, to be found alike in the visitation-books of the bishops and in popular literature, show that the concomitant *conversio morum* was rare.

The Church, too, was developing an aristocratic standpoint in an age of democracy. The philosophical activities of the twelfth century had led to a theolgy of speculative subtleties which could only be comprehended by trained minds. The later developments of the Gregorian movement engrossed the

Papacy in a policy devoted to the establishment of papal supremacy in temporal as in spiritual things. But if the Church was monarchical at its summit, it was democratic at its base, and in the thirteenth century this lay democracy became conscious of its individual and collective power. To many the spheres of dominion, judicature, and administration were closed, but every man had a sphere of expression in his spiritual life. Laymen became conscious of the power of judging their priests by standards which were Christian and which should have been priestly. St. Bernard expresses his sense of the corruption of the hierarchy of the church : ' The cardinals are full of avarice and evil living; without faith or religion they sell God and his Mother, and betray us and their fathers. Rome sucks and devours us, Rome kills and destroys all.' Almost for the first time men ventured to hold the opinion that the man may pollute the office rather than that the office must inevitably ennoble the man. The majority of men were filled with a profound conviction of the emptiness of sacerdotal Christianity and were ready to cry with Guiot de Provins : ' A congregation is made by charity, and should be full of charity. A monk may suffer much, read, chant, work, and fast; unless he has charity, in my opinion it counts for nothing. He is like an empty house in which spiders spin their webs, but quickly destroy what they have spun. To chant and to fast does not save souls : only faith and charity.' Hugues de St. Cher preaches that ' this pompous religion shall be reduced to great usefulness, so that the monks shall sometimes be compelled to beg their kinsfolk for food and raiment, to disperse their communities, to pawn their croziers and crosses, and to sell their books '.

The earlier institutions of the Church no longer fulfilled the needs they had once served; a new task called for workers of another kind. If the earlier centuries are the age of the Benedictines, and the twelfth century of the secular priests, the thirteenth century, in many ways the culmination of the Middle Ages, is the age of the friars.

Mystics such as Joachim of Flores, awaiting the coming of the Gospel of the Spirit; thinkers such as Arnold of Brescia, wishing either so to spiritualize the Church as to make it worthy of its Master or else to transfer the sacerdotal power into the hands of those prepared to follow Him ; Amaury of Chartres, declaring, 'Now the sacraments of the New Testament are at an end, and the reign of the Holy Spirit becomes each day incarnate in each of us'; the Lombard Humiliati, penitents who went about the world preaching repentance and lowliness of spirit, crying *Pax et bonum* as they went—these are all precursors of Francis and Dominic. There grew up an ideal of individual striving for perfection, which is the common note of Franciscan and Dominican, of Albigensian and Vaudois; but it was recognized that such perfection lay not in cloistered seclusion but in leading a life at once pure and fruitful in the crowded highways of the world.

The French spirit of Crusade and chivalry had so beautified the lives of ordinary men that it was felt to be possible even for those under vows to seek perfection while working in the world. Francis, who knew the poetry and chivalry of Provence, thus dedicated his troubadour's spirit in the service of Christ, and so brought the glamour and romance of Provençal *courtoisie* into an ascetic Order in setting before the world the example of the *Joculatores Dei.*[1]   Love and peace were their watchwords; courtesy and forgiveness their duties; absolute poverty and chastity their vows.   But so far his Order was nothing but a chance confraternity, offering dangerous similarities with such heretics as the Pauvres de Lyon.[2]   Before it could work in a Christian community it must be taken into the Church and be, as it were, ordained.   The Roman Curia saw in its rules a dangerous resemblance to the innovations of the reformers, but Cardinal John of St. Paul overruled their prejudices.   'If we reject the petition of this poor man as something novel and too hard to fulfil', he declared, 'when all he asks is that the Law of Life of the Gospel be confirmed to him, let us beware lest we offend against the Gospel of Christ.   For if any one shall say that in the observance of evangelical perfection and the vow to observe it, there is anything new or irrational or impossible of observance, such a one is convicted of blasphemy.'   Recognition by the Church was thus secured in 1217; organization within the Church had then to be achieved.   First, the friar's

---

[1] He had a habit of singing French songs which he composed himself in the langue d'oil, and knew and loved the *Chanson de Roland.*

[2] In Germany, Hungary, and France the first Franciscans were taken for *Cathari.*

vows of chastity and poverty were confirmed. Next, the second monastic duty—obedience—was expressed in the image of parenthood, and all idea of lordship one over another was disclaimed. Then—and it is here that a great difference is apparent between the Benedictine and the Franciscan Rules— instead of being bound to a communal life within the walls of his monastery, the friar was allotted to his province, Spain, Portugal, France, Germany, Hungary, England, Italy, or Syria. The government of the Order lay with a general chapter of the whole confraternity; the whole organization of the society was designed to weaken neither its democratic basis nor its ideal of the nomadic life. Though affairs in Italy prevented Francis himself from heading the French mission, as he had wished, by 1219 the Order was established at Paris, and by 1233 it had innumerable branches all over France. But as the reins of government ceased to be held by Francis alone, a tendency away from poverty and simplicity began to make itself felt, and in spite of opposition from one party in the Order, the conventual gradually superseded the nomadic life.

St. Dominic unconsciously began the foundation of his Order when, as a canon of the French Order of Prémontré at the cathedral of Osma in Spain, he undertook the mission of preaching to the heretics of Languedoc. Spain, like France and Italy, had felt the stirrings of the movement towards a return to simple Christianity, and the *Pauperes Catholici*—a sect which managed to remain orthodox though having a distinct affinity with the Vaudois of Aragon—are the precursors of the Dominicans. It was through their example that Dominic set out to destroy heresy, following the apostolic example as a pilgrim with wallet and staff, preaching the Gospel. Gradually a confraternity developed from his work, offering close parallels with the Franciscan Order. It was formally incorporated at Prouille in Languedoc. The first Friars Preachers numbered six Spaniards, one Englishman, and seven men from the provinces of France: the Île de France, Provence, Toulouse, Navarre, Lorraine, and Normandy.[1] Its rule was that of Dominic's own Order of

---

[1] It was decided as early as 1220 that the general assembly should be held alternately in the University centres of Paris and Bologna. The Order was established in Lyons 1218, Rheims and Limoges 1219, Poitiers 1220, Metz and Montpellier 1221, Bayonne 1222.

Prémontré, without the obligation to lead a cloistered life. Dominic and Francis became friends; and Dominic, who had not originally intended the vow of poverty to extend to the Order as well as to the individuals composing it, was persuaded by Francis to adopt the Franciscan principle of communal poverty. But in spite of their general similarity in aim and constitution, the two Orders preserved in a remarkable degree the stamp impressed upon them by the personality of their founders. The Dominican and the Franciscan mind are to this day marked and distinguishable. The Dominican love of souls accompanies a fiery zeal for conservative orthodoxy, which the more emotional temper and more democratic sympathies of the Franciscan have constantly threatened. It has been the maxim of the Dominican *Ordo Predicatorum* to preach the Gospel by word and example—*verbo pariter et exemplo*, and the Franciscan to exhort *plus exemplo quam verbo*. Further, the Dominican trusts first to reason, and the Franciscan first to feeling; as St. Bonaventura says, ' Praedicatores principaliter intendunt speculationi . . . et postea unctioni; Minores vero principaliter unctioni et postea speculationi'. Each remained faithful to the spirit of their founder :

> L' un fu tutto serafico in ardore,
> L' altro per sapienza in terra fue
> Di cherubica luce uno spendore.

The specific function of both Orders was and is to preach the Gospel : every friar was a missionary to his province. Nor was this missionary effort confined to Christendom. Francis himself at the time of the Crusade went to Damietta and strove to prevent battle between the Christian and Paynim hosts. He went unarmed to the camp of the Sultan and explained his mission to convert the world, and as the Eastern mind always respects the religious fanatic, he was received and dismissed with courtesy. He then went to found a province of his Order in Syria. By 1245 missionaries of the Mendicant Orders had reached Persia, and in 1252 St. Louis sent the Franciscan Guillaume de Rubriquis to the Great Khan, at whose court he held disputations with Nestorian Christians, Moslems, and Buddhists. In 1253, at the request of St. Louis, Innocent IV founded the Society of *Peregrinantes propter Christum*, recruited from the Franciscans and Dominicans. By 1276 the Dominican mission to Bagdad under Ricold de Montecroix had reached considerable proportions; a bishopric was founded there in 1318, embracing twenty-five churches in the new capital of Sultaniyeh. Meanwhile a Franciscan mission under John of Montecorvino had penetrated to India, and thence reached China in 1298. They were well received by the Khan, and were allowed to preach and build a church. Learning the Tartar language, they translated the Psalms and the New Testament, founded a missionary college, and by 1304 had secured more than five thousand converts. In the early fourteenth century Pope John XXII corresponded with missions in Georgia, Persia, China, Tartary, and Turkestan, and in 1329 founded the bishoprics of Lesser Armenia, Tauris, and India.

Thus the Mendicant Orders became to the Papacy of the later thirteenth century what the Jesuits were to be to that of the sixteenth. Further, they helped the Papacy to combat heresy at home. The Mendicant Orders themselves had in their origin something in common with the heretical sects they were to combat, in their desire to return to a simpler Christianity. The Vaudois, or Poor of Lyons, show the most obvious parallel. About 1170 a rich merchant of Lyons, Pierre Valdo, had certain books of the Bible and of the Fathers translated into the vulgar tongue,[1] and basing his teaching upon them strove to return to the conditions of the primitive Church. But it was a lay reform that never received ecclesiastical sanction: he was excommunicated and the *Pauvres de Lyon* were denounced as heretics by Lucius III. More definitely heretical were two sects of the South of France; the Petrobrusians, founded by Pierre de Bruis in the early twelfth century, as a sect opposed to infant baptism, worship in churches, reverence for the Cross, the doctrine of the Real Presence, and the saying of masses for the dead; and the Cathari or Albigensians, who inherited from the Eastern Manichaeans a dualistic religion steeped in morbid and fanatical asceticism. Theirs was a definite schism from the Church; for them the God of the Old Testament was the devil, the Roman Church 'the Synagogue of Satan'. Such sects threatened the Church, and though the Papacy resisted the appeal to force against them until 1207, even before then

[1] It is interesting to note how many of the 'heresies' within the mediaeval Church were based on a Biblical Version in the vernacular.

conversion had passed into persecution. With papal and popular support the Albigensian Crusade of 1209 was carried out with almost incredible cruelty. At Beziers alone 7,000 persons were massacred; Provençal civilization, already weakened, received its death-blow. The *Besant de Dieu*, written about 1230, says,

> Quant Franceis vont sor Tolosans
> Qu'il tienent a popelicans
> E la legacie romaine
> Les i conduit et les i maine,
> N'est mie bien, ceo m'est avis.
> Bons e mals sont en toz pais.[1]

All this was secular action, but the Church preached that mercy to those who rejected the true faith could be nothing but disobedience to God. The Mendicants very gradually made the Inquisition their own. They were bound by no ties of locality, they were free from episcopal dominion, and were directly dependent on the Holy See. Consequently some of the functions of the papal courts were delegated to them. The Inquisition was never formally founded and never formally vested in the friars, but its powers gradually passed into their hands, and by 1258 two Dominicans held commissions as Papal Inquisitors of Albi, while others were working in France and Aragon in a similar capacity.

By the later thirteenth century the living force in the Church was a didactic force. The canons of the cathedrals, the doctors of the universities, the Friars Preachers, the Mendicant missionaries, even the Inquisitors are all there to teach men the truths of the Gospel. In face of the opposition of his chapter the then Abbot of Cîteaux opened a Cistercian college in Paris in 1227, and by the end of the century there are Cistercian houses at all the great universities. By knowledge shall men reach salvation, and on the portal of the thirteenth-century cathedral Christ stands as the Teacher of the world.

---

[1] 'When men of France attack the men of Toulouse, whom they consider heretics, and the Roman Legate leads them and drives them on, in my opinion it is not at all a good thing. There are good and bad men in every country.'

V

PILGRIMAGE AND CRUSADE

MEN can never altogether forget their nomadic past; even when necessity no longer drives the tribe, they do not rest quietly for all their lives in the corner of the earth they have made their own. Beyond the next hill lies always a new Jerusalem: such is the romance of life.

Christian Rome turned to Syria to find in Jerusalem itself the sanctity of a vision. Constantine excavated to find the grotto of the Holy Sepulchre and the site of Calvary; the piety of Helena was rewarded by the Invention of the True Cross. Pilgrims came to the basilicas of the Sepulchre, the Mount of Olives, and Bethlehem from all the Christian countries of the West. Devout men desired, as Paula wrote to St. Jerome: 'To put the finishing touch to virtue by adoring Christ in the very place where the Gospel first shone forth from the Cross.' As early as 333 a native of Bordeaux made the pilgrimage and wrote an account of all the stages of the journey from Bordeaux by way of Constantinople to Jerusalem.[1] Some fifty years later St. Jerome founded a convent and monastery on the Egyptian model with a dependent hospice for pilgrims, and the first settlement of Western Christians in the Holy Land was established. Not even the barbarian invasions of the fifth century could put an end to pilgrimage; the attraction of the Holy Land had grown strong enough to survive the strain and stress of the most troubled years of the Dark Ages. Even after the establishment of Arab power in Syria after 633, the pilgrimage was occasionally undertaken as a penance, though it sometimes took as much as seven years to perform.

As the imperial power weakened, so did the glamour of Rome's past glories strengthen. To go *ad limina sancti apostoli* was to go to the chief city of the world:

> Roma nobilis, orbis et domina
> Cunctarum urbium excellentissima,
> Roseo martyrum sanguine rubea . . .

[1] Other early pilgrims are: Silvia of Aquitaine, *c.* 380; the Frankish Bishop Arculf, *c.* 680; Prince Willibald of Kent, *c.* 730; Bernard of Mont St. Michel, *c.* 870.

When Charlemagne went to Rome for the first time in 773, he got down from his horse on Monte Mario, the Mount of Joy, from which the city first appears, and entered it on foot as a humble pilgrim.[1] In his day the way thither came to be marked by hostels for pilgrims, and the *via Cornelia* from the Tiber to St. Peter's was lined by *Scholae peregrinorum.*

Charlemagne was himself not only a pilgrim, but a defender of pilgrims. With him the Frankish Emperor became in the eyes of the world the champion of Christendom. The Arab invasion had been checked at Constantinople in 718 and at Poitiers in 732, and a certain balance of power between East and West had been attained. Charlemagne was therefore able to employ the diplomatic relations with Bagdad established by Pepin the Short for the confirmation of the Western Emperor's right of protectorate over Christians in the Holy Land.[2] Since it involved no diminution of his political power, Haroun-el-Raschid confirmed Charlemagne in this privilege, and further made him an absolute gift of the Holy Sepulchre. As early as 870 the square in front of St. Mary Latina at Jerusalem was known as the Frankish Market.

So to the pilgrimage to Rome in a friendly country was added the pilgrimage to Jerusalem in a neutral country under friendly protection; and to these was later added a third pilgrimage, this time under arms. The Arabs of Spain were beaten at Poitiers, but through the centuries that followed they remained a perpetual menace to France. To keep them back had been the struggle that helped to make France a nation; there is political truth behind the cry of Charlemagne in *Aymeri de Narbone* :

> Ralez vos en, Borguignon et François,
> Et Hennuier, Flamenc et Avalois,
> Et Angevin, Poitevin et Mansois,
> Et Loherain, Breton et Herupois.
> Je remendrai ici en Nerbonois,
> Si garderai Nerbone et le defois!

In 1015 the Norman Roger I de Toéni, Seigneur de Castillon, led the first French expedition against the Moors since the

---

[1] M. Bédier has ably shown (*Légendes Épiques*, vol. ii), how far the later Carolingian cycle is linked up with the stages of the pilgrimage to Rome.
[2] To the conservative Orient Europeans are still *Franks* in the Levant.

time of Charlemagne, and this was quickly followed by other hosts from Burgundy and the south.[1] It is a Burgundian who becomes King of Portugal after seventeen victories against the Moors; and another mounts the throne of Castille.

For them the shrine of St. James at Compostella, which at first had been of merely local importance,[2] became the goal of a pilgrimage under arms. This, the First Crusade, undertaken by Frenchmen of the north, the east, and the south, brought a new element into Christian life; for the early Church, unlike Islam, had no tradition of Holy War. The Church of France by the land-peace and the *Truga Dei* had sought to check the abuse of war in feudal society; in the Crusade the fighting instincts of Christian feudalism were directed to a Christian end. With Turpin before Roncesvaux, the Church 'par penitence les cumandet a ferir'. With Roland she said to those who died fighting:

> Seignors barons, de vos ait Deus mercit!
> Tutes vos anmes otreit il pareïs!
> En seintes flurs il les facet gesir!
> Meillors vassels de vos unkes ne vi.[3]

The crusading spirit is a French impulse, and only keeps its vitality so long as it is in close touch with France. There is little doubt that its first inspiration came from the Burgundian monastery of Cluny and its daughter-houses; by 1015, Raoul Glaber tells us, Cluniac minds were already haunted by the idea of leading men to seek glory and martyrdom in Saracen lands. Pilgrim and crusader were one and the same; the one

---

[1] There were no less than thirty-four such expeditions. Among the most important are :

1033. Odilo of Cluny enrols Burgundian army.
1063. Expedition from Aquitaine.
1065. Expedition under Thibaut de Semur.
1073. Eble de Rouci, with support of the Pope.
1078. Hugues de Bourgogne.
1085. Eudes de Bourgogne, Raimond de Bourgogne, Raimond de St. Gilles, Robert de Bourgogne, Savaric de Donzy, Humbert de Joinville. On the whole question see Boissonnade, *Du nouveau sur la Chanson de Roland*, pp. 3–68.

[2] The tomb called that of St. James was only discovered about 830.

[3] 'Lord Barons, may God have mercy on you! May he grant all your souls rest in Paradise! May he set them amidst the Holy flowers! Never have I seen better vassals than you.'

defended himself, the other attacked his enemies in order to reach his goal.

They had the same rallying cries:

> Cunctae gentes, linguae, tribus,
> Illuc vunt clamantes
> Sus eja! Ultreja!

And the crusaders set out on the first stage of the journey unarmed and in pilgrim's garb. So Joinville begins his journey: ' Then I departed from Joinville on foot barefoot in my shirt, not to re-enter the castle till my return; and thus I went to Blécourt, and St. Urbain, and to other places thereabouts where there are holy relics. And never while I went to Blécourt and St. Urbain would I turn my eyes towards Joinville for fear my heart should melt within me at thought of the fair castle I was leaving behind, and my two children.' So Fra Salimbene meets St. Louis at Sens ' in a pilgrim's habit, with the staff and scrip of his pilgrimage hanging about his neck '.

With the establishment of feudal order after the tenth century pilgrimages became more and more frequent, whether undertaken in expiation of sin, in fulfilment of a vow, or as a holy end to life. Peter, Abbot of Josselin, says there are three sorts of pilgrims: ' the first is of those who seek the holy places for the sake of piety; the second of penitents, on whom a pilgrimage has been imposed as a penance, or who undertake it of their own free will; the third of those near death, who desire sepulture in holy ground '. In the sculpture of the Last Judgement at Autun all the dead are naked except two who have died on pilgrimage, who still have their wallets, one with the cross of Jerusalem and the other with the shell of St. James.

Pilgrimage first appears as a penalty in the legislation by which the Church strove to modify feudal warfare; any one who killed a man during the *Truga Dei* was to be exiled from his province and to go on pilgrimage to Jerusalem. Later it become a punishment that was also decreed by the civil authority; a royal ordinance of 1371 decrees, ' we will that our said échevins shall be able to enforce and commit those who by them shall be condemned for their offences to make any journeys or pilgrimages by penalty of fixed sums of money '. Such a punishment might even be imposed on a community through its representatives. A treaty signed at Arcques near St. Omer on Christmas Eve 1356, between the King of France, Count

XXIX. The Tomb of Philippe Pot, Grand Seneschal de Bourgogne

1473–1493

Louis of Flanders, and the Flemish cities, stipulates that 300 men of Bruges and Cambrai must go on pilgrimage, a hundred to St. James at Compostella, a hundred to St. Gilles in Provence, and a hundred to Rocamadour.

By the end of the eleventh century pilgrimages were divided into two categories; the greater pilgrimages to Rome, Compostella, and Jerusalem, and the lesser pilgrimages within a man's own country. The departure for each was hallowed by the Church; the *Coutume de Normandie* describes the ceremony, which usually took place at nightfall. 'Then the pilgrim, having received his scrip with cross and holy water in the parish church, is conducted in procession outside the parish, to seek Jerusalem, Rome, or St. James, or to go on another pilgrimage " per cruce signationem ".' The *Roman du Mont St. Michel*, written between 1154 and 1186, describes the pilgrims two hundred years before Chaucer:

> Li jorz iert clers e sanz grant vent.
> Les meschines e les vallez
> Chascuns d'els dist verz ou sonnez.
> Neis li viellart revunt chantant
> De leece funt tuit semblant;
> Qui plus ne seit si chante *outree*
> E *Dex aie* u *Asusee.*
> Cil jugleor la u il vunt
> Tuit lor vieles traites unt
> Laiz et sonnez vunt vielant.
> Li tens est beals, la joie est grant.
> Cil palefrei e cil destrier
> E cil roncin e cil sommier
> Qui errouent par le chemin
> Que menouent cil pelerin,
> De totes parz henissant vunt
> Par la grant joie que il unt.
> Neis par les bois chantonent tuit
> Li oiselet grant et petit . . .
> Entor le mont el bois follu
> Cil travetier unt tres tendu
> Rues unt fait par les chemins.
> Plentei i ont de divers vins,
> Pain e pastez, fruit e poissons,
> Oisels, obleies, veneisons,
> De totes parz aveit a vendre
> Assez en ont qui ad que tendre.[1]

---

[1] 'The day was clear, without much wind. The maidens and the young

Besides Mont St. Michel there were innumerable pilgrimages within France itself: to Chartres, to see the Tunic of the Virgin; to Ste. Geneviève at Paris, to Saint Denis, to Notre Dame de Puy, to St. Martial at Limoges, to St. Martin at Tours, to St. Sernin at Toulouse, to Ste. Marie Madeleine at Vézelay. The last named gained far more than local importance through its geographical position at the crossing of the route from Channel to Mediterranean and from Central France to Rome; thousands came to it three times a year, at Easter, Whitsun, and on July 22. But such pilgrimages, like that to Mont St. Michel, were easy and happy: ' Li tens est beals, la joie est grant ': and they tended to degenerate into attendance at fairs in pilgrimage places, and to become one with travel that lacked a religious purpose.

Indeed, the spiritual value of a pilgrimage and the consequent strength of its tradition would seem to depend upon its difficulty. Thus the three major pilgrimages—to Rome, to Compostella, and to Jerusalem—have the greatest importance. To go to Rome was by custom the duty of a bishop upon his consecration, and many humbler pilgrims followed. The Pilgrims' Way from France lay over the St. Bernard or the Mont Cenis; the roads they used still bear in many places the name of ' via francesca '. They brought back to France a memory of the troubled greatness of Rome, though for them it was a city of ghosts speaking an unknown tongue. History might be lost in legend; the emperors and poets might figure as magicians; but it is none the less the Capitoline statue of Marcus Aurelius—whom they believed to be Constantine—which reappears upon the church façades of Southern France; and the French battle-cry ' Montjoie! ' comes from the *Mons Gaudii* whence the pilgrims first saw Rome.

men each of them said verse or song; even the old start singing again: all have a look of joy. Who knows no more sings ' Outree ! ' or ' God help ! ' or ' Asusee ! ' The minstrels there where they go have all brought their viols, and go playing lays and songs. The weather is fine and joy is great. The palfreys and the chargers, the hackneys and the packhorses which amble along the road that the pilgrims follow, go neighing on all sides for the great joy that they have. Even in the woods all the little birds sing, great and small. . . . About the mount, in the leafy wood, the victuallers have set up tents and turned the paths into streets. Plenty was there of divers wines, bread and pasties, fruit and fish, birds, cakes and venison; everywhere was there for sale enough for him who had the means to pay.'

XXX.   The Portal of the Church of the Madeleine

Vézelay

Yet, though from April to July the long files of 'romieux' and 'paumiers' might pass along the roads, the pilgrimage to Rome lacked the heroic tradition. Cluny, it is true, did its best to supply it; but even their stories of the pilgrimage of their Abbot St. Maieul, of his being attacked by Saracens, and his miraculous escape, failed to do more than make his tomb at Souvigny a local centre of pilgrimage.

The pilgrimage to Compostella held the romance and purpose that were lacking from the pilgrimage to Rome: French monks of Cluny had inspired the knights of Burgundy and Aquitaine to conquer it from the Moors and had peopled Spain with Cluniac colonies. It was through the influence of Cluny that the Bishop of Compostella had obtained first the pallium and then the dignity of metropolitan; the Abbot of Cluny was proud to bear St. James's shell upon his shield.

Cluniac monasteries marked the stages of the four great roads to Compostella, from Tours, Vézelay, Le Puy, and Arles. St. Gilles, St. Pierre de Moissac, St. Jean d'Angély, St. Eutrope de Saintes offered hospitality and sanctity, and the chain of Cluniac monasteries was continued over the frontier into Spain along the 'Camino francés' to Compostella. In the twelfth century Cluniac monks compiled a guide book for the journey, the *Liber Sancti Jacobi*. It gives the hymns to the saint, recounts his history and his miracles, and describes the roads and the stages. The 'Advice to the Traveller' includes a brief Basque vocabulary, a list of rivers of which the water is wholesome, and of relics that should be seen on the way. A Latin poem of the same date, composed by monks of the abbey of Roncesvalles, describes the hospitality it offered; all who came were welcomed. At the door a man offered bread, and took no price; within, a barber and a cobbler were at the service of the pilgrims.

> Si videres pauperum ibi sobtulares
> Resarciri corio, tunc Deum laudares.

There were two hospices for the sick, with beds and baths; the cellars were reported to be full of almonds, pomegranates, and other fruit. Even if the pilgrim died there, his salvation was assured by sepulture in holy ground. In 1161 the Order of St. James of the Sword was founded—with the device *Rubet ensis sanguine Arabum*—in order to protect the pilgrims; and

by its care, and that of the innumerable confraternities of
St. James, hostels to give shelter for the night arose at all the
stages of the road.

The eleventh-century French Crusade in Spain and the sub-
sequent pilgrimages had a double influence on the art of France.
When Raymond of Burgundy re-peopled Avila in 1090, he
summoned not only ninety French knights, but also twenty-two
masters of *piedras tallar*, and twelve of *jometria*. These built
the walls, the cathedral, and the churches, and left the stamp
of France upon them. With more settled times the workmen
came as pilgrims; men from the Île de France form the architectural style of Leon; men from Chartres leave their handiwork in passing on the door-jambs of Sangüesa. The monasteries on the *Camino francés*—such as those of Las Huelgas and
Villa Sirga—show the influence of French workmen. Indeed,
from the eleventh to the fourteenth century there was a wave
of French architecture into Spain along the pilgrim's way;
and if the French workmen gave much, they received something in return. In the eleventh century Moorish architecture
was perhaps the most advanced in Europe; and the crockets
and arcadings of the Romanesque style of Cluny and her
daughter-churches on the roads to Spain show the lobes, the
framing to the arches, and the parti-coloured stone of the Moorish
style which is reflected in the eleventh-century architecture of
the church of St. James at Compostella.

The pilgrims of France did more than this for art. All
epics are at bottom journey-songs; and behind the measures of
the *chansons de geste* sounds the rhythm of the pilgrims' march.
Monsieur Bédier has proved that the whole cycle of Guillaume
d'Orange owes its historic basis to documents of monasteries—
St. Julien de Brioude, St. Honorat des Aliscamps, St. Guilhem
du Desert—on the *via Tolosana* to Compostella; and that the
Chanson de Roland and others of the Carolingian cycle arise out
of the Crusades of the men of Burgundy and Provence who
followed in Charlemagne's footsteps to fight the Saracens. So,
instead of a Teutonic epic tradition three centuries old, we
have the immediate past of France as the inspiration of the first
French classic, and the chivalry of France as the indirect
creator of the first *style noble*.

Thus Roland and Oliver appear as Christian heroes on the

sculptures of the twelfth-century cathedrals, and even the jongleurs who sing them find a place.[1] The jongleurs, indeed, were pilgrims for life,[2] and in their hands the traditions of the road were safe. Bertrand de Bar-sur-Aube tells how he got the story of his *Girard de Vienne* from such a pilgrim:

> A un juedi, cant dou mustier issi,
> Ot escoute un gaillart pallerin
> Qui ot Saint Jacque aoré et servi
> Et par Saint Piere de Rome reverti.
> Cil li conta ce que il sot de fi,
> Les aventures que a repaire oï
> Et les grans poines que dans Girars soufri
> Ains qu'il eüst Viane.[3]

The development of the pilgrimages to Rome and Compostella in no wise detracted from the importance of the pilgrimage to Jerusalem. All the mediaeval maps give the Holy City as the centre of the world; for all nations the difficulties of the journey and the glamour of the Holy Places made it the greatest pilgrimage of all. The conversion of the Hungarians to Christianity at the end of the tenth century made it possible to travel by land, by way of Constantinople and Asia Minor. At the end of the century the first band of pilgrims arrived from Iceland; the confines of Europe acknowledged the claims of the Holy Places. But at the beginning of the eleventh century the position of the Franks in the Holy Land was rudely changed. The Caliph Hakem, in a sudden attack of Shiite fanaticism, ordered the demolition of the Holy Sepulchre, the confiscation of its treasure, and the destruction of all Christian relics and symbols. The majority of the Christians were massacred, and the survivors heavily penalized: they were not only under legal disabilities, but had to wear a copper cross ten

[1] Jongleurs appear on the portals of the churches of Ferrières, Souvigny, and Bourbon-l'Archambault; the jongleresse walking on her hands at Amboise; the acrobat with his head between his legs at St. Martin de Tours.

[2] St. Julian, the traveller's saint, was their patron; witness the church of St. Julien les Ménétriers at Paris.

[3] 'One Thursday, as he came out of church, he listened to a lusty pilgrim who had worshipped and served St. James and had come back by St. Peter's at Rome. He (the pilgrim) told him what he knew of a truth, namely the adventures he heard of on his way home, and the hardships which Girard endured before he captured Viane.'

pounds in weight. Though this persecution came to a sudden
end in 1020 it destroyed the Frankish protectorate, which was
succeeded by the Byzantine power. The basilicas were rebuilt
and the Christian quarter was fortified, but though the position
of Christians in Jerusalem might be more secure, the schism
between Eastern and Western Churches involved the western
pilgrim in difficulties under a Byzantine protectorate. Hence,
though the number of pilgrims increased, they no longer came
individually, but in armed and organized companies. In 1016
the company of Normans coming back from Syria is strong
enough to help the Salernitans against the Saracens, and so to
begin the Norman settlement of Southern Italy. In 1027,
again, the Norman band that sets out at the expense of Duke
Richard II numbers seven hundred, and is followed the next
year by another led by the Bishops of Poitiers and Limoges.
With the progress of the century the difficulties increased.
Gerbert, Pope under the name of Sylvester II, made the pilgrimage and returned to make an appeal to Christendom against
pagan persecution. In 1064 the Seljuk Turks began to threaten
both the Byzantine Empire and the Fatimite Caliphate, and by
1081 they held the East and had destroyed the churches of Asia
Minor.

Already the crusading spirit was abroad in France; and when
at the Council of Clermont in 1095 Pope Urban II—himself a
Cluniac monk and a Frenchman from the diocese of Soissons—
besought men to come to the deliverance of the Holy Sepulchre
and the Christians of the East, the cry went up through France,
' Diex lo vot! Diex lo vot!' and many thousands took the
cross. The vow was irrevocable; the Church, in the person
of the local bishop, became responsible for the protection of the
goods of those absent on Crusade. The *Chanson d'Antioche*
pictures the return of a baron from the assembly at Clermont:

> Li quens Robers de Flandres part de la baronie
> A Arras est venus a Climence sa mie,
> Souavet li conseille doucement en l'oïe:
> ' Dame, jou ai la crois, ne vous en poise mie!
> De vous voel le congié; s'en irai en Surie
> Delivrer le sepulchre de la gent paienie.'
> Quant l'entent la contesse, s'a la coulor noircie:
> ' Sire,' ce dist la dame, ' pour moi, n'irés-vous mie;
> Vos avés dui biaus fis que Jhesus beneïe!

Grant mestier ont de vous et de la vostre aïe.'
Quant li quens l'entendi, si l'a estroit baisie:
'Dame,' ce dist li quens, 'tenés, je vous afie,
Si tost com au sepulcre iert m'ofrande coucie,
Et je l'aurai baisié et m'orison fenie,
Dedens les quinze jors vous afi, sans boisdie,
Me metrai al retour, se Diex me donne vie.'
La dame tent sa main et li quens li afie;
N'i a cel de plorer n'ait la face moillie.[1]

The wives had to accept their husbands' vows, and could only ask to be remembered oversea:

Lor seigneurs en apelent a cui sont espousées:
'Seigneur, a la foi Dieu somes-nous mariées,
Loiautés vous avons plevies et jurées;
Por Dieu! quand vous arés les terres conquestées,
Et vous verrés la vile ou Diex soufri colées,
Souveigne-vous de nous, n'i soions oubliées!'
Ha Diex! Adont i ot maintes larmes plorées.[2]

The Pope's appeal was repeated by many itinerant preachers, one of whom—Peter the Hermit, a native of Amiens—took in later legend the place of the Pope as the originator of the Crusade. These appeals were primarily directed to the feudal classes whose position and military training fitted them to become the defenders of Christendom, but the call to Crusade was unexpectedly answered by the organization among towns-men and peasants of contingents pledged to go to the deliverance

[1] 'The count Robert of Flanders left the assembly and is come to Arras, to his dear Clémence; gently he tells her in her ear, "Lady, I have taken the cross; do not let it make you sad! I wish you farewell, for I am going to Syria to deliver the Sepulchre from the pagan folk." When the countess heard him, her colour changed; "My lord," said she, "for my sake, do not go! You have two fair sons, whom may Jesus bless; they have great need of you and of your help." When the count heard her, he kissed her close; "Lady," said he, "Hold my hand, and I give you my troth, that as soon as my offering is laid on the Sepulchre, and I have kissed it and finished my prayer, within a fortnight, I swear to you without deceit, I will set out to return, if God gives me life." The lady held out her hand and the count gave his troth; no one was there but had his face wet with tears.'

[2] 'They cry to their lords to whom they are wed: "My lord, we are married in the faith of God; we have engaged and sworn loyalty to you; for God's sake, when you have conquered the land, and you see the city where God suffered on the Cross, remember us, let us not there be forgotten!" By heaven, then were many tears shed.'

of Jerusalem. They set out to fight the 'gent mescreue' as they might have set out on any other pilgrimage. The spirit of adventure was no longer the prerogative of the knightly class, but offered even to the villein an escape from the monotonous round of his existence. The appeal to Crusade had special force at a time when general scarcity encouraged emigration. Urban himself said: 'The land in which you dwell, shut in on all sides by mountain and sea, holds too straitly your over-great numbers; she is stripped of riches and barely yields nourishment to those who cultivate her soil. For this reason you hate and destroy one another in envy, and slay your brethren. Appease your hatred, and take the road to the Holy Sepulchre.'

The warlike spirit of feudalism was as yet in no wise subdued; Fulcher of Chartres, in his account of the First Crusade, *Gesta Dei per Francos*, says, 'Christianity was growing fearfully worse in both clergy and people; war was preferred before peace by all the Princes of the earth, who quarrelled ceaselessly'. Guibert de Nogent gives a vivid picture of the movement.

'The French at that time', he says, 'suffered from famine; bad harvests year after year had raised the price of corn to a great height, and avaricious merchants according to their wont took advantage of the general misery. There was little bread, and that was dear; the poor had to eke it out with roots and wild herbs. Suddenly, the cry of Crusade, sounding everywhere at once, broke the locks and bars that closed the granaries. Provisions that had been beyond price when every one stayed where they were, sold for nothing when every one was stirring and anxious to depart. Famine disappeared and was replaced by abundance. As every one hastened to take the road of God each hurried to change into money everything that was not of use for the journey, and the price was fixed not by the seller but by the buyer. It was strange and marvellous to see every one buying dear and selling cheap: everything that was needed for the journey was very costly, but the rest was sold for nothing. . . . It touched the heart to see these poor crusaders shoeing their oxen as if they had been horses, and harnessing them to two-wheeled carts on which they put their small belongings and their little children. At each castle and each city they passed on the road they stretched out their hands and asked if they had not yet reached that Jerusalem which all were seeking. I have heard that men speaking an unknown tongue came to our seaports; they put their fingers together in the form of a cross, to show that they wished to be enrolled in the cause of the Faith.'

This crowd of peasants, ignorant and ill-organized, straggled across Bohemia and Hungary ravaging the country like an invading army. By the time they reached Hungary the inhabitants were up in arms against them, and many were slain. On August 1st, 1096, Peter the Hermit and a remnant of his followers reached Constantinople, and tried to plunder it, having lost all they had ever had. By the time they reached Asia they were demoralized and disbanded; the Crusade of the People had come to a miserable end.

But in the same month that Peter the Hermit reached Constantinople with the broken remnant of his followers the first armies of the real Crusade—the Crusade of Feudalism—set out for Constantinople on their way to the Holy Land. The army was divided into three hosts: the first, composed of men of Flanders and the Rhineland, subjects of the Emperor, under Godfrey of Bouillon, Duke of Lower Lorraine; the second of men of Normandy, the royal domain, and Burgundy, under the King's brother Hugh the Great of Vermandois, Robert of Normandy, Alan of Brittany, and Stephen of Blois; the third of men of Gascony, Aquitaine, and the Midi under Raymond of Toulouse. Unfortunately, on their arrival at Constantinople, the Emperor Alexis did not welcome them as deliverers of the Holy Sepulchre, but was not content until with much difficulty he had persuaded them to take an oath of allegiance to him and to make the reconquest of his Empire their first charge. Thus they embarked upon a perilous campaign in Asia Minor, culminating in the siege of Antioch. After three years they were in a position to lay siege to Jerusalem in June 1099. Many attacks were made in vain; finally a solemn procession all round the walls of the city was followed by a valiant and successful assault, and after an appalling massacre of its inhabitants Jerusalem was in Christian hands.

The dawn of the twelfth century saw the foundation of the Latin principalities of Jerusalem, Tripolis, Antioch, and Edessa. The story of the crusaders' success brought reinforcements from Europe, and helped to establish a European colony fed without intermission by new immigrants and visited by innumerable pilgrims and merchants. The foundation of this European settlement in the East is of importance for the social, political, and economic history of the West. It was definitely

international in character : not only was it an expression of
the Oriental idea of the 'Empire of the Franks', but the
Eastern merchants of every race who thronged its bazaars made
it a cosmopolis of the Middle Ages. The Italians were an
important element in its sea-coast towns, as they still are in
the Levantine ports; the Teutonic nations were represented;
but the predominant national element was French. They
furnished the largest contingent of the crusaders who captured
it; they secured the election of Godfrey de Bouillon as King—
or, since in humility he forswore the title, as 'Advocate of
the Holy Sepulchre'—and theirs was the official language of
a kingdom whose fiefs spread between Egypt and the Euphrates
and from the Euphrates to the Peloponnese. So French rose
above the rusticity and diversity of its dialects to the creation
of a literary language; and so the rhythms of poets such as
William of Poitiers, who went on Crusade in 1103, started
a lyric tradition which was followed not only by the Latin
countries, but also by Germany and Scandinavia and even by
Iceland. So, too, did the French style in architecture become
international; Eudes de Montereau went to Palestine with
St. Louis and stayed to do much building there; Jean Langlois,
the architect of Troyes, went on pilgrimage to Jerusalem in
1267, and to his journey may be due the fact that the cathedral
of Famagusta is in the style of Troyes.

The political and constitutional development of the Latin
Kingdom is remarkable. The Emperor had neither part nor
lot in it; since there was never any question of his suzerainty,
the growth of public spirit and public power is witnessed here
even earlier than it is in England and Sicily. The power
lay less in the hands of the King than in the Court of Lieges or
High Court established by Godfrey of Bouillon, which enabled
vassals and even under-vassals to exercise a permanent control
over the royal power, and even to determine the succession to
the throne.

But this kingdom, outwardly prosperous and progressive, had
one fatal weakness : political necessities, arising from lack of
real political unity, weakened its military organization. The
claims of merchants, burgesses, and settlers weakened one side
of feudalism as an elected monarch with greatly limited powers
weakened another. The recognition of the need for greater

XXXI. St. Theodore as a Crusader

Chartres Cathedral. 13th Century

military strength in a kingdom so precariously situated led to the institution of Orders of Chivalry. The French Church of the eleventh century in its attempt to bring all classes of men and all branches of social activity into conformity with the *lex evangelica* had attempted the difficult task of the moralization of war. As early as 1100 a Church service at the initiation of young knights sought to impress on the feudal world the lesson that its weapons must be used in Christian ways and consecrated to Christian ends, such as the defence of the weak. At about the same time a band of French lords, led by the Provençal Pierre Gérard, founded the Order of Hospitallers by making themselves responsible for the Amalfitan Hospital at Jerusalem. By 1113 their military organization was developed; by 1118 all members took vows of obedience, chastity, and poverty : the fighting layman had become a *religiosus*. In this year Hugues de Payens and Geoffrey de Saint Aldemar came oversea, with nine other Frenchmen, and obtained from Baldwin II the grant of a house near the Temple of Solomon. Thus the Order of Templars came into being, to receive its Rule, written under the direction of St. Bernard, in 1228.[1] Their life was to be one of perpetual exile and Holy War till death; they were never to refuse combat, even of one against three; they were never to ask quarter and never to give ransom. Besides these, they took the monastic vows of chastity, poverty, and obedience. The Prologue to their Rule states :

'Our word is primarily directed to all those who despise their own will, and with purity of mind desire to serve under the one true King; and with minds intent choose the noble warfare of obedience and persevere therein. We therefore exhort you who until now have embraced secular knighthood in which Christ was not the cause, you whom God in his mercy has chosen out of the mass of perdition for the defence of Holy Church, to hasten to associate yourselves perpetually together.'

At the first chapter-general, held about 1160, there were already three hundred knights and as many serving-brethren, nearly all French. The first chivalry, the result of the clerical

---

[1] The Spanish knights of Calatrava were also under Cistercian influence ; founded by Raymond, Abbot of Citeaux, they simply added military duties to the Cistercian Rule.

consecration of war—clearly to be distinguished from the thirteenth- and fourteenth-century lay chivalry—had reached its zenith.

The Orders rapidly acquired by papal and royal gifts great riches and power, all dedicated to the service of the Cross. Their military strength brought real support to the Kingdom of Jerusalem, but their power only intensified its lack of political unity, since their Grand Masters were not under the King, but acknowledged obedience only to the Pope. Thus the middle years of the twelfth century witnessed a time of internal strife and disorganization, which once more permitted Saracen inroads into Christian territory. So serious was the situation after the fall of Edessa in 1144 that St. Bernard preached a new Crusade at Vézelay, at Easter, when pilgrims from every part of France were assembled there. The immediate response was enthusiastic: all the crosses provided were not sufficient, and he had to cut up his own vestments to furnish enough.

The jongleurs seconded his sermons with their *chansons de croisade :*

> Pris est Rohais,[1] ben le savez,
> Dunt crestiens sunt esmaiez,
> Les mustiers ars e desertez:
> Deus n'i est mais sacrifiez.
> Chivalers, cher vus purpensez,
> Vus ki d'armes estes preisez;
> A celui voz cors presentez
> Ki pur vus fut en cruiz drecez.
> Ki ore irat od Loovis
> Ja mar d'enfern avrat pouur,
> Char s'alme en iert en pareis
> Od les angles nostre segnor.[2]

But the ultimate response proved unexpectedly limited, and the armies were accompanied by bands of non-combatant pilgrims. St. Bernard's grandiose scheme of attacking Islam simultaneously in Portugal, in Syria, and on the coasts of Elba

---

[1] Er-roha, Edessa.

[2] 'Edessa is taken, you know it well, at which Christians are dismayed; the churches are burnt and desolate, and God is no more sacrificed therein. Knights, think well of it, you who are prized for arms, give your hearts to Him who was lifted up upon the Cross for you. He that shall now go with Louis, shall nevermore have fear of Hell, for his soul shall go to Paradise with the angels of Our Lord.'

XXXII. The Knights of the Holy Spirit starting on Crusade

14th Century

fell before the political ill-feeling existing in Europe, notably between Byzantium and the Normans in Sicily, and his Crusade came to nothing.

The second half of the twelfth century sees the gradual decline of the Latin Kingdom of Jerusalem, in spite of a close alliance with Byzantium, before the growing power of Saladin. By 1179 he had made serious inroads, gradually surrounding the Christian territory. In 1187 Jerusalem and the Holy Places fell into his hands, and the Christians held only Tyre, Antioch, and Tripoli of all their former possessions. A new army of crusaders had to be found to step into the breach.

To preach this Crusade was the first act of Gregory VIII (1187); but hardly had he proclaimed a *Truce of God* to last for seven years before he died, leaving the organization of the Crusade to his successor, Clement III. The news of the loss of Jerusalem stirred Europe to real emotion. The Pope's adversary, Barbarossa, acknowledged his duty to the Church and joined the Crusade; Philip Augustus and Henry II were reconciled and took the cross; Pisa made peace with Genoa, Venice with Hungary, William of Sicily with the Byzantine Emperor. All the countries of Europe played their part; at the Diet of Mainz alone thirteen thousand Germans took the vow of Crusade, while twelve thousand crusaders came from Scandinavia. The crusading spirit had passed beyond France into Christendom. There was real enthusiasm for the defence of Christianity in the East and the recovery of the Holy City, but the century that had elapsed since the First Crusade had so added to the complexity of European politics that this enthusiasm was bound and limited by political interests. Christendom could still be conscious of itself as a united body face to face with a united Islam, but its unity was no more than the temporary federation of individual nations.

How little strain such a federation could stand soon became painfully evident, when all the crusading hosts were concentrated at their rallying-point to besiege the city of St. Jean d'Acre. In the course of a two-year siege violent quarrels broke out between the crusaders of different nationalities, and loss of discipline among the troops made it difficult to face disasters of famine and flood. Such disasters and the length of the siege meant not only that each army felt a certain respect for its opponents but also that the siege was at moments relaxed and followed by a tacit truce. The crusaders recognized a kindred chivalry to their own in their heathen enemies, just as their ancestors had done in the *Chanson de Roland*. The author of *L'Estoire de la Guerre Sainte* wrote:

Fierre iert la gent et orgoillose
En la cité e merveillose;
Se ço ne fust gent mescreue,
Onques mieldre ne fut veue.[1]

The influence of *courtoisie* upon chivalry had begun. The other side of this influence is manifest in the lament of Conon de Bethune, starting upon the Third Crusade: 'Alas, love! What a cruel leave I must take from the best lady who was ever loved and served! May the good God restore me to her, as surely I leave her with sorrow. What have I said? If the body goes to serve the Lord the heart remains entirely in her power. On to Syria, sighing for her.'

Jerusalem might be lost, but the effects of intercourse between East and West in the territories of the Latin Kingdom had brought about a better understanding that in some sense could survive even open warfare. This feeling was shown in marked degree when St. Jean d'Acre at last fell in 1191. On the departure of Philip Augustus, Coeur de Lion had become the leader of the crusaders, though his temperament ill fitted him to keep peace between them. When Acre had fallen, after much dissension in the crusading hosts, he arranged a truce of three years with Saladin. Ascalon was to be destroyed, and English crusaders were to be allowed to make pilgrimages to the Holy Sepulchre. Jerusalem remained in Moslem hands, but for the first time an attempt was made to regain it by negotiation when force had failed. European influence was modifying the French idea of a Holy War, and the conflict was now one between equals in civilization, terminable by honourable negotiation.

The death of Saladin in 1193 and the consequent division of his Empire plunged the East in civil war and altered the balance of power between Orient and Occident. At the same time the Emperor Henry VI, the one powerful sovereign in

[1] 'Brave and proud and wonderful were the folk in the city; if they were not unbelievers, better men would never have been seen.'

Europe, extended his ambitious schemes to include a project of Oriental sovereignty. The Holy Lands were no longer to be the patrimony of the Church but of the Empire; as Emperor he laid claim to the common conquests of the faithful in the East. The Crusade which he was to lead might well have permanently extended the frontiers of Christendom and of the Empire, had it not been stopped by his sudden death in 1197, at a time when his son was an infant and there was no monarch competent to succeed to his policy and his power.

The end of the twelfth century, then, marks a profound modification of the idea of Crusade. It was no longer a French, but a European idea. Its centre was no longer the Holy City, but the coast towns of Syria; once these were held, it was felt, Jerusalem could be negotiated for. The economic interests of the Italian cities had become one of the most important elements in Christian policy in the East, and had modified the French idea of a war of extermination. National pride and national piety played a lesser part, and the Christian princes received with indifference the appeals to Crusade circulated by Innocent III and his encyclicals after the death of Henry VI. A change of policy and of ideal is manifest in the story of the Crusade under Thibaut de Champagne made familiar by the narrative of Villehardouin. His account shows the extreme importance of political negotiation in the organization of the Crusade, the part played in it by the merchants of Venice, Pisa, and Genoa, and its divagation from its true purpose to the taking of Zara and Constantinople. The establishment of a Latin Kingdom in Constantinople and the Balkan peninsula at the expense of Byzantine power crowned the acropolises of Corinth, Mistra, Kalamata, and Athens with French feudal castles, and established Louis of Blois at Nicea, Hugues de St. Pol at Demotica, Geoffroi de Villehardouin and Guillaume de Champlette in the Morea, and the Burgundian house of La Roche at Athens; but such successes are proof of the failure of a Crusade originally directed against the forces of Islam. Such an end to the enterprise did not satisfy Innocent III; he was steadfast in his aim of the restoration of the Christian States in Syria. In 1212 he therefore again preached a Crusade, but the state of Europe prevented the realization of his dream: instead, Christendom itself witnessed Crusades against the Albigensian heretics, the Moors in Spain, the excommunicate John of England, the heathen in Prussia, and the Greeks of Constantinople. Yet still Innocent persevered. The Emperor Frederick II took vows of Crusade after his coronation 'to show his gratitude to God for all the benefits he had received'; a general peace was proclaimed for four years, to be kept under penalty of excommunication; every one was to help either in service or in money. Everything was prepared and on the point of fruition when Innocent died in 1216. Without his master-hand to steer it, the project failed through lack of unity of leadership or plan. Frederick II refused to join in the Crusade of 1218, remarkable only for its aim—Egypt, not Syria—and for its complete failure. But with his coronation at Rome in 1220 he renewed his vows, to fulfil them in a spirit strangely different from that of the earlier crusaders. When he finally set out in 1228 the purely political character of the expedition was sufficiently evident; Saracen soldiers were included in his army; he himself was excommunicate and brought every place to which he went under an interdict: the Military Orders were expressly forbidden to obey him. Yet he did not underrate the knowledge of Eastern diplomacy he had gained in his half-Eastern kingdom of Sicily, and by playing off one Eastern power against another he found himself, without serious warfare, in possession of Jerusalem, Bethlehem, Nazareth, and the road to Jaffa. No better contrast between the earlier and later Crusades can be found than that between Godfrey of Bouillon refusing to wear a temporal crown in the city where his Master had worn a crown of thorns, and Frederick II, excommunicate from the Church, himself taking the crown from the altar of the Holy Sepulchre, and with no religious ceremony crowning himself King of Jerusalem.

The death of Frederick II changed the political balance of Europe; and in the middle of the thirteenth century the rise to power of a nomadic Mongol tribe under Jenghiz Khan upset the stability of Asia. By 1216 he held Pekin; by 1219 the road to the West lay open. By 1223 he was in Armenia, having destroyed the Seljuk power. His death failed to put an end to the Mongol invasion, for his admirable organization survived; by 1237 they held Moscow and Kieff, and by 1240 they reached the borders of Hungary. Such a menace completely overshadowed the Moslem domination of Syria, though fugitives from the Mongol inroads strengthened the armies of the Sultan of Egypt and enabled him to recapture Jerusalem in 1244.

The loss of Jerusalem, the Tartar menace to Europe, and the imminent peril of the Byzantine Empire made some action inevitable. Baldwin II of Constantinople and the Patriarchs of Constantinople and Antioch came to the Council of Lyons in 1245, and a Crusade was preached. But the conflict between Guelf and Ghibeline was at its height, and popular feeling was against the Crusade. England resisted the imposition of forced levies, and the burgesses of Ratisbon showed their imperial sympathies by a decision to punish by death any who took the cross. The only king in Europe whose piety and whose position was sufficiently strong to make it possible for him to lead it was St. Louis, and it remained a purely French Crusade. Like the Franciscan and Dominican missions into Asia, the Crusade of 1248 is the expression of an age of idealism. Like the first French Crusades in Spain, it brought new life to French literature. Who can forget Joinville's account of the departure?

' In the month of August we entered into our ship at the Roche-de-Marseille. . . . When the horses were in the ship, our master mariner called to his seamen, who stood at the prow, and said, " Are you ready?" and they answered, " Aye, sir; let the clerks and priests come forward ". As soon as these had come forward, he called to them, " Sing for God's sake!" and they all, with one voice, chanted: " Veni Creator Spiritus." Then he cried to his seamen, " Unfurl the sails for God's sake!" And they did so.

' In a short space the wind filled our sail and had borne us out of sight of land, so that we saw naught save sky and water, and every day the wind carried us farther from the land where we were born. And these things I tell you, that you may understand how foolhardy is that man who dares, having other's chattels in his possession, or being in mortal sin, to place himself in such peril, seeing that, when you lie down to sleep at night on shipboard, you lie down not knowing whether, in the morning, you may find yourself at the bottom of the sea.'

Who can forget the gallantry of the landing at Damietta? They found

' all the power of the Soldan—a host fair to look upon, for the Soldan's arms are of gold, and when the sun struck upon them they were resplendent. The noise they made with their cymbals and horns was fearful to listen to. . . . But I caused my people to land in front of a great body of Turks, at a place where there were full six thousand men on horseback. So soon as these saw us land, they came towards us, hotly spurring. We, when we saw them coming, fixed the points of our shields into the sand and the handles of our lances in the sand with the points set towards them. But when they were so near that they saw the lances about to enter into their bellies, they turned about and fled. . . . At our left landed the Count of Jaffa, who was cousin-german to the Count of Montbéliard, and of the lineage of Joinville. It was he who landed in greatest pride, for his galley came all painted, within and without, with escutcheons of his arms, which arms are *Or, a cross patée gules*. He had at least three hundred rowers in his galley, and for each rower there was a targe with the count's arms thereon, and to each targe was a pennon attached with his arms wrought in gold. While he was coming it seemed as if his galley flew, so did the rowers urge it forward with their sweep; and it seemed as if the lightning were falling from the skies at the sound that the pennants made, and the cymbals, and the drums, and the Saracenic horns that were in his galley.'

But neither the faith of St. Louis nor the honourable chivalry that followed him sufficed to bring success to the Crusade; after the fall of Damietta disaster followed disaster. St. Louis himself suffered imprisonment in Moslem hands, and the Crusade ended in retreat to Syria after the Christian prisoners had been ransomed at great cost. Joinville, who had seen and survived the Egyptian *débâcle*, had yet enough faith and courage left to support St. Louis in his desire for a fresh campaign, but there was no response from Europe, and on the death of Blanche of Castille in 1252 the crusading host left Syria and the remains of the Christian power there to a time of conflict and insecurity. The second Crusade of St. Louis was more disastrous than the first, and in it he met his death at Tunis. As he died his pilgrim thoughts turned back to Compostella, and he said St. James's prayer: 'Keep, Lord, Thy people, and sanctify them, that fortified by the help of Thine Apostle St. James, they may please Thee in their works and serve Thee with a quiet heart. Amen.'

The crusading enthusiasm died with St. Louis; there was no response to an appeal from Syria in face of fresh Mameluke inroads in 1289. Finally, St. Jean d'Acre, the last remaining Christian possession in the East, was taken in 1291 after a gallant resistance from its garrison of military knights; of the Latin Kingdom of Jerusalem nothing but the memory lived on

XXXIII. The Walls of Aigues-Mortes

into the fourteenth century.[1] It is significant of the changed spirit of feudalism that the loss of Acre, instead of impelling men to undertake a fresh Crusade, caused nothing but discouragement, in spite of the efforts of the Church. It is perfectly true that hardly a year passed without some prince taking vows of Crusade, but nothing came of it beyond taxation to pay for it and occasional diplomatic negotiation. To Philippe le Bel indeed, taxation for the purpose proved a regular source of revenue. But such vows never led to action; war in their own country monopolized men's energies, and the idea of re-establishing the Latin Empire of Constantinople was politically more important than the deliverance of the Holy Sepulchre.

The crusading spirit was dead, but a fresh movement turned men's spiritual forces into a new channel. The idea of the *conversion* of the heathen began to supersede that of their *extermination*: the conquest was to be not of territory but of souls. It was as natural a reflection of the age of Dominic and Francis as the initiation of the Crusade was of the age of Cluny, but it involved a real change of attitude toward the East. This was made possible by the fact that the Mongol hordes included followers not only of their national religion, but also of all the religions of the East, including Nestorian Christians. When the Venetian merchants of the Crimea made this known to Europe, Innocent IV sent Franciscan and Dominican envoys to the Great Khan, and an interview took place at Karakorum in the presence of Yaroslav, Grand Duke of Russia, the vassals of Georgia and the Caucasus, the Seljuk Sultan of Asia Minor, Mongol generals, Chinese men of learning, and lamas from Tibet.

St. Louis in 1253 sent Rubriquis to the Khan of Tartary, at whose court he found not only a Parisian goldsmith, but also a Nestorian monk who spoke of setting out on pilgrimage to St. James of Galicia. The pioneers were such Mendicants as these, but the man who gave real force to the movement was a man who came from the *Camino francés* that leads to Compostella: Raymond Lull, the son of a Catalan lord who had helped to conquer Majorca from the Moslems. After a stormy youth he handed over his property to his wife and went to the

[1] The Christian kingdoms of Cyprus and Armenia survived.

sanctuary of St. James, where he bought a slave from whom he
learnt Arabic. Then he persuaded the King of Majorca to
found a monastery at Miramar where thirteen friars minor were
to learn Arabic. In 1285 he began his voyages: to Rome,
Paris, Tartary, Armenia, Ethiopia, Africa, and Tunis, everywhere disputing with the Moslems in their own tongue, until
he was eventually martyred in North Africa. It was through
him that the Council of Vienna in 1311 decided to found six
schools of Oriental languages in Europe. The Crusades had
been the Christian policy of the past, but Raymond Lull formulated the policy of the future. 'I see the knights going over-
seas to the Holy Land thinking to take it by force of arms, and
in the end exhausting themselves without achieving their aim.
Then I think that this conquest should be made as Thou madest
it, Lord, with Thine apostles : that is by love, by prayer, and
by shedding of tears. Then let the holy knights of religion
set forth, let them arm themselves with the sign of the cross,
let them be filled with the grace of the Holy Ghost, let them
preach to the heathen the truths of the Passion.' *Peregrinantes
propter Christum* were to take the place of crusaders on 'the
road of God'.[1]

The early fourteenth century found Europe, and particularly
France, so bound and limited by constraint of circumstances
that men's mental activities found an outlet not in action but
in theory. No Crusade was undertaken, but many treatises
were addressed to the Pope and to the monarchs of Europe on
the best way of delivering the Holy Land from the Moslem
yoke. Some of these treatises were the work of visionaries;
others, of which the best known is Marino Sanudo's *Secreta
Fidelium Crucis*, were written by men with real experience of
the Levant gained in missionary or commercial enterprise. All
kinds of views were current; in 1303 an ecclesiastical judge of
Aquitaine suggested besides the more usual preparations for
Crusade, that a certain number of girls should be taught the
practice of medicine and surgery, grammar, logic, and the
elements of mathematics, in order to make good wives for the

[1] Lull was a Majorcan, and it is the Aragonese Popes who did much for
Christian missions. Christianity, much of it the Nestorianism indigenous to
India, was more widely spread in Asia in the fourteenth than in any other
century.

princes of the East. The Armenian Prince Haiton, who had taken monastic vows at Poitiers, two years later expounded a plan of which the basis was the recovery of his own country.

The French theorists of the time of Philippe le Bel—notably Pierre du Bois and Guillaume de Nogaret—continued to put forward Ghibeline views : the conquest was to be monarchical and not papal. The Empire was to be hereditary in the French dynasty ; the Pope was to live in France; Papacy and Church alike were to give up their temporal possessions to furnish funds for the Holy War. All the theorists recognized that the greatest difficulty lay in the political disunion of Christendom and many proposed the establishment of an international board of arbitration, of which half the members should be laymen and half ecclesiastics. A further difficulty was recognized in the rivalry between the Templars and Hospitallers, and various plans were put forward by which they and the other Orders of Chivalry were to be united under a single head, the King of Jerusalem.

The basis of all the plans of action was a commercial blockade of Egypt, and an alliance with the Mongols, but nothing was done to put them into execution. The Military Orders were not united; commerce with Egypt did not cease; no lasting alliance was formed with the Mongols; and the princes who took the cross made no effort to fulfil their vows.

Meanwhile the Holy Land lapsed into a state comparable with that of the century before the Crusades. The Ottoman invasions of the early fourteenth century added a new element to the complex of Eastern politics, and the only Christian settlements in the Levant were those of the Hospitallers at Rhodes and in the Sporades and of the French dynasty of Lusignan in Cyprus. Pierre de Lusignan was conscious of his position as defender of an outpost of Christendom, but his romantic journey across Europe in search of aid failed to stir men to action, and the taking of Alexandria was the only success—and that a passing one—of his expedition. His was the last serious effort at Crusade, yet the idea of the deliverance of the Holy Sepulchre was not quite dead : we find it haunting the minds of Henry V and Joan of Arc. Rutebeuf wrote:

> Tornoieor, vous que direz
> Qui au jor du juyse irez?

Devant Dieu que porrez respondre?
Quar lors ne se porront repondre
Ne gent clergies, ne gent laies,
Et Diex vous monstrera ses plaies!
Se il vous demande la terre
Ou por vous vout la mort soufferre,
Que direz vous? . . .
Ha! Antioche, terre sainte,
Com ci a dolereuse plainte
Quant tu n'as més nus Godefroiz!
Li feus de charité est froiz
En chascun cuer de crestien.[1]

But the age was too troubled for any such enterprise; from East to West the balance of empire was shaken. The Mongol dynasty fell in China, and with it the Christian missions;[2] Islam triumphed in Central Asia under Tamerlane, and by 1390 Bajazet was master of the Balkans and the Byzantine Empire was in dire peril, while Serbian independence lay dead upon the field of Kossovo. An attempt to check the Turkish advance ended in the disastrous defeat of Nicopolis; and in spite of the journey of the Emperor Manuel to Venice, Paris, and London beseeching help, nothing could have saved Constantinople had not Tamerlane invaded the territory of Bajazet and defeated him at Ancyra. This defeat prolonged the existence of Christian power in the East into the fifteenth century, but the crusading spirit was dead. French power in the East had fallen to the commercial cities of Italy, and the question of commercial advantage had become more important than that of religious conquest, whether territorial or spiritual. In 1415 Mahomet I entered into alliance with the Grand Master of the Knights Hospitallers of Rhodes. The fall of Constantinople in 1453 is the last episode of the relations of mediaeval Christendom with the East. It was made possible by the inability of the sovereigns of the fifteenth century to take common action and by their indifference to everything not tangible and immediate.

[1] ' Jousters, what will you say who will come to the Day of Judgement? What will you answer before God? For then neither clerk nor layman will be able to conceal himself, and God will show you His wounds. If He asks of you the land where for you He was willing to suffer death, what will you say? Oh, Antioch, holy land, what sad complaining is there when thou no longer hast a Godfrey! The fire of love is cold in the heart of every Christian.'

[2] Bishops of Pekin are heard of till 1456, but were non-resident.

It marks the beginning of that Eastern question which still awaits solution.

The relations of France and the Moslem peoples of Spain and the East fill six hundred years of the Middle Ages : what effects did they have upon French civilization? Few aspects of mediaeval life—political, artistic, intellectual, commercial, or domestic—escaped their influence.

Indeed, the dominating fact of French mediaeval history—the gradual centralization of power in the hands of the monarchy—owed something to the Crusades. The prestige of the King spread beyond his own domain, and the absence of his barons, and their death by mischance of war, famine, pestilence, or the hardships of the journey, did much to increase the power of the royal officers who were in the meantime entrusted with the administration of his kingdom. Moreover, when the lords returned, not only were their sympathies insensibly democratized by their absence from feudal conditions, but they were also financially poorer, and therefore willing to sell much of their land and many of their rights. Thus service was commuted for a money payment, and another step was taken towards the emancipation of the rural classes and the enfranchisement of the bourgeoisie. Indeed, even lords such as Joinville began to enrol themselves in service in return for a money payment and not for a fief; the land-basis of feudal society was seriously shaken.

So, too, the Crusades affected the basis of men's dreams. A new life, a new country, new contact with other races, provided a stimulus to their imagination that is reflected in their literature : it is no mere coincidence that vernacular epic and vernacular history appear simultaneously with the Crusades, nor is it accident that makes the *Chansons d'Antioche* and *de Jerusalem* unique as epic histories written by a contemporary.[1] Contact with the East gave the mediaeval poet many traditional themes —stories of Solomon, of the Trojan war, of Alexander the Great;[2] but it was the inevitable shock of romance in the

---

[1] It is not till later that such cycles as the *Chevalier du Cygne* are fathered on Godfrey de Bouillon and spangled with irrelevant marvels and incongruous romantic episodes under the influence of *courtoisie*.

[2] Aimon de Varenne in 1188 got the story of his *Florimont* from a Greek source ; the *Eracle* of Gautier d'Arras, the *Athis et Porphirias* of Alexandre

strangeness of the Crusades themselves that made him realize
that he was living in an epic world. For the first time men
felt that their own *mémoires* were worth writing; and Villehardouin and Joinville are the first autobiographers writing in
French. Further, the Crusades—*Gesta Dei per Francos*—helped
to make French a universal language, spoken at the courts of
England, Portugal, Sicily, Constantinople, Athens, Cyprus,
Antioch, and Jerusalem; so that French songs spread through
Christendom and became a part of the literary heritage of all
nations. With her poetry spread French lay music, a monody
in strict time accompanied on instruments of many countries,
Northern, Byzantine, Latin, and Arab. Guillaume de Machaut's
list of musical instruments shows how varied is the list:

> Orgues, vielles, micanons,
> Rubebes et psalterions,
> Leus, moraches et guiternes
> Dont on joue par ces tavernes,
> Cymbales, citoles, naquaires,
> Et de flaios plus de dix paires . . .
> Cors sarrasinois et doussaines,
> Demi-doussaines et flaüstes
> Dont droit joue quand tu flaüstes,
> Trompes, buisines et trompettes,
> Guigues, rotes, harpes, chevrettes,
> Cornemuses et chalemielles.

To take but one, and that the most familiar, *lute* is derived
from the Arabic al'ud, and is a legacy of the Crusades.
Heraldry, again, that seems to us the typical accompaniment of
European chivalry, is an Eastern institution. The Arab Emirs
used heraldic bearings before the eleventh century, and it is
from them that European knighthood took the custom.[1] The
double-headed eagle, adopted by the German Emperors in 1345,
was in the eleventh century the badge of the Ortokid family.
The thirteenth-century roman d'aventure of *Galeran* describes
the knights arming themselves before a tournament:

de Bernai, and the *Empereur Constant*, all come from Oriental or Byzantine
sources.

[1] Raymond of St. Gilles, Count of Toulouse, was the first to bear blazon;
he bore the cross of Constantine, ' croix clichée, vuidée et pommettée '.

Chascun de soy armer se peine
D'armeures neufves et fresches.
Li un y porte unes bretesches
En son escu reluisant cler,
Cil un lyon, cil un cengler,
Cil un liepart, cil un poisson.
Cil porte son heaulme en son
Boote ou oioel ou flour aucune,
Cil porte une baniere brune,
Cil blanche, cil ynde, cil vert.
L'autre y poez veoir couvert
D'armes vermeilles foillollées.[1]

Such a description is true of the court of Philip Augustus, but it would have been equally true of the court of any Sultan of Bagdad. Not only did the knights of Europe adopt the heraldry of the East, but they also wore its dress: the Arab *kouffieh* round the helmet (the origin of heraldic mantling) and the flowing robe. Saladin in 1192 sent Henry of Champagne an Arab tunic and turban, and Henry in his reply wrote: ' You know that your robes and turbans are far from being held in scorn among us. I will certainly wear your gifts.' In *Galeran* the hero, after being dubbed knight, puts on a robe of silk and gold, lined with ermine, ' qui sont faites en la terre aux Maures'. The only place where the shoes with turned-up points of the noble of thirteenth- and fourteenth-century France are still in use is the East, and it was from the East that France borrowed them. The knights thence brought back the custom of bathing in tubs, and a liking for enclosed gardens; mediaeval domestic architecture also owed a debt to the East. The leper-houses of the Orient are the ancestors of the hospitals of Europe. The breed of horses was improved; silkworms and dyeing became French industries, and windmills (in Normandy called *turquois* or Turkish) came to the help of the miller.

The *Assizes of Jerusalem*, drawn up in Cyprus, the legal focus of the Latin kingdoms, with their numerous clauses on the regulation of industry and commerce, attest the importance

---

[1] ' Each strives to arm himself with new clean coat-armour. One has a tower shining brightly on his shield, one a lion, one a boar, this man a leopard, and the other a fish. One has a beast or bird or flower on the peak of his helmet. This man bears a sable banner, another white, another azure, and another green. You can see another blazoned with a red coat covered with leaves.'

of Levantine trade. This trade was far earlier than the Crusades; as early as the fourth century colonies of Eastern merchants, generically called Syrians, were established in Gaul, Italy, Africa, and even Britain. In France their chief settlements were at Bordeaux, Lyons, and Narbonne, always important commercial centres. The establishment of Latin settlements in the East in the tenth and twelfth centuries made their position more secure, and the establishment of the Kingdom of Cyprus and the taking of Constantinople in 1204 made the commerce of the Eastern Mediterranean of great importance in the thirteenth century. Narbonne, Montpellier, Arles, and Marseilles had their consulates and agencies in the Levant as well as the merchants of Genoa, Pisa, Venice, and Amalfi. Marseilles, indeed, as the centre of transport from France to the Holy Land, had in 1253 and 1255 to pass statutes to regulate the traffic. Not more than fifteen hundred pilgrims were to be taken in any one ship. First-class passengers, with deck cabins, were to pay 60 sous; second-class, between decks, 40; third-class, on the lowest deck, 35; and fourth-class, in the hold, 25. Each pilgrim received a numbered ticket, after inscribing his name and that of his guarantor in a register. This was kept in duplicate, one copy being preserved in the communal archives of Marseilles.

The most perfect mediaeval market still extant is the Souk of Jerusalem, with three great twelfth-century arcades in French Gothic, communicating by lateral galleries. Here, and at the great annual fair outside the walls, every kind of Eastern merchandise was sold either for use in the Latin Kingdom or to export to Europe; cotton, linen, and silk (*taffetas, chiffon*, and *muslin* are all of Arabic origin, muslin from Mosul); dyes, indigo, madder, saffron, and the blue we still call ultramarine, from *oultremer*; spices from the Far East; sugar, rice, and all kinds of produce. From Damascus, always important commercially as the starting-point of the caravan routes to the Holy Places of the Mahommedan world, came pottery of all kinds, much glass—the Venetian glass factories were founded by workers from Syria—damask silks, Damascus swords, damascened metal work of all kinds, as well as furs from the Caspian ports of the Volga and ostrich feathers from the East. For such Levantine trade, nineteen centuries earlier, money had first been coined in Ionia; in the Latin Kingdom the Lombard system of banking was elaborated and an international system of exchange revived. Such a trade called for a more highly developed organization than did the local markets of France: commercial treaties were drawn up, a court to regulate the mercantile marine was instituted; and those 'merchant's marks' that take the place of the knight's armorial bearings among the merchants of the cities were instituted to serve as trade-marks among people who could not read a European script.

The main current of Eastern learning reached Europe not through the Crusades and the Latin Kingdom, but from Sicily and Spain. Yet one of the most important branches of Arab learning was the science of geography, and it is through the commercial activities of the Latin Kingdom that this was shared by Europe. The studies of Arab scholars of the eighth century in geometry, in astronomy in the ninth, in trigonometry in the tenth, had given a great impetus to Arab navigation. The use of the sextant and the astrolabe supplemented that of the compass, itself an Eastern discovery, and from an Arab table of longitudes drawn up in 1230 we find they had a very exact idea of Mediterranean distance. More than this, since the eleventh century they had known the coasts of India, Ceylon, Indo-China, and the islands of Java, Sumatra, and Borneo, and it is thanks to them that the Eastern half of a mediaeval map of the world is not wholly blank.

Moreover, it was the Sultan's part to encourage learning among his subjects. While on Crusade St. Louis heard that a Saracen Sultan had collected the books of Moslem philosophy at his own expense, and had formed a library for his subjects' use. St. Louis was inspired to follow his example on his return to Paris by 'diligently and generously' giving money for the copying of the works of Doctors of the Christian Church; and the library thus formed is the direct ancestor of the Bibliothèque Nationale.

VI

LEARNING

ALL knowledge is based on tradition; we inherit not only a mass of received opinion that it is easy to accept, but also a mass of refuted hypotheses which it is easy to set aside. Neither empiricism nor experiment can be independent of this tradition, even when their relation to it is contradictory. The more we are conscious of the historic past, the more are we indebted to our heritage of knowledge; the more the past transcends the present in congruity, in splendour, or in force, the blinder is our faith in its doctrines and its beliefs.

Thus mediaeval thought is based on a classical heritage, and its history is the story of the acceptance, the comprehension, and the transmutation of that tradition. Latin was its vernacular: in that language alone could the seven liberal Arts be studied—the Trivium, the study of speech, in Grammar, Logic, and Rhetoric, and the Quadrivium, the study of number, in Arithmetic, Geometry, Music, and Astronomy. It is only through Latin paraphrase and Latin transmutations that Greek thought was known in mediaeval Europe until the Renaissance.[1]

Thus freed from the boundaries of language mediaeval learning was international; to distinguish the *nuances* of nationality in the learned literature of the Middle Ages is one of the most delicate tasks that the critic can set himself, for not only must he consider the nationality that men inherit, but the modifications that they acquire through education and work in a foreign land. French thought and learning have their beginnings in the scholars whom Charlemagne called to his court in 781, and yet not one of them was French; Alcuin was English, Leutrad Norman, Peter Pisan, Agobard Spanish, and Theodulf an Italian Goth. Throughout the Middle Ages the learning of France

[1] For instance the logic of Aristotle was taught at Rheims about 980 from translations made by Boethius at Rome about 510. Certain exceptional men like Grosseteste and John of Salisbury may have known some Greek, but it was not a common instrument of knowledge until the sixteenth century.

was an integral part of the learning of Europe, and the rise of
Paris to be the intellectual centre of Christendom only served
to raise French learning still further above the limits of
nationality.

The Dark Ages were inevitably conscious of the overwhelming greatness of the past. Men approached the classics not as
critics, but as docile pupils. For them they were the only
storehouses of knowledge; poetry, eloquence, history, philosophy, natural science, law and polity were to be found therein.
As Richard de Fournival writes in his *Bestiaire d'Amour*, 'cil
qui ont esté cha en arrière ont seu tel chose que nus qui soit
orendroit ne le conquerroit de son sens, ne ne seroit seu, s'on
ne le savoit par les anciens'.[1] Century by century mediaeval
learning not only added to its independent store but also drew
more deeply from classical sources. It is convenient to speak
of the Renaissance of classical learning as coming at the end of
the Middle Ages, but the phrase is false in its assumption that
classical learning had ever died. There is a continuous and
steadily growing tradition; the new birth is rather one of freedom of thought, at a time when the classics had at last become
thoroughly assimilated.

But if the Middle Ages inherited the lore of Greece and Rome,
they turned it to fresh ends. Every mediaeval book that is
more than a translation is inspired by the idea of man's salvation. The desire of the mediaeval scholar was not only a
desire to know, for the sake of knowledge, but a desire to be
saved, and to that end to possess knowledge in its saving forms.
This purpose, early made clear in Ambrose's *Hexaëmeron*, is again
evident in Charlemagne's open letters of general admonition,
de litteris colendis and *de emendatione librorum*: it is to advance
the easy and true understanding of the mysteries of Scripture
that learning is to be cultivated and encouraged. Even the
sources of ancient history were apologetic, and not written for
history's sake alone: the *Civitas Dei* was written to refute those
who laid Alaric's sack of Rome in 410 at the Church's door,
and Orosius's *Seven Books of Histories* are *adversus paganos*.
The Scriptures rightly interpreted held the sum of saving

[1] 'Those who have already lived before us have known certain things of
which no man who lives now could acquire knowledge by his own intellect, nor
would they be known did we not know them from the men of old.'

knowledge and therefore there was no question with a valid claim to human curiosity which the Scriptures, through their interpreters, could not be called upon to answer.

It is because of this primary importance of scriptural interpretation that the Fathers of the Church are so important an element in mediaeval thought. St. Augustine permeates the Middle Ages. The Christianized Platonism which they owed to him exercised an even stronger influence than the Aristoteleanism they gained from Latin translations and commentaries. The idea of the seven Arts (on which Augustine began a treatise) is itself Platonic. With him Christian learning reached a compass which it was not to pass for a thousand years. It has been said that he 'brought all intellectual interests into the closure of the Christian faith, or discredited whatever stubbornly remained without'. He catholicized the pagan virtues, which Ambrose had borrowed from Plato's *Republic*. With him the substance of Christian doctrine was defined; the principles of symbolism and allegory were set; the part to be played in man's salvation by the human will was reasoned out; and the great truths of man's dependence on God were uttered in words which men still use. Succeeding generations had not to add to his work, but to learn to comprehend it and to make it a part of their own thought. Classical learning and the memory of the Empire might play an important part in the Middle Ages, but they were dominated by patristic learning and the vision of the *Civitas Dei*. It is the Augustinian tradition which is handed on, with little change but re-classification, by Isidore of Seville; and there are few learned books of the Middle Ages that do not owe some of their material to his *Etymologiae*.

But if classical and patristic learning form a part of the intellectual heritage of France, they were not the only element in its tradition. An examination of the literary art of the Dark Ages reveals an element that is definitely not classical: an heroic treatment of national history, in which Teuton, Scandinavian, and Celt alike find an expression of their peculiar heritage; systems of mystic thought, ways of imagination, tunes of poetry, that are alien to the Latin mind; just as an examination of the art of the same period reveals motives of ornament, fantastic creations of the imagination, and a balance and proportion that utterly changes the whole, though it be made of material that dates from Rome itself. It is this elusive element of nationality which in combination with the traditional classical element bears fruit in mediaeval France ; it is through its action that there is a truly mediaeval literature and not merely a decadence of classicism.

The first phase of mediaeval learning is one of mystic allegory, but these elaborations of Augustinian exposition are not a French but a German development. The first allegorical work of any importance is that of Hrabanus Maurus (d. 857), a native of Mainz, and his contemporaries and compatriots Honorius of Autun and Walafrid Strabo.

Gradually, as this mass of material was acquired, construction of a kind arose, that attempted to classify and to systematize even though it did not question. In this development France played a part, and the impress of French thought was set upon a formless tradition. The most important of these systematic expositions of a symbolical or sacramental plan of the universe is the *Rationale of the Visible World* written in the first half of the twelfth century by a Saxon monk of a convent near Paris, Hugh of St. Victor. He argues that the world is made for man, and that to understand man the world must be understood ; but man's body exists for his spirit's sake, and thus the material creation has a spiritual meaning. Symbolism is then rooted in the character and purpose of material creation ; and therefore the allegorical interpretation of the Scriptures can alone reveal their true meaning. A sacrament is *sacrae rei signum*, and so the whole world has a sacramental significance. The sacraments of natural law are ' umbra veritatis ', those of written law ' imago vel figura veritatis ', and those under grace ' corpus veritatis '. He begins with an exposition of the six days of Creation, corresponding to the six ages of restoration ; for a more minute treatment his *De Arca Noë morale* and *De Arca Noë mystica* must be studied. There every detail of the Ark, typifying the Church, is allegorically applied to the Christian scheme of life and salvation. For instance, he considered the dove as the symbol of the Church. ' It has two wings, since there are for the Christian two kinds of life, the active and the contemplative. The grey-blue feathers of its wings show heavenly thoughts. The changing colours of the rest of its body, like a troubled sea, symbolize the sea of human passion on which floats the Church. Why are a dove's eyes golden yellow? Because yellow, the colour of ripe fruit, is the colour of experience and maturity. The yellow eyes of the dove symbolize the glance of wisdom which the Church casts on the future. Finally, the dove has red feet, for the Church progresses through the world her feet reddened by the blood of martyrs.' To his work much of the allegorical inspiration of mediaeval literature is due ; Dante gratefully gives him a lofty seat in Paradise.

Hugh of St. Victor, though he wrote in France and bears the stamp of French training, was not French by birth. The next great mediaeval symbolists, Guillaume Durand and Adam of St. Victor, belong altogether to France ; they naturalize Hugh of St. Victor's symbolism by transmuting it into terms of art. The *Rationale divinorum officiorum* of Durand takes the office of the mass as containing the greater part of what was fulfilled by and in Christ from His descent to earth to His Ascension, and all the sacrifices of the ancient law, and then explains every part of the edifice of the church in which mass is performed as typifying one or another of these aspects of it. Here it is that symbolism is accepted by art, for the *Rationale divinorum officiorum* is mirrored in the sculpture and architecture of the French cathedrals, for instance at Chartres and Bourges.[1]

The second great French symbolist was a pupil of Hugh of St. Victor, but was a Breton by birth. Adam of St. Victor received the symbolism of Hugh, but embodied it in sequences of hymns for church use; in his turn he transmuted it to imagery. His work can only be appreciated in its Latin form, but it is purely French in the vividnesss and clarity of its style. With him, as with the French cathedral builders, symbolism serves a true artistic purpose :

> O Maria ! Stella maris !
> Dignitate singularis,
> Super omnes ordinaris
>   Ordines coelestium !
> In supremo sita poli
> Nos commenda tuae proli,
> Ne terrores sive doli
>   Nos supplantent hostium !

[1] It is through such works, and not through the Bestiaries themselves, that bestiary animals enter Gothic decoration.

But artistic symbolism is not the most important intellectual activity of mediaeval France. Its fundamental interest was the study of logic; that reasoning science by which men can proceed from fact to abstraction, from abstraction to principle, from principle to law. In this sphere not only did France recreate mediaeval science, but she also gave new life to its language. Latin was of necessity the language of learning, which cannot be trammelled by the bonds of dialect; and Latin in French hands was given a new subtlety, a new flexibility, and a new power of dealing with the matter of abstract thought. Scholastic Latin is a living language that owes its vitality to France.

The process of civilization often consists in substituting a conscious method for a half-conscious process, and this is what the dialectic of Paris did for European thought in the Middle Ages. It is no doubt true that method was in some sense developed at the expense of content; we find Robert de Sorbon asking, 'Does not he who day and night practises the tortures of dialectic walk in the way of vanity and darkness of the mind? Is not the labourer mad who is for ever sharpening his ploughshare without ever ploughing the field? The art of dialectic should sharpen the mind, but in order to prepare it for greater things.' Yet even if mediaeval logicians were not in a position to use their dialectic so fruitfully as later ages have done, they built up a system of clear thinking that has ever since been the foundation of science not only in France but also in Europe.

The central problem of mediaeval thought was the problem of the priority of the universal over the particular. Two schools of thought endeavoured to answer it; the Realists believed universals—let us say the Church, Humanity, Divinity —to be prior to the particular—the churchman, the individual man, the Persons of the Trinity—and held that the universal must first be comprehended in order to comprehend the particular. Further, the universal had existence as a thing, *res*: the Church is an entity; humanity exists; the Unity of the Deity is: hence came their name of Realists. The most complete Realist is Anselm. He held with Plato that universals exist eternally in God, and are the interior discourse of His mind: models and types after which particulars are created. Anselm used Realism as the servant of the orthodox faith: his motto was the Augustinian *credo ut intelligam*: I believe in the God of Revelation, in order that in the light of that belief I may understand the world. His most famous thesis was the ontological argument in proof of the existence of God: God is the highest being of which the human mind can conceive; and the mere fact that such a conception is attainable and permanent is the proof of the existence of a Being corresponding to such a conception.[1]

The second answer was given by the Nominalists, who upheld the importance of the particular: *post rem universalia*. What had to be comprehended was the concrete uniqueness of the particular: the universal to them was *nomen*; it had a grammatical existence only. Their inspiration was ultimately Aristotelean; but they exaggerated the Aristotelean view that universals were concepts of reason predicable about particulars, and instead of emphasizing the importance of such concepts, and of reason in furnishing them, reduced them to what their leader Roscellinus called *flatus vocis*. Like all Aristoteleans they ended by paying attention to the particular itself and thus furthered the progress of scientific observation.

The typical French mediaeval logician is Abelard. He began as a student of logic, and remained a logician pure and simple up to 1113. He inclined to nominalism; he started from the individual, and believed that by the effort of thought we rise from it to the universal. But he approximated to the Realists in his belief that universals are not merely names, but are creations of the mind, necessary in the sense that thought is impossible without them, and real in virtue of their necessity. This conceptualism combines the analytic and the synthetic points of view, and is remarkable in two ways: that it approximates to the doctrine of Aristotle in the Posterior Analytics, which were not known in Paris till twenty years after Abelard's death,[2] and that it emphasizes the creative power of reason. The reasoning mind arrives at universals, and thus constitutes the universe as thought.

Abelard not only created a fresh philosophical point of view,

[1] Cf. Descartes' ontological argument in proof of the existence of God.

[2] In his *Theologia* he declares he has gathered his citations of pagan authors from the Fathers, and not from the books of the philosophers ' quorum pauca novi '.

but extended philosophy's sphere of vision. France is never content to let discovery in one province of knowledge be without influence upon other kinds of learning. Even in the eleventh century Berengar of Tours had argued that 'true courage lies in flying to dialectic in all things, since to fly to it is to fly to reason'; and had accordingly treated the doctrine of Transubstantiation in logical fashion. But with Abelard the fusion of the reasoning methods of dialectic with theology is more complete; he sought to rationalize in categories of formal logic every matter apprehended by his mind, and when he went to become Anselm of Laon's pupil in theology he crossed a dangerous threshold. He rapidly passed from pupil to master; as he tells us in his *apologia pro vita sua*, fitly called *Historia Calamitatum*:

'Then it came about that I was brought to expound the very foundation of our faith by applying the analogies of human reason, and was led to compose for my pupils a theological treatise on the Divine Unity and Trinity. They were calling for human and philosophical arguments and insisting upon something intelligible, rather than mere words, saying that there had been more than enough of talk which the mind could not follow; that it was impossible to believe what was not in the first place understood, and that it was ridiculous for any one to set forth to others what neither he nor they could rationally conceive (*intellectu capere*).'

It was impossible to believe what was not in the first place understood: Abelard reversed the Augustinian motto, and made *intelligo ut credam* his starting-point. 'By doubting we are led to inquire: by inquiry we perceive the truth.' It is impossible to rely entirely upon tradition, for tradition has inconsistent elements; two inconsistent things cannot be believed simultaneously, for it is the mark of truth that it is self-consistent. Reason and intelligence must do the preparatory work of solving or reconciling inconsistencies before faith can have a consistent body of belief which alone is credible. This is the fundamental idea of Abelard's method of marshalling his theological arguments: the method of *Sic et non*, by which he clarified the inconsistencies of Church tradition by opposing contradictory statements of the Fathers on a hundred and fifty-eight theological questions. His purpose is thus constructive and not destructive; it is to point beyond the inconsistencies of tradition to a reconciliation, and not to destroy faith by a mere exposure of inconsistencies.   Yet this was the light in which his work struck traditionalists and mystics like Bernard and Norbert; not only could they point to single sentences, like that famous one in Abelard's lost *De Trinitate*, 'that a thing is not believed because God said it, but received as true because proved to be so', but they could and did object to the whole tone, spirit, and method of his theological teaching.   He had presumed to try to understand and to explain the mystery of the Trinity, and had dared to bring all things in heaven and earth to the test of reason.

The proof of the constructive character of Abelard's method is the influence it exerted in the succeeding generation.   The disciple of Abelard was Peter Lombard, Bishop of Paris in 1159, the *Magister Sententiarum*, whose *Sentences* were the received text-book of theology for the later Middle Ages.[1] Here was carried on the positive work made possible by the negative criticism of Abelard: Peter followed his master in stating the *pro* and *contra*, and then harmonized them by distinctions or inferences.   His work is not so much original in itself as progressive in its systematization.

This systematization was due to Abelard, but as a logician Abelard died thirty years too soon.   Of the treatises of the Aristotelean *Organon* he only knew the first two, the *De Interpretatione* and the *Categories*, the first treating of the constituent parts and kinds of sentences and the second of the classes of logical propositions.   Not until the latter half of the twelfth century was the whole *Organon* known to the West; the introduction is probably due to another Frenchman, Thierry of Chartres.[2] The discovery of the laws of the syllogism, of logical demonstration, and of the refutation of false conclusions enlarged the intellectual horizon and advanced the method of scholastic thought.   The centre of study was still Paris; the Parisian doctor Gilbert de la Porrée is for the generation of Dante the master of the Six Principles of Logic for Christendom as a whole.

---

[1] In the thirteenth century Dominican convents always had a *Sententiarus* to lecture on the Sentences as well as a *Biblicus* to lecture on the Bible.

[2] By the eighth century Aristotle and his Greek commentators had been translated from Syriac into Arabic, and with the growth of learning in Spain this was translated by the Spanish Jews into Hebrew and thence in 1128 into Latin.

But if the scholars of the thirteenth century recovered the ancient principles of logical reasoning, they also discovered fresh material on which to exercise them. Greek mathematics, medicine, and science came back to Europe, both from Moslem Spain and from the Byzantine East. Knowledge once more took an encyclopaedic turn; but the pioneers were not Frenchmen, but foreign doctors of Paris—the English Alexander of Hales and the Swabian Albertus. Albertus, an active Dominican, vowed to strict poverty and unable to own even his own manuscripts, fulfilling his duty as Provincial of Germany by walking barefoot through the province under his supervision, yet found time and energy to serve science. At the beginning of his exposition of Aristotle's *Physics* he says that substantial philosophy has three parts, physics, mathematics, and metaphysics, and 'it is our intention to make all the said parts intelligible to the Latins'. The marvellous thing is that he accomplished it, and that he lived in an age that could understand his work. He took and made his own the Aristotelean view that the love of knowledge is natural to man, and though he is mediaeval in his reliance on his sources, he yet recognizes that even Aristotle may be fallible. He is the link between Abelard and Roger Bacon, for he says, ' experiments should be made not in one way only, but according to all the circumstances'. Moreover, for him the compass of knowledge was not yet complete: 'It must be stated that not all the demonstrative sciences have been established, but that many still remain to be discovered.' He does not test the opinions of others by experiment, but he does observe natural phenomena and incorporate his observations in his work.[1] The twenty-one books of his work cover Logic, Physics, Metaphysics, Ethics, Politics, and the main branches of natural science—Botany, Mineralogy, Zoology, and so forth.

The new body of learning thus began to be systematized, and as this happened it had simultaneously to be incorporated in the Christian scheme of the universe. St. Louis, who had been impelled by the example of the Sultan to collect a library, furthered this incorporation by lending Vincent of Beauvais twelve hundred manuscripts, from which he and his staff

[1] His book *De mineralibus*, for instance, contains a number of first-hand observations, and is the first mediaeval lapidary to do so.

compiled an encyclopaedia.[1]   This was composed of four parts—
three, the *Speculum Naturale*, the *Speculum Doctrinale*, and the
Speculum Historiale, forming the *Imago Mundi*, and the fourth,
the *Speculum Morale*—a later work—dealing with the spiritual
world.   The *Imago Mundi* is arranged in scriptural order :
it treats first of the Creator, next of the creation, then of man's
fall and reparation, and then of events—*rebus gestis*—chronologically.   The history, however, is still that of the *City of God*,
of saints of the old and the new law.   Ancient history is ' historia
filiorum Cain ' ; but Vincent none the less shows a sound knowledge of Virgil, Horace, Ovid, Lucan, Cicero, and other authors
in the episodes he admits.   There are three evils in the world ;
ignorance, sin, and mortality, for which there are three
remedies ; wisdom, represented by philosophia theorica, virtue,
represented by philosophia practica, and action, by philosophia
mechanica.   ' Theorica,' he says, ' driving out ignorance,
illuminates wisdom ; Practica, shutting out vice, strengthens
virtue ; and Mechanica,[2] providing against penury, tempers the
infirmities of the present life.   Theorica, in all that is and that
is not, chooses to investigate the true ; Practica determines the
right way of living and the form of discipline, according to the
institution of the virtues ; Mechanica, occupied with fleeting
things, strives to provide for the needs of the body.   For the end
and aim of all human actions and studies, which reason regulates,
ought to concern either the reparation of the integrity of our
nature or the alleviation of the needs to which life is subjected.
The integrity of our nature is repaired by wisdom, to which
Theorica relates, and by Virtue, which Practica cultivates.
Need is alleviated by the administration of temporalities, to
which Mechanica attends.   Last found of all is Logic, source
of eloquence, through which the wise who understand the
aforesaid principal sciences and disciplines may discourse upon
them more correctly, truly, and elegantly ; more correctly
through Grammar ; more truly through Dialectic ; more

---

[1] He was thus the first man to earn the right to be called a bookworm :
librorum helluo.
[2] Thus it is that the labours of the field of each month appear on the façades
of Notre Dame de Paris and at Amiens.   His divisions may be compared
with this threefold division of the three worlds of Pascal—monde des corps,
monde des esprits, monde de la charité.

elegantly through Rhetoric.' Mediaeval philosophy still keeps the liberal arts within its synthesis: education is still based on the Trivium and still lies within the province of religion. On tombs of the thirteenth century no one is represented in pursuit of his calling but the priest with the chalice, since the Church says 'tu es sacerdos in aeternum', and the professor seated teaching from his chair, for he teaches the truth which is also eternal.

It remained for one not a Frenchman, but a doctor and teacher at Paris, to wed the whole of the recovered Aristotle to the teaching of the Fathers and the traditions of the Church, as Abelard had wedded Aristotelean logic to theology. Aquinas strictly follows the scholastic method of *Sic et non*, and never forgets to consider any side of the question; he expounds syllogistic argument within syllogistic argument with unfailing lucidity; he, the Angelic Doctor, constructs an ideal universe that by reason springs from the Christian faith. A true syllogistic structure supersedes the plan of the *Sentences* in setting one excerpted opinion against another, to the end of arriving at an adjustment. His conclusion is that final and perfect beatitude can only be in the vision of the Divine essence. 'For perfect beatitude it is necessary that the intellect should attain to the very essence of the first cause. And thus it will have its perfection through union with God as its object.'

Thus philosophy and theology were made one in the dialectic processes of the Aristotelean syllogism. It remained for Dante to show the congruity of mediaeval humanity and mediaeval Christianity in his symbolic transmutation of material to spiritual, mortal to eternal. His is the true ability to *reducere ad unum*, for he makes his *Divina Commedia* not only a *summa salvationis* but also a poem.[1]

All the learned books so far described were clerical, professional, and for the ordinary man abstruse. Written in Latin, they were intended for the clerk and not for the layman. But since learning was a part of religion, the friars helped to bring it as part of religion down to the popular level. It is true that St. Francis was on the whole opposed to learning and that the Dominican constitutions of 1228 forbade the brethren to study 'books of the gentiles and secular sciences'. But the new

[1] The way was paved for it by Raoul de Houdan's *Voie d'enfer* (a vision of Hell) and *Voie de Paradis*.

religious movement attracted men of intellectual energy, who
leading an uncloistered life could not escape the influence of
the new learning. We have seen the importance of the
encyclopaedic work of the great Dominican Doctors Albertus
and Aquinas, and in the same century we find the facts, if not
the philosophical structure, of these Latin works reproduced in
œuvres de vulgarisation in the vernacular. Such works were
in real demand; even a German Franciscan with a strong dislike
of France confesses in his *Notitia Seculi* of 1288 that the
French are filled with the 'amor sciendi', and Etienne de
Bourbon records that Robert d'Auvergne, who died in 1234,
made out of historical curiosity so large a collection of books
'concerning heresy and heretics', to which he devoted forty
years of his life, that his own orthodoxy became suspect. The
thirteenth century witnessed a considerable production of quasi-
scientific treatises in French, usually translated from Latin:
books on astronomy and astrology, on animals (*bestiaires*), birds
(*volucraires*), stones (*lapidaires*), and plants (*herbiers*), on weather,
on medicine, on physiognomy, and on world history. Some are
merely descriptions of the 'proprietez des choses'; some cater
for the romantic with 'merveilles', and some for the pious with
allegorical 'senefiances'.

The most interesting are the treatises with an encyclopaedic
scope, and of these the *Image du Monde*, written by a friar of
Metz in 1247, is one of the earliest. It is based on Honorius's
Imago Mundi, Cardinal Jacques de Vitry's *Historia Hiero-
solymitana*, and the *Anticlaudianus* of Alain de Lille, and is
divided into three books; the first concerned with God, with
human intelligence, and the cosmogony of the universe; the
second with earth and the four elements that compose it; and
the third with the Heavens, and a good many discursions
which found no other place.

The friar begins by describing the ancients, who

> Ne penserent pas comme bestes
> Qui ne quierent fors la pasture . . .
> Ainz veillierent par mainte nuit . . .
> N'orent de nul autre avoir cure
> Fors d'aprendre science pure.[1]

[1] 'They did not think like the beasts, who only seek for food, but watched
through many a night, nor had heed of anything but to learn pure knowledge.'

' By their efforts the seven Arts were established, and many were martyred in the cause of knowledge. We shall only make like progress in our time if we are equally disinterested. In these days men think only of riches, and only at Paris does learning survive. There, thank God, the Mendicants have lately come and " retiennent or la flour de clergie ".'

The author proceeds to describe a globular, geocentric universe. Earth is the heaviest of the four elements, and so our world is at the centre,

Quer qui pluz poise plus bas tret
Et quanque poise a lui atret.[1]

Men should remember that as the earth is tiny in relation to the heavens, so is earthly life petty in comparison with the heavenly. The earth is divided into four parts. Asia is the earthly paradise where is the tree of life and the fountain whence rise the four great rivers: the Indian Phison, the Egyptian Nile, the Tigris, and the Euphrates. India is surrounded by the great sea, where is the Isle Taprobane (Ceylon). There summer and winter come twice in the year, but so mildly that the trees are always green. There are found gold and precious stones guarded by dragons and griffins; there too are cannibals. India is divided into four and twenty provinces, all very populous. There are pygmies, who live in tribes; ' brahmanes ', who throw themselves into the fire; and others who worship the sun. There are hairy people who eat raw fish and drink salt water, as well as hordes of monstrous creatures. In India are serpents that can eat deer, and many terrible beasts. The Indians and Persians are used to fighting on elephants, seated in little towers.

Europe can be dismissed in a string of names, since all men know them. Africa is a dark continent. Then come the islands—Colchis, where Jason went for the Golden Fleece; the island where St. Denis was born; Delos, that first appeared above the waters of the Flood; Paros, with its white marble; Samos, whence came the Sibyl who prophesied the coming of Christ; Sicily, where Pythagoras was born, and where pottery was first made; Sardinia, the Balearics, Meroes, where there

---

[1] ' For that which is heaviest falls lowest, and draws to it all things which have weight.'

is no shade, and the lost land that Plato knew that sank beneath the sea.

Then to the north, Ireland where there are no snakes, and Thule with its evergreen trees, and its division of the year into one long day and one long night.

Then follows a long description of the marvels of nature; every-day things that none the less cannot be explained.

> Quar il n'est si petite chose
> Dont nus hom puist savoir la glose
> Veraiement por coi ele est
> Fors si com a Damnedieu plest.[1]

From the exterior of the earth the author passes to a vivid description of hell. This concludes the section on earth, and the author proceeds to deal with the other elements: water, with a consideration of mineral springs; the air, with a description of the reasons why the weather changes; and fire, which is a kind of air, noble, subtle, and shining, with no trace of humidity. Thence the author passes to astronomy: day and night, the phases of the moon, and the hidden forces of the heavens on earthly things. Ptolemy of Egypt was the first to make great progress in the study of the planets, and he invented clocks. These are a great help to man, since God loves order and regularity.

> Si sont ore maintes gens mors
> Qui, se lor afferes eüssent
> Ordenez si com il deüssent
> Chascun jor a heure establie,
> Qui encore fussent en vie.[2]

It is to Ptolemy that we owe the calendar, revised by Caesar, the next great astronomer. So we come to a general consideration of Philosophy. What is it?

> Philosophie est connoissance
> Et fine amour de sapience . . .
> Dont Platon respondi aucun
> Qui li demanda en commun:
> 'Sire Platon, avez apris
> Qui tant avez vostre tans mis

---

[1] 'For there is no thing so small that man can know the meaning of it truly for what it is unless it pleases God.'

[2] 'How many men are dead, who if they had ordered their business as they ought, each day at a fixed hour, might still be alive?'

Et estudié por aprendre? . . .
Quar nous dites aucun bon mot.'
Et Platons, qui plus que nus sot,
Lor dist, si comme a cuer dolant,
Qu'il n'avoit rien apris fors tant
Qu'il se sentoit et jour et nuit
Ausi com un vaissel tout vuit;
Tant leur en respondit Platons.[1]

There also exists a second version of the *Image du Monde*, written a few years later. To this the author has added a certain amount of information drawn from personal experience, including an account of the ascent of Etna:

Je, qui cest livre fis ici,
Celes .ii. monteignes je vi
Et montai en son la plus grans
Pour veïr ce qu'ist de leans.
La bouche vi de la fumée
Qu'adès fume sanz reposée . . .
U feu ting ma main nuement:
Suer la me fist doucement . . .
Grans esté fu; si oi grant soif,
Si bui de l'engelee noif . . .
Au descendre oï la tonnierre
Plus bas de moi desouz mon erre
Pour la nue en quoi il tonnoit,
Qui plus basse de moi estoit.[2]

It is evident that writing in the vernacular makes the book more personal and in closer touch with common life. This directness may have influenced Brunetto Latino, who, while passing three or four years in French lands after 1263, wrote his encyclopaedic *Livre du Trésor* in French 'porce que la

[1] 'Philosophy is knowledge and a noble love of wisdom. About which Plato answered one who asked him in company: "Sir Plato, what have you learnt, who have studied and spent so much time in learning? Pray tell us something witty." And Plato, who knew more than any one, said to him as if his heart was heavy, that he had learnt nothing but that he felt night and day like an empty vessel. That is what Plato answered.'

[2] 'I who made this book have seen these two mountains, and have climbed the larger to the top, to see what comes forth there. I saw the mouth of the smoke that always smokes without ceasing. . . . I held my naked hand near the fire, and it made it sweat gently. . . . It was high summer, and I was very thirsty, and drank from the frozen snow. Coming down I heard the thunder, beneath my path lower down, out of the cloud in which it thundered, which was lower than I.'

parleure et plus delitable et plus commune a toutes gens'.   His
book, too, makes no claim to originality, it is 'compilés seule-
ment de mervillus diz des autors qui devant nostre tens ont
traitié de philosophie'.   Its philosophic aim is to show that the
function of nature is to accord the discordant principles—
hot and cold, wet and dry—so that 'totes diversités retornent
en unité'.

The next encyclopaedia was written in Latin by an Englishman, Bartholomew Glanvil, who is said by Salimbene to have
first delivered its substance as a course of lectures at the
University of Paris. It was, at all events, popular there; not only
was it on the official list of books on hire from the university
booksellers to the students, but it was also owned in duplicate by
the Sorbonne.   It is intended for the use of preachers who
need illustrations for their sermons, and lacks the philosophic
scope of the earlier encyclopaedias.   It is significant that it was
almost immediately translated into French by Jean Corbichon,
and that it is in the translated form that it was most used.

The very popularity of Bartholomew's book shows a certain
decline.   The *Summa Theologiae* of Aquinas is the true crown
of French scholastic thought.   The aim of such thought, both
in detail of method and in breadth of aim, was *reducere ad unum*;
with the next generation the aim was changed, and the French
systematization of thought went to pieces in English hands.
The aim of Roger Bacon and Duns Scotus was not to lead
thought back to unity but to find out new truths.   Yet Gerson
could still call the University of Paris 'the Paradise of this
world, where is the tree of knowledge of good and evil', and
for the later Middle Ages she was still the fountain to which
all streams of knowledge could eventually be traced.

The work of the Frenchmen of the later Middle Ages was
less to increase the sum of learning than to make that sum more
generally profitable.   The gradual assimilation of learned and
popular writings, no longer definitely divided by the test of
the language in which they were written, marks the growth
of a class of enlightened laics, and the transformation of learning
from the prerogative of the Church into a national possession.
A leading part in this transformation was taken by Charles V,
who was, like the rich amateur Philippe le Bon of Burgundy,
the elegant René of Anjou, and the poet Charles d'Orléans,

XXXIV.   Jean Miélot
translating the Miracles of Notre-Dame
c. 1456

both a student and a collector of books. Christine de Pisan is a witness to his learning: 'Shall we not also speak of the wisdom of King Charles, of the great love he had for study and knowledge? He clearly showed it by his fair array of notable books, and his fair library of all the most notable volumes which had been compiled by sovereign authors, whether of Holy Scripture, theology, philosophy, or the sciences, all well written and richly adorned; and the best scribes who could be found ever employed by him in such work; and whether his study was well ordered and well planned, since he wished all his possessions fair and clean, well kept and well ordered, it behoves not to ask: for a better could not be.'

Nor was it only by the collection and study of books that Charles forwarded the growth of a learned literature in French; it was due to his patronage that Pierre Bersuire translated Livy into French, Nicholas d'Oresme Aristotle, and Raoul de Presle Augustine's *City of God*, 'for the public utility of the realm and of all Christendom'. His library contained a considerable number of French translations of the classics of the two preceding centuries, such as the *Rationale* of Guillaume Durand and the works of Hugh of St. Victor. He possessed remarkably few works of scholastic theology, and among the legal books only one Latin text of the Institutes of Justinian as compared with numerous—and often duplicated—French works: translations of the Institutes, the Digest, the Code, and commentaries on them; the *Coutumier de Normandie* (three copies), Pierre de Fontaines, and French translations of six works on Canon Law. In science, besides the library of a specialist in astrology, we again find a marked preponderance of French works—the encyclopaedias are all French translations from Latin, Aristotle appears in French translation, and all the rest but a few old texts are in that language. In history there was not a single Latin book without a translation appended, and not a single example of a history of France written in Latin is mentioned in an inventory of very considerable length, including a large number of rhymed chronicles. The library of Charles V was not confined to learned literature,[1] but was

---

[1] It also included twenty-four romances of the Carolingian cycle, seventeen *Romans de la Table Ronde*, fifteen romances of classical subjects, seven *Romans d'aventures*, several collections of satirical compositions, and fifteen of lyrics.

rather a collection of the literary work of the French nation among which works of erudition took their place. Even at the university heavy punishments were being decreed in vain against the students who spoke French; and with a generation accustomed to think in French, succeeded by a generation that read from printed books, a new chapter in the history of learning began.

VII

EDUCATION

THE mediaeval view of man set his function and end before any other aspect of his being: 'the proper function does not come into existence for the sake of the being, but the latter for the sake of the former'. Consequently it was natural that mediaeval education should be definitely fitted to the function that the child was eventually to perform, whether as noble, as cleric, or as artisan. So it can be divided into three kinds —the practical, the speculative, and the technical—each of which was so to prepare the child to do his duty in his station that his existence might be justified and his function fulfilled.

The training of the noble child was rather *éducation* in the French sense than instruction of an academic kind. He had to carry on the practical work of feudal government; to fight, to be a courtier, to learn the self-control and the decision that befit a member of the governing class. A thirteenth-century sermon tells us: 'Peasants spoil their children and make them little red frocks, and then, when they are a little older, they put them to the plough. On the other hand, the nobles first set their children beneath them and make them eat with the serving lads; and then, when they are grown up, set them on high.' All the writers of the Middle Ages agree that to spare the rod is to spoil the child. It is a mistake also, to begin too late—the bough should be bent while it is still green. Philippe de Novare in his *Quatre Ages de l'homme* explains that after the age of ten children have the 'franc arbitre' between good and evil, and too much allowance must not be made for them. Rather are they to be corrected when young: 'N'avient pas sovent que anfant facent bien se ce n'est par doute ou par ansaignement.' Punish them first with words, then with rods, then, if you must, with imprisonment. Make them learn the Credo, Pater Noster, and Ave Maria; then the

two first commandments of the law : ‘Aimme ton Seigneur ton
Dieu de tout ton cuer et de toute ta pensée et de toute ta langue
et de touz tes manbres et de toute t’ame’, and ‘Aimme ton
proïme si comme toi meïsme’.

Such religious education seems usually to have been the
parent’s prerogative ; we have still the psalter from which
Blanche of Castille taught St. Louis his letters, and Joinville
describes St. Louis teaching his own children in his turn :
‘Before he lay down in his bed he would cause his children to
come to him, and bring to their minds the deeds of good kings
and good emperors, telling them that it was of such men they
should take example. And he would bring to their minds also
the deeds of great men who were wicked, and by their ill-
doing, and their rapine, and their avarice, had brought their
kingdoms to ruin. . . . He made them learn the Hours of Our
Lady, and say before him the Hours of the Day, so as to ac-
custom them to hear the Hours when they ruled over their
own lands.’ Much of the moral training thus received rested
upon the idea that the man of noble birth should in every
thought and deed set a good example to others. So we find
St. Louis reminding Joinville that if he would be honoured in
this world and go to Paradise in the next, he should keep himself from knowingly doing or saying anything which, if the
whole world knew of it, he would be ashamed to acknowledge.
So, too, good manners were a duty. The romance of *Urbain le
Courtois* tells us :

> Li bon enfant deit ester
> Devant son seigneur a manger.
> Il ne se doit apouuer
> Ne nul membre de doit grater . . .
> Si homme vous doigne petit u grant
> Tant com vous este joesne enfant
> En genouillant le recevez
> Et doucement lui merciez.[1]

and the child was brought up to speak politely to clerks and
not to make a noise in church.[2] France was early aware—and

[1] ‘The good child ought to stand upright before his lord at meals, and not
lean against anything or scratch his limbs with his finger. . . . If any one
gives you anything, great or small, while you are still a young child, receive
it kneeling and thank him nicely.’

[2] *Doon de Mayence*, thirteenth century.

XXXV. The Family

15th Century

has never forgotten—that good manners are based on consideration for others, and are thus a part of morality. By 1247
the author of *Sidrach* teaches that you should listen, even if
you are bored; 'car si est un grand sens de courtoisie de
regarder a celui qui parle, car il li fait plaisir'. You must show
neither haughtiness nor shyness; every one has a right to play
a part in society, and if from either of these reasons a man is
silent, 'il pert sa raison et son droit'. It is selfish to show
your feelings: when Galeran is in love he is reproved by his
chaplain-tutor for looking miserable:

> Tout le monde blasme et reprent
> Jeune varlet et riche et hault
> Qu'en ne voit envoisié et baut . . .
> S'en vous voy faire chiere mate
> En vo pays repris serez.[1]

And in another romance Joufroi has to hide his feelings when
he hears of his father's death:

> Car n'avient pas a nul baron
> Qu'il face dueil outre raison.[2]

Even St. Louis had occasionally to be reminded of this duty
of self-control. Joinville tells us that when he lost his mother
he 'made such lamentation that, for two days, no one could
speak to him. After that he sent one of the varlets of his
chamber to summon me. When I came before him in his
chamber, where he was alone, and he saw me, he stretched out
his arms, and said: "Ah, Seneschal, I have lost my mother!"
"Sir," said I, "I do not marvel at that, since she had to die;
but I do marvel that you, who are a wise man, should have
made such great mourning; for you know what the sage says:
that whatever grief a man may have in his heart, none should
appear in his countenance, because he who shows his grief
causes his enemies to rejoice and afflicts his friends."'

There was much for the child to learn besides religion and
good manners. *Les Quatre Ages de l'Homme* expounds the
typically French view that the whole function of life is to be
able to follow one's profession well; to do this the child must

---

[1] 'Every one blames and rebukes a young man, rich and well born, who
does not look gay and gallant. . . . If they see you looking sad you will be
rebuked in your own country.'
[2] 'For it befits not a baron to mourn beyond reason.'

next learn its ' métier '. ' Clergie et chevalerie ' are the most
honourable callings, and both must be learnt young. ' A poines
puet estre bon clers qui ne commance dès anfance, ne ja bien
ne chevauchera qui ne l'aprent jones.' The thirteenth-century
romance of *Aiol* describes the ideal education for a boy of noble
birth :

>   Il n'ot valet en France mieus dotriné(s),
>   Ne mieus a .i. preudome seust parler.
>   Del ceval et des armes seut il assés,
>   Si vos dirai comment, se vous volés :
>   Car ses peres l'ot fait sovent monter
>   Par la dedens le bos ens en .i. pré
>   Et le boin ceval core et trestorner,
>   De dit et de parolle l'en a moustré,
>   Aiols le retient bien comme senés ;
>   Et des cours des estoiles, del remuer,
>   Del refait de la lune, del rafermer,
>   De chou par savoit il quant qu'il en ert :
>   Avise la ducoise l'en ot moustré ;
>   Il n'ot plus sage feme en .x. chités.
>   Et Moisès l'ermite l'ot doctriné
>   De letres de gramaire l'ot escolé :
>   Bien savoit Aiols lire et enbriever,
>   Et latin et romans savoit parler.

In the early fourteenth-century romance of *Sone de Nansai* the
hero learns to read and write, to play chess and backgammon,
to hawk, hunt, and fence; to study geometry, ' magic ', and
law; and has as many as four masters.[2] Fencing was learnt
not so much for its own sake as to develop the lungs; in
L'Escoufle Guillaume studies it :

>   Por combatre nel fait il mie,
>   Mais por avoir grignor alaine.
>   Et c'est une chose certaine

---

[1] ' There was no youth in France better brought up, nor who knew better
how to speak to a gentleman. He knew enough about horses and arms, and if
you like I will tell you how : for his father made him often ride through the wood-
land and in the meadow and learn how to trot and turn the horse, and showed him
by word and deed, and Aiol remembered it well as a sensible youth. He knew all
about the courses of the stars, the changes of the moon, . . . Avice the duchess
had shown him ; there was no wiser woman in ten cities. And Moses the
hermit had taught him, and schooled him in letters and grammar. Well did
Aiol know how to read and write, how to speak in Latin and French . . .'

[2] A similar account is given in *Galeran*.

Que hom va plus bel et plus droit
Et si en est on mout plus droit :
To cis biens vient de l'escremie.[1]

Of his other studies, chess and backgammon, hawking and hunting, were knightly occupations; Law befitted one who had judicial powers; and fair speech was a necessity. Writing was less important, and went more against the grain. *Sidrach* describes how difficult it is: the man who writes labours with his body and his eyes and his brain, and dare neither think nor look nor laugh nor speak nor listen while he is writing. Only the scribe knows what an art it is.

Yet reading, writing, and a little Latin were useful for a man of high birth, and by 1454 we find Charles, Duke of Berry, aged eight, owning five school books—an ABC, a copy of the Seven Penitential Psalms, Donatus on the eight parts of speech, Cato's moral distichs with a French translation, and a rhymed abstract of Priscian's Latin Grammar.

On the other hand it was, generally speaking, better for womenfolk to be unlettered. *Urbain le Courtois* gives good advice :

Si femme volez esposer
Pensez de tei, mon fils chier.
Pernez nule por sa beauté
Ni ki soit en livre lettrié ;
Car sovent sunt decevables.[2]

What women must know is how to spin and sew, to embroider and sing ; and above everything to acquire 'la bele contenance et simple'; to look straight in front of them, quietly and unaffectedly, and to learn to behave without either prudery or over-familiarity.

Social condition was the directive force in education among the lower classes as among the nobility. Children learnt their *métier*, most often from a parent or near relative ; and they had other schooling, chiefly in learning to read in the Psalter, for which time is usually claimed in the indentures of their

---

[1] 'He does not do it for fighting, but to have deeper breath ; and it is a certain thing that one is fitter and more erect and much straighter for it. . . . All these good things come from fencing.'

[2] 'If you wish to marry a wife, dear son, consider your own good ; take none for her beauty, nor any that have book learning, for they are often deceitful.' A similar view is expressed in *Les Quatre Ages de l'Homme.*

apprenticeship. Even girls got a certain amount of such teaching; the nunnery of Prouille, near Castelnaudary, was founded by St. Dominic for the special purpose of training nuns to act as village school-mistresses. A certain number of mistresses worked in Paris under the control of the Precentor of Notre Dame, who gave them the licence to teach *in litteris grammaticis.*

Yet since each exists to fulfil a specific function in society, men and women of noble or artisan birth had little concern with the sphere of learning. That sphere was the province of the clerk; it was his heritage as much as his land was the knight's or his trade the craftsman's; and, like them, he had to learn his *métier* young.

Mediaeval clerkly education in France begins with Charlemagne. Alcuin's school was migratory and followed the court, but it did much to establish a tradition, which was strengthened by the enactments of 787 and 789 that every cathedral should have a school for young clerks. Down to the beginning of the eleventh century the chief educational centres were the monastic schools. Rheims was the most important; here Gerbert did much to found the French educational tradition. Towards the end of his life he wrote to the abbot of the monastery of Tours:

' I am not one who . . . would sometimes separate the good from the useful, but rather . . . would mingle it with everything useful. . . . And as morality and the art of speech are not to be severed from philosophy, I have always joined the study of speaking well with the study of living well. . . . In preparing for such a business (of establishing a school) I am eagerly collecting a library; and as formerly at Rome and elsewhere in Italy, so likewise in Germany and Belgium, I have obtained copyists and manuscripts with a mass of money and the help of friends in those parts. Permit me likewise to beg of you also to promote this end. I will append at the end of this letter a list of those writers whom I wish to have copied. I have sent for your disposal parchment for the scribes and money to defray the cost.'

It is to Gerbert that we owe the musical stave and the scale that takes its notes from the hymn to St. John:

> *Ut* queant laxis
> *Re*sonare fibris
> *Mi*ra gestorum
> *Fa*muli tuorum

*So*lve polluti
*La*bii reatum
*Sa*ncte Johannes.

At Rheims, as at most of the monastic schools, there were two departments, one for the monastery's own *oblati* and one for external pupils. The oblates—who were usually received into the community at about the age of seven were under a strict discipline. The fourteenth-century custumal of St. Bénigne at Dijon, for instance, decrees,

At Nocturns, and indeed at all the Hours, if the boys commit any fault in the Psalmody or other singing, either by sleeping or such like transgression, let there be no sort of delay, but let them be stripped forthwith of frock and cowl, and be beaten in their shirt only. . . . Let the masters sleep between every two boys in the dormitory, and sit between every two at other times. . . . When they lie down in bed, let a master always be among them with his rod and (if it be night) with a candle, holding the rod in one hand and the light in the other. If any chance to linger after the rest, he is forthwith to be smartly touched; for children everywhere need custody with discipline, and discipline with custody. . . . When they wash, let masters stand between each pair. . . . When they sit in cloister or chapter, let each have his own tree-trunk for a seat, and so far apart that none touch in any way even the skirt of the other's robe. . . . Let them wipe their hands as far as possible one from the other, that is at opposite corners of the towel. . . . Nor doth one ever speak to the other, except by his master's express leave, and in the hearing of all who are in the school. . . . One reporteth whatsoever he knoweth against the other; else, if he be found to have concealed aught of set purpose, both the concealer and the culprit are beaten.'

But if the cloister had its terrors for the schoolboy destined for the Church, so had the alternative, the private tutor. Guibert de Nogent, who was born in 1053, has left a sad little picture of his childish education under a tutor at home :

'When I was set to learning, I had indeed already touched the rudiments, yet I could scarce put together the simplest elements when my loving mother, eager for my teaching, purposed to set me to grammar. . . . The man to whom my mother was purposed to give me over, had begun to learn grammar at an advanced age, and was so much the more rude in that art, that he had known so little thereof in his youth. Yet he was of so great modesty that his honesty supplied his lack of learning. . . . When therefore I was set under his care, he taught me with such purity and guarded me so sincerely . . . that he kept me altogether from the general games, never suffering me to go forth unaccompanied, nor to eat away from home, nor to accept any gift without his leave . . . whereas the others of my age wandered everywhere at their own will. . . . I for my part was shackled by constant restraints, sitting in my little clerical cloak and watching the bands of playing children like some tame animal. . . . But while he lay so hard upon me, and all who knew us thought that my little mind must be sharpened to its keenest edge by these incessant pains, all men's hopes were none the less frustrated. For he himself was utterly ignorant of the arts of composition, whether in verse or in prose ; so that I was smitten with a grievous and almost daily hail of fierce words and blows, while he would have compelled me to learn that which he himself knew not. . . . Weary nature should sometimes find her remedy in some diversity of work. Let us bear in mind how God formed his world, not in uniformity, but with vicissitudes of day and night, of spring and summer and autumn and winter, thus refreshing us by the change of the seasons.'

To almost every boy the elements seem to have been hardly taught, and it is the hardship and not the method that is recorded for posterity. Only Anselm's voice is heard to remind the teacher that his boys are human like himself, and have need 'of loving kindness from others, of gentleness, mercy, cheerful address, charitable patience, and many such like comforts '.

School education developed slowly and gradually, changing not with any change of view but to meet the slow development of the national life. The oblate schools survived, but Bec was the last of any great importance, and in the eleventh century the control of education passed into the hands of the secular clergy in the cathedral schools. Of these, Chartres, Laon, Auxerre, Sens, Rouen, and Clermont were the chief; and at all these cathedrals, as at Notre Dame de Paris, the sculptured figures of the Seven Liberal Arts appear on the façade : Grammar as an old woman with the rod of correction, Dialectic with the serpent of wisdom, Rhetoric with the tablets of the poet, Arithmetic counting on her fingers, Geometry with the compasses, Astronomy with the astrolabe, and Music striking a peal of bells with a hammer.

Grammar, the science of words, was followed by the sciences of thought ; Logic, which Vincent de Beauvais says argues from theses, that is from abstractions, and Rhetoric, that argues from hypotheses, or circumstantial evidence. Rhetoric, indeed, covered both poetry and law ; Brunetto Latino gives an account of all its ' couleurs ' : ' aornemens, tourn, comparaison, clamour, fainture, trespas, demonstrance, adoublement ',[1] and the *Image du Monde* says that from Rhetoric

> sont li Droit estrait
> Par coi li jugement sont fait
> Qui esgardé sont par raison
> En court de Roi et de Baron . . .
> Qui Retoricque bien sauroit
> Il connoistroit et tort et droit.[2]

The cathedral schools rose to importance by virtue of the ability of the teachers who ruled them—Fulbert, St. Ives, Gilbert de la Porrée, and their peers—and therefore it was natural that they should mark a real development of pedagogic method. The best teachers found themselves in a position to teach as they pleased, and to link their own learning more closely to the teaching of their scholars. Fulbert, appointed Bishop of Chartres in 1006, was the direct heir of Gerbert's learning and helped firmly to establish his educational system. Not only were pupils of all ages instructed in the Trivium— Grammar, Logic, and Rhetoric—but the higher faculties were also included. The improved methods of arithmetical computation which Gerbert had brought from Spain, including a use of Arabic numerals if not of the cipher; music; astronomy, with clear teaching on Greek lines on the horizon and the parallels; medicine—Fulbert himself cast the Hippocratic receipts into verse for memorizing; much theology of a traditional kind, based on the study of Augustine, and the study of some Canon and Roman Law and the Capitularies of Charlemagne, made Fulbert's school at Chartres representative of the extreme compass of learning in eleventh-century France.

At Chartres John of Salisbury, about 1140, received his classical training from William of Conches on the method invented by Bernard Sylvester—a method which is the direct ancestor of the *lecture expliquée* which still forms the basis of French teaching. Most of the available classical authors were studied in turn. After questioning his pupils on parsing,

---

[1] ' Paraphrase, form, comparison, apostrophe, imagination, metaphor, description, and repetition.'

[2] ' Does Law come forth, by which judgements are made which are rightly considered in King's and Baron's courts. . . . Who well knows Rhetoric knows both right and wrong.

scansion, construction, grammatical figures, and 'oratorical tropes' in the passage read, the lecturer commented on the varieties of phraseology which there occurred, and pointed out possible alternatives. Then the subject-matter was analysed and annotated. The next morning the students, under threat of the severest penalties, had to repeat what they had been taught the previous day. Such study of texts was supplemented by teaching in verse and prose composition in imitation of the authors read, and by frequent discussions on set themes. It is obvious that teaching such as this inevitably leads to more advanced work ; it is thus that the transition from school to university teaching was insensibly effected.

It is almost accidental that a succession of great teachers of law—Irnerius for Roman Law and Gratian for Canon Law— at Bologna, and a succession of philosophers, William of Champeaux, Hugh of St. Victor, and Abelard at Paris, should have given Bologna and Paris permanent importance as the two great seats of mediaeval learning. But though the University of Paris, even in its most rudimentary state, did not exist until a generation after Abelard, and there was nothing in Abelard's schools to distinguish them from any cathedral school made famous by a single master, it must not be forgotten that he helped to inaugurate the intellectual movement out of which the University of Paris sprang. His career at Paris exactly coincided with the first steps of its rapid rise to commercial and political importance ; his renown drew thither crowds of students from the remotest parts of Europe. For a century and a half his method of teaching and inquiry was the method that essentially characterized the university, and for the same length of time the stream of students contributed to make Paris the Mistress City of Transalpine Europe, and enabled Eudes de Chateauroux to declare that France was the oven where the intellectual bread of the whole world was baked.

Constitutionally speaking, the university was an outgrowth of the cathedral school, administered by the bishop and canons. Gradually the right of granting the licence to teach was transferred from the bishop to the chancellor of the cathedral. The need of organization among those thus licensed led to the formation of a guild of masters, and thus the university itself arose.

A university is far more closely allied to a guild than we usually remember. *Universitas vestra* is the polite form of address to any corporate body, whether it be a corporation of teachers or of cobblers, and in the Middle Ages *universitas* is therefore never used absolutely, but is always qualified: 'The University of Paris' is a convenient abbreviation for the University of the Chancellor, Masters, and Scholars of Paris. The mediaeval phrase for the place where higher studies are pursued was *studium generale*, but this did not mean a place where all subjects were studied, but a place where students from all parts could pursue their studies.

The University of Paris first came into being about 1160.[1] By the thirteenth century it was full grown; it was no longer a question of chapter-schools and wandering teachers, but of an organized university with regular doctors teaching permanently, where the student could proceed to the higher faculties of theology, law, and medicine after taking his degree in arts. Their guild of masters had taken its place in the city.

The earliest written statutes—which arose like so many university regulations out of a town and gown row—date from about 1208 and are guild regulations of the simplest kind. Members of the university are to wear a plain round black cloak, reaching to the heels, 'saltem dum nova est'; they are to follow the 'accustomed order' in lectures and disputations, and are to attend the funerals of deceased masters. The first statutes confirmed by the Pope, dating from 1215, lay down regulations for the actual teaching: Grammar and Logic are to be studied on ordinary days, and Rhetoric and Philosophy reserved as a treat for festivals. The next versions of the statutes—those of 1228 and 1244—give the university the legal right of suspending lectures as a protest against any injustice done to its corporation or to any of its members.

Since all lectures were in Latin, the student had to be able to read, write, and understand it, and necessity took the place of an entrance examination. A Statute of Paris makes the ability of a petitioner to state his case before the rector in Latin, without any 'interposition of French words', a test of his *bona fide* studentship. The university curriculum was in its

---

[1] The author desires to express her indebtedness to Rashdall's account of the University of Paris in his *Universities of the Middle Ages*.

turn inherited from the cathedral school. The Seven Liberal Arts—the more advanced of which hardly formed part of school training—comprised the whole sphere of education, not only in France, but in every civilized country. But then, as now, each university tended to focus its efforts on a single aspect of knowledge ; in Italy Grammar and Rhetoric received much attention, and Logic was studied with them for its importance on the legal side : Canon Law, indeed, came to be the aim of much Italian education. In Paris the goal proved to be Theology, and this is the dominating interest towards which all other studies, notably the study of Dialectic, were consciously or unconsciously bent. Further, the sphere of intellectual interests was extended through the re-discovery of Greek thought through Arabic translations. Aristotelean logic is the basis of the structure of scholastic thought as Aristotelean science is of the content of its *Summae*; and, in addition, the mathematical sciences also received a new impetus from the same source. The elements of Euclid were translated from Arabic into Latin by Adelard of Bath after a voyage in the East about 1130, and in 1202 Leonard of Pisa published his *Liber Abaci*, giving not only the Arabic numerals, but also the use of the cipher in a decimal notation. At the same time the great teachers come from a new source. Just as about 1100 the monks were displaced in education by the secular clergy, so in the thirteenth century the seculars began to be supplanted by the friars.

The older monastic orders did not produce a single great theologian after St. Bernard until scholastic theology was superseded by learned ' professional ' theology. Monasteries only needed a few members able to preach an occasional sermon and to instruct the novices in elementary theology, and a few canonists to transact their legal business. The real services of the monks to literature in the later Middle Ages lie in the production of histories, a field quite alien to the studies of the universities.

All the great doctors belonged to the Mendicant Orders. The Dominicans were the first to reach the universities ; as friars preachers their function was to combat heresy, and to this a course of study was a necessary preliminary. Thus they were drawn to the universities, where they gained two ends—the training of those who were already in the Order, and the opportunity

XXXVI.   The Students of Paris
Cathedral of Notre-Dame de Paris
Middle of 13th Century

of recruiting into it students and even teachers of the university. The Dominican centre in each country was at the seat of its chief university : Bologna, Paris, and Oxford.

Francis in the beginning had been opposed to learning. 'These brethren of mine', he declared, 'who are led away by curiosity of knowledge, in the day of tribulation shall find their hands empty. . . . Books are a temptation; the brethren who cannot read shall not seek to learn.' The Franciscans, however, like the Dominicans, had to be competent to combat heresy, and thus had to have some intellectual training, though for some time their studies were confined to the Bible and its commentaries, and did not include the Sentences or philosophy. But while the university was still a scattered community of seculars, without colleges or community life outside the lecture-room, the convents or halls of the Mendicants, communities within the community, inevitably acquired considerable importance. Further, the dispersion of the university of Paris by its masters in 1229 as a protest against the action taken by the provost in a town and gown quarrel, not only drove many of the secular masters to the rising universities of Oxford and Cambridge and to the smaller *studia generalia* of France—Toulouse, Orléans, Rheims, and Angers—but also changed the relations of the Mendicants and the university. They did not migrate, but established schools of theology of their own. On the re-opening of the university these were brought under its control, but a struggle was inevitable between the university as a guild of secular clergy and the corporate Orders of the friars. It began, as might be expected, with the Orders' claim to immunity from the rules of the guild, that is from the statutes of the university. The friars of Paris decided it was inconsistent with their profession of humility to supplicate for the Doctorate, yet they wanted the degree. Therefore in 1250 they procured a Papal Bull declaring that they should be admitted to the degree without supplicating. The struggle lasted for eight years. With the support of the Papacy the friars gained their point, but while the university was able to insist that no friar should be a member of the faculty of arts leading to the M.A., and that secular doctors should have a monopoly of teaching secular students theology, the university had to give in to the papal view of its work, and discourage as heretical those wider studies which the increasing knowledge of Greek thought was reviving. So the struggle had certain ill effects. In the first place the intellectual activities of the Orders came to be to a great extent self-contained; there was little outside contact to check the Dominicans in their tendency to be inflexible adherents of their doctor Aquinas, and the Franciscans were divided between their own doctors, the mystic Bonaventura, and the realist Alexander of Hales. Further, the support given by the Papacy to the friars against the guild of secular masters tended to make the university as a whole anti-papal. Finally, the university was no longer free to develop humanistic studies to their full extent. The exclusion of Civil Law from its curriculum by Honorius III in 1219 made it less truly a *studium generale*, though it did much to develop the legal universities of the southern provinces where the tradition of Roman Law was always strongest. The important school of Orléans, where the classical traditions of Chartres had been perpetuated, even in an age of dialectic, developed into such a university at a convenient distance from the capital.

But the Papacy did more than this; it is through its intervention that a French university was first formally founded. Toulouse was the centre of the religious and intellectual ferment of the Albigensian heresy, and therefore the Pope decided that it should be the home of a great school of orthodoxy. On Maundy Thursday 1229/30, the final treaty between the conquered Count Raymond of Toulouse and St. Louis was signed before the great door of Notre Dame de Paris. By an article of that treaty it was provided that for ten years Raymond should pay the salaries of fourteen professors: four Masters of Theology with fifty marks a year, two Decretalists with thirty, six Artists with twenty, and two Grammarians with ten. The theological faculty was to be in the hands of the friars— a *Propaganda Fide*—and the masters of the other faculties were to come from Paris.

Students flocked to every university in France, but most of all to Paris. About 1210: ' Never before in any time or in any part of the world, whether in Athens or in Egypt, had there been such a multitude of students. The reason for this must be sought not only in the admirable beauty of Paris, but also in the special privileges which King Philip and his father

before him conferred upon the scholars.'[1]   Seventy-five years
later we are told:

> Clerc vienent as estudes de toutes nations
> Et en yvier s'asanlent par plusuers legions:
> On leur lit et il oient pour leur instructions;
> En esté s'en retraient moult en leurs regions.[2]

Soon after 1219 the students of the university had to be
divided into four nations: France, England, Picardy, and
Normandy.   The French nation was further subdivided into
five ' tribes ', corresponding with the five ecclesiastical provinces
of France.   When the English Wars made the name of England
too hateful for use, her ' nation ' was re-christened *Nation
d'Allemagne*, but the title was never really accepted.

Since there was a total absence of organized amusement—to
play ' ad pilam vel ad crossiam vel ad alios ludos insultuosos ' is
forbidden by the 1379 statutes of the Collège de Narbonne—
the students were apt to take their exercise not only in studious
walks in the Pré aux Clercs but also in fighting the men of
other nations.   Jacques de Vitry tells us:

' Because of the differences of their homes they disagree, are
envious and insulting, and without shame offer each other much insult
and contumely, saying that the English are drunkards and have tails;
that the French are proud, soft, and womanish; the Germans mad
and indecent in their feasting; the Normans stupid and boastful; the
Picards traitors and fair-weather friends.   Those who come from Burgundy they hold to be brutish and slow, and thinking the Bretons fickle
and unstable, they often throw the death of Arthur in their faces.   The
Lombards they call avaricious, full of malice, and unwarlike; the
Romans given to sedition, violent people who bite their nails; the
Sicilians tyrannical and cruel;   the men of Brabant men of blood,
incendiaries, freebooters, and robbers; the Flemings wasteful, prodigal,
given over to feasting, and soft as butter.   And because of such
wrangling they often proceed from words to blows.'

The student was under little restraint; coming into residence
about the age of sixteen or rather later, he was free to arrange
most of the conditions of his life as he liked.   Unless his parents

[1] Guillaume le Breton.
[2] ' Clerks of all nations come to study, and in winter assemble in their
legions; they are lectured to and listen for instruction, and then in summer
many go back to their homes.'

had settled it beforehand, he chose the master whose lectures he was to attend, and the hall or hostel to which he was to be attached. By 1290 statutes had to be passed forbidding masters to tout for work among the freshmen. Jacques de Vitry warns them against the young professors, ' who draw their teaching not from memory and experience, but from notebooks and cupboards'.

No freshman escaped some kind of initiation ceremony that varied with the university. At the logical university of Paris the *bejaunus* or *bec-jaune* seems to have been treated as a fool, and hoaxed; in the legal universities of the south he was treated as a criminal and given a mock trial. At Paris he was finally driven through the streets on a donkey, and then ' purged ' by a bath. History is silent as to the details of the ceremony. Once made free of the community, the freshman had still to submit to the yoke of student etiquette. At Avignon the seniors held a court twice a week under their ' abbot' to enforce their regulations. The freshmen were to serve them at table, not to stand between them and the fire in Hall, to give place to them on all occasions, not to sit at the first table in Hall, and not to call one another ' Sir '. The decisions of the Court were enforced by a certain number of blows with a wooden spoon; in addition the freshmen had one blow each all round whenever the Court met. In the early years of the university such student rule was the more important as there was no proper residential organization. The principal of a hall was often a student himself, and held an office like that of the president of a modern junior common room. Not until the fifteenth century were the halls organized under a master, with doors locked at night and formal requirements for residence: it was only after the endowment of colleges had made studentship a privilege that discipline could be enforced.

The colleges of Paris were initiated by the charity of a burgess of London, who on his return from Jerusalem bought a room in the Hôtel-Dieu and endowed it to be a dormitory for eighteen students, who in return were to watch by the dead of the hospital and assist at their funerals. This Collège des Dix-huit was followed by those of the Bons-Enfants St. Honoré in 1208, of Ste. Catherine du Val des Écoliers in 1229, of the Bons-Enfants St. Victor in 1248, of the Collège de Prémontré in 1252, the Collège du Trésorier in 1268, and the Collège de Navarre in 1304. In all sixty colleges were founded at Paris between 1137 and 1360.

Robert de Sorbon, who founded his great college in 1250, with the help of St. Louis, was indebted for some details of his organization to the Mendicant Orders; his 'pauvres maîtres' have something of their discipline as of their nomenclature. But his advice to his scholars is full of inspired common sense based on the views of St. Bernard. The scholar, he says, who wishes to profit by his studies must observe six essential rules: first, to dedicate a fixed hour to each kind of reading, as St. Bernard advises in his letter to the brothers of Mont Dieu. Second, to concentrate his attention on what he is reading, and not merely to skim over it. 'There is as much difference between reading and study, says St. Bernard, as there is between an acquaintance and a friend, between bows exchanged in the street and an unchanging affection.' Third, to extract from his daily reading some thought or saying of truth, and to store it in his memory with especial care. Seneca has said, ' Cum multa percurreris in die, unum tibi elige, quod illa die excoquas '. Fourth, to write an abstract of everything he reads, since words which are not committed to writing vanish like dust in the wind. Fifth, to discuss his work with his fellow students, whether in formal disputation or in friendly talk. This is even more important than reading, for it leaves no loop-hole of uncertainty or misunderstanding. ' Nihil perfecte scitur, nisi dente disputationis feriatur.' Sixth, to pray, for Prayer is the true road to understanding. St. Bernard teaches that reading should stir the soul, and that then, without ceasing from study, the heart should be lifted up to God. Robert de Sorbon at the same time condemns those scholars who, ' so as not to seem to have wasted their time, bind up many sheets of parchment into thick volumes, full of blank pages inside, but bound in fine red leather; and so go home with a little bag stuffed with a learning that rats and bookworms may eat, and that fire and water may destroy '.

The student, indeed, was not always a deep scholar. Even by the end of the thirteenth century his critics were singing:

> Iam fit magister artium
> qui nescit quotas partium
> de vero fundamento;

habere nomen appetit,
rem vero nec curat nec scit,
    examine contento.
Iam fiant baccalaurei
pro munere denarii
    quam plures idiotae;
in artibus, et aliis
egregiis scientiis
    sunt bestiae promotae.

Yet Paris had already become a paradise of books for the scholar. The *Stationarii* who employed the writers, and the *Librarii* who sold their productions,[1] were both under the control of the university, which appointed a joint board of four masters and four chief booksellers to supervise them. No book might be sold or, as was more usual, hired out, until the board had tested its correctness and fixed its price or rate of hire. A book might not be sold to a stranger until he had informed the Congregation of the University of his purpose, so that they might, if they wished, take measures to prevent its going out of their reach.

To those who could not afford to buy or hire the library of Notre Dame was always open, while the Sorbonne soon acquired an excellent library, since from its earliest days its doctors, at their death, left their books for the common use. It is not surprising that Richard de Bury should write,

'O Holy God of Gods in Sion, what a mighty stream of pleasure made glad our hearts whenever we had leisure to visit Paris, the paradise of the world!... There are delightful libraries, more aromatic than stores of spice; there abundant orchards of all manner of books ... there, indeed, opening our treasures and unfastening our purse strings we scattered money with joyful heart and bought books without price.'

It is, perhaps, harder to recover a clear idea of the life of the student than of the doctor; undergraduates' letters rarely say much about their curriculum. Rather, like the student who writes to Christian of Stommeln about 1280, do they tell us that they have not been well for the whole of Hilary Term, but, now that Easter is come, they are so far recovered that

---

[1] By 1323 there were twenty-eight booksellers besides keepers of open-air bookstalls. When the Rector of the University attended the Foire du Lendit in state it was officially to buy parchment for university use.

they can eat even College eggs; or else they write in the strain immortalized by Eustache Deschamps some hundred and twenty years later:

> Lettres des escoliers d'Orliens:
> Treschiers peres, je n'ay denier,
> Ne sanz vous ne puis avoir riens;
> Et si fait a l'estude chier,
> Ne je ne puis estudier
> En mon Code n'en ma Digeste:
> Caduque sont. Je doy de reste
> De ma prevosté dix escus,
> Et ne treuve homme qui me preste:
> Je vous mande argent et salus!
>
> Trop fault, qui est estudiens;
> Se son fait veult bien advancier,
> Il fault que son pere et les siens
> Lui baillent argent sanz dangier,
> Par quoy cause n'ait d'engagier
> Ses livres, ait finance preste,
> Robes, pannes, vesteure honneste,
> Ou il sera un malostrus;
> Et qu'om ne me tiengne pour beste,
> Je vous mande argent et salus.
>
> Vins sont chiers, hostelz, autres biens;
> Je doy partout; s'ay grant mestier
> D'estre mis hors de tels liens:
> Chiers peres, vueillez moy aidier.
> Je doubte l'excommunier,
> Cité suy; cy n'a n'os n'areste:
> S'argent n'ay devant cette feste
> De Pasques, du moustier exclus
> Seray. Ottroiez ma requeste
> Je vous mande argent et salus.

L'Envoy

> Treschiers peres, pour m'alegier
> En la taverne, au boulengier,
> Aux docteurs, aux bediaux, conclus,
> Et pour mes colectes payer
> A la burresse et au barbier,
> Je vous mande argent et salus.[1]

---

[1] 'Thus runs the Orléans scholar's letter: "Well beloved father, I have not a penny, nor can I get any save through you, for all things at the university are so dear; nor can I study in my Code or my Digest, for their leaves have

Numbers rose and fell; in 1350 Gilles de Muisis complains that once the schools of Paris were full of scholars, 'gens de plusieurs estats', who were sure of an honourable career. Now the benefices go to hunting parsons, and except among the Mendicants there are fewer scholars. Among the seculars only lawyers and doctors can be sure of a livelihood, and then, when they have saved money enough, of securing a benefice. But Dr. Rashdall has made a calculation to show that the numbers a hundred years later were very considerable. About 1450 there were, he thinks, at least 2,500 members in residence, of whom about 800 were graduates; and in 1464 a record of dues paid shows that there were at least 3,000 members in residence.

Jean de Jandun, writing in 1320, said that to be in Paris was to exist in the absolute sense, *simpliciter*, but to be anywhere else was to exist relatively, *secundum quid*. Yet the intellectual life of Paris gradually weakened, in spite of a temporary revival which owed its impulse to Oxford, and in 1452 the university had to have its curriculum reformed. Earlier statutes had required masters to lecture *extempore* instead of dictating; they had even gone so far as to prescribe the exact pace at which he was to speak; not drawlingly, *tractim*, but rapidly, *raptim*, 'bringing out the words as rapidly as if no one was writing before him'. Indeed penalties were prescribed for students who by hissing, groaning, or throwing stones tried to make him go

the falling sickness. Moreover, I owe ten crowns in dues to the provost, and can find no man to lend them to me; I ask of you greetings and gold.

"The student has need of many things if he will profit here; his father and his kin must needs supply him freely, that he be not compelled to pawn his books, but have ready money in his purse, with gowns and furs and decent clothing; or he will be damned for a beggar; wherefore, that men may not take me for a beast, I ask of you greetings and gold.

"Wines are dear, and hostels and other good things; I owe in every street, and am hard bestead to free myself from such snares. Dear father, deign to help me! I fear to be excommunicated; already I have been cited, and there is not even a dry bone in my larder. If I find not the money before this feast of Easter, the church door will be shut in my face; wherefore grant my supplication. I ask of you greetings and gold.

Envoi.

"Well beloved father, to ease my debts contracted at the tavern, at the baker's, with the professors and the bedels, to pay my subscriptions to the laundress and the barber, I ask of you greetings and gold." '

slower. But by 1452 the lecturing tradition had greatly changed; the new statutes of that year only prescribe that the master should read the lecture himself, and not hand its manuscript to a student for him to dictate it to the rest. Similarly, though the regulations for undergraduates of the Sorbonne were strict—they had to ask leave to go out, and might only walk the streets in couples—the fifteenth-century register of the College suggests that discipline was not much above its usual level. Clerks are sconced a pint for 'very inordinately' knocking at the door during dinner; for being very drunk, for 'confabulating' in the quad late at night, and refusing to go to their chambers when ordered, and for asking for wine at the buttery in the name of a master and drinking it themselves.[1]

The University of Paris gradually lost its international character with the growth of the English, Italian, and German universities, and in France itself Montpellier, Toulouse, Orléans, and Angers flourished in spite of war. It is true that on the side of scholastic theology Paris was the theological arbiter of Europe, 'Ratio dictans in ecclesia'; and it is largely due to her performance of this function that Northern Europe was spared the horrors of the Inquisition. But as far as real intellectual activity was concerned Oxford was in the fourteenth century more important than Paris. The University of Paris, however, in losing her international character gained national importance. She was the only great mediaeval university in a capital city, and that city was more like a modern capital than any in Europe. Thus in that city she came to play a political part not unlike that of the Corporation in London. She was immune from secular justice: in France all students were assumed as a matter of course to be clerks and enjoyed the privileges of clerkship. She had the right of public meeting and free debate. Thus when Paris under Étienne Marcel became the real seat of power and the only counteracting force to corrupt government, the university became a political power, and under the Valois policy of depressing the nobility and conciliating the support of the clerical and legal classes she gained a place in the councils of the National Church and in the States General.

[1] A D.D. is sconced a quart of wine for picking a pear off a tree in the College garden, again for forgetting to shut the chapel door, and again for taking his meals in the kitchen. Finally, the head cook is sconced for cooking the meat badly and not putting enough salt in the soup.

VIII

WORK AND RELIGION [1]

For the men of the Middle Ages work was not servitude, but a way of enfranchisement for the soul. The preface to the *Speculum doctrinale* of Vincent de Beauvais tells us ' ipsa restitutio sive restauratio per doctrinam efficitur ', and what follows proves that labour of every kind—manual, intellectual, and spiritual—was included in ' doctrina '. In the monasteries work and prayer were the two essentials of life, and in the world the relation between them was little less close. The twelfth century was not only an age of monasticism but also an age of lay corporations—guilds of citizens, guilds of teachers, guilds of traders, and guilds of craftsmen—whose purpose was work and prayer as a community. The monk retired within the cloister and combated spiritual evil; the guildsman stayed in the world and struggled with earthly evil.

His dangers were many. Plague and pestilence were endemic in the narrow and crowded streets; in 1129, 1206, and 1233 the plague was so serious that the châsse of Ste. Geneviève was carried in penitential procession through the streets of Paris. There was danger of flood: in Paris both bridges went in 1196; and, worse than this, there was danger of fire. Between 1200 and 1225 Rouen was burned six times; in 1198 Rouen, Troyes, Beauvais, Provins, Arras, Poitiers, and Moissac were burned. There was danger of fire not only from accidental causes, but in course of war; men expert in firing houses were attached to every army, and Philip Augustus in the course of his campaigns burnt Châtillon-sur-Seine, Dreux, le Mans, Évreux, Dieppe, Tours, Angers, and Lille. Earth offered no security : nothing availed but the protection of heaven.

In the twelfth century the saints begin to appear in monumental art. Nearly always it is the local saint who is repre-

[1] The author desires to express her indebtedness to M. Émile Male's *Art religieux en France.*

sented; the holy man who is responsible for the town or the province, who will intercede for the people of his *pays* in all their troubles: St. Sernin in Languedoc, St. Martial in Aquitaine, St. Hilaire in Poitou, St. Ursin in Berri, St. Denis in Paris, St. Bénigne in Burgundy, and a whole local hierarchy in the Auvergne. The first saint to become national is the travellers' friend, St. Martin of Tours; and then, with the growth of the nation in the thirteenth century, the local saints come to be aided by strangers who have power over special forms of evil and misfortune. So figures of protecting saints appear carved on the towers and walls of the city: as at Amiens, where they were protected by figures of Michael, Peter, Christopher, Sebastian, Barbara, Margaret, and Nicholas, all considered especially to protect men from battle and murder and sudden death; on the walls of castles—Peter, Anne, and Susanna protected Chantelle—and on the houses of its burgesses: at Luynes, for instance, a citizen's house still bears the figures of the Virgin, Ste. Geneviève, patron saint of the city, St. Christopher, who defends from sudden death, and St. James, who never forgets those who have made pilgrimages to his shrine. But if the province has its tutelary saint and the city its patrons, the communities within it must in their turn find heavenly defenders. So every corporation had its patron saint, chosen for some kind of affinity with the *métier*—St. Éloi, a goldsmith, to the goldsmiths; St. Crispin, a shoemaker, to the shoemakers; St. Martha to the maidservants; St. Julian, who housed even the lepers, to the innkeepers; St. Bartholomew, who was flayed, to the tanners of hides; and St. Blaise, who was tortured with an iron comb, to the wool combers. Thus, too, every member of the guild was in relation with the Church not only as an individual, but also as a member of his community. In Rouen, for instance, each trade had a street to itself, and each had the church of its corporation: St. Étienne des Tonneliers, Sainte Croix des Pelletiers, and so on. It is clear that the trade guild was a religious confraternity. As such they undertook *œuvres de piété*: the increase of hospitals in the fifteenth century was largely due to their benefactions. There were fifteen such hospitals in Arras alone. Corporations who had not a church of their own had a chapel in one of the great churches. Towards the end of the Middle Ages there was not a chapel in any of the churches of Rouen that was not the home of a confraternity, whether pious, commercial, military, or artistic. Thus the guilds came to play a double part in the history of French art: in secular art, through their control of their own craft, the standards they maintained for its *maîtrise*, and the teaching they gave their apprentices; and in religious art, in the part they played as religious confraternities. As such they had their share in the religious theatre of the Middle Ages; Gringoire wrote *La Vie de Monseigneur St. Louis* for such a confraternity, and the *Mystère de Saint Crépin et St. Crépinian* was written for a guild of shoemakers. Further, as religious confraternities they took their part in the building and beautification of churches. At Chartres, in particular, windows were given by nineteen guilds; the figures of the donors at the bottom of the windows—craftsmen with their trowels, hammers, carding combs, shovels, and knives—show what an important part the artisan class had come to play in the life of the Church. Work was a divine law; work was necessary to human salvation; and therefore work in itself was worthy to be represented in the decoration of the church. At Semur one window, given by the corporation of clothmakers, is entirely taken up with pictures of the processes of cloth making, and no saint or religious scene appears in it, yet it was in no way incongruous with a religious edifice. In this congruity with every side of life lay the true greatness of the religious art of the Middle Ages.

The basis of every style of architecture is its adjustment of roof to walls. Classical architecture solved the problem by a flat or slightly angular roof resting on walls supported by colonnades; Roman architecture of the later empire introduced the rounded barrel vault; but in the eleventh century a new solution to the problem was attempted, and from this Gothic architecture arose. The Roman barrel vault had great solidity and little elasticity, but it was found that by spanning the space to be roofed by two or more intersecting arches and filling in the spaces of this skeleton with lighter stone, there was obtained not only greater ease of construction, and considerable diminution of weight and of consequent thrust against the walls, but also a great extension of the space and variety of forms that could be vaulted. Quicherat has said, 'l'histoire de l'architec-

VII. The Annual Audit of the Confrérie de la Charité-Dieu et
Notre-Dame de la Recouvrance of Rouen

1466

ture du moyen âge n'est que l'histoire de la lutte des architectes contre la poussée et la pesanteur des voûtes '; and it is thanks to the invention of this system of vaulting, which in the intersection of its arches makes the pointed arch a constructive element in the whole building, that the mediaeval cathedral became more lofty, more airy, more luminous, so that even in ages in which its art was entirely foreign to men's minds such an observer as Montesquieu could find in it the obscure beauty of a poem in a foreign tongue. All the architectural features of the Gothic style depend upon this principle of vaulting. The piers and pillars are there to bear the direct weight of the intersecting arches of the vault, and the indirect thrust of the vaulting upon the walls is counteracted by the counter thrust of the flying buttresses outside, of which the piers take the thrust safely into the earth again. Thus is built up an edifice which has a latent energy comparable with that of a living body. The walls remain necessary for shelter, but cease to be an essential part of the constructive system; the equilibrium and solidity of the building are independent of their support. Thus the natural tendency of the new architecture is to pierce them with windows till they eventually become little more than the splendid frame of a mosaic of stained glass, as in the Sainte Chapelle of Paris. To harmonize with this the heavy pillars of the earlier style develop into a clustered group of colonnettes, until by the time of Philippe le Bel the whole is of filigree delicacy.

Now this invention of the Gothic vault (the French *croisée d'ogives*) is an invention of Royal France, of the Île de France, Picardy, and Champagne. During the Middle Ages it was, indeed, designated as *le style français*: Gothic is a term of opprobrium invented during the Renaissance. Between 1150 and 1180 a great number of churches were built in the royal domain of Louis VII: Noyon, Soissons, Sens, Arras, Cambrai, and others, and there was a similar though less important movement under the Plantagenets in Anjou, Touraine, Maine, and Poitou. Who was chiefly responsible for this growth? Undoubtedly the bishops: it is another example of the growing importance of the provincial capitals in the twelfth century. Cathedral building became the peculiar activity of the episcopate ; the funds were drawn partly from the seigneurial revenues of the diocese, partly from the bishop's private fortune, partly from contributions from the members of the chapter, partly from offerings from the inhabitants of the See, whether given as free-will offerings, as payment for indulgences, or in endowment of masses for the dead. Men gave not only money but labour; Archbishop Hugh of Rouen found in 1145, when the cathedral of Chartres was built, that

'The inhabitants of Chartres have combined to aid in the construction of their church by transporting the materials . . . the faithful of our diocese and of other neighbouring regions have formed associations for the same object; they admit no one into their company unless he has been to confession, has renounced enmities and revenges, and has reconciled himself with his enemies. That done, they elect a chief, under whose direction they conduct their waggons in silence and humility.'

Bernard's strictures on the elaboration of monastic architecture have already been quoted. Even he admits that for the bishops it is a different question: 'We know that they, as debtors alike to wise and foolish, when they cannot rouse the sense of religion in the carnal multitude by spiritual means, must do so by ornaments that appeal to the senses.'

The first great church built in the new style is that of the abbey of St. Denis, 1140. For the next fifty years Gothic architecture was employed in many churches, but it was not until the cathedral of Chartres had to be rebuilt after a fire in 1194 that the style was fully formulated, to be developed later at Rheims in 1210 and Amiens in 1220. In this series of three cathedrals it is possible to see an ascending scale: at Chartres the proportions seem to restrain a force that wishes to lift the whole building higher; at Rheims there seems to be the perfect balance of rest; and at Amiens something beyond this, something above human equilibrium, beyond which—as was proved at Beauvais—a loftier proportion is impossible of attainment.

Another series of developments is to be traced in the detail of the sculpture. Gothic architecture is primarily the creation of the Île de France; and the *flora* of its decoration nearly all grows there. But about 1150 the early style treats only the flowers of spring, in bud; in the thirteenth century the buds open and the leaves are unfurled; and by the fourteenth century the spray has grown into a complete branch.

XXXVIII. Chartres Cathedral : the South Porch

It is true that Gothic architecture is the creation of the Île de France, but as it spread over Western Europe and beyond, the provinces and countries that employed the style set their several seals upon its character. There are Burgundian, Angevin, Anglo-Norman, and Provençal Gothic styles, all differing in detail, but all employing the Gothic vault. In the West this vault suffered a transformation by which eight or more ribs were employed instead of the classic four; it is from this development in the English provinces of France that we inherited the characteristically English tradition of fan-vaulting. But Gothic passed far beyond the boundaries of France and England; the cathedrals of Upsala in Sweden and Nicosia in Cyprus are imitated from Notre Dame de Paris, and the cathedrals of Burgos and Toledo in Spain from that of Bourges.

Gothic architecture is much more than a finely constructed system based upon a scheme of vaulting. The difference between any early Romanesque church and a great Gothic cathedral is the sum that mediaeval France added to the Christian religion. As early as the eleventh century the Synod of Arras stated, 'Simple and unlettered souls find in the church what they cannot know from writings: they perceive it through the lines of the building'. Every important thought found expression in stone. The twelfth century was the age of monasteries and mystic thought; Cluny turned the symbolism of Honorius of Autun into stone, and based its architecture on his mystical use of number. The thirteenth century was the age of the universities and of the great mediaeval encyclopaedias as well as the age of cathedrals. While the doctors built up their intellectual cathedrals to shelter the multitude of all faithful people, the bishops and the people built up their cathedrals of stone, to be as it were mirrors of the other. Therein all the articles of their faith were expressed: they were *Summae, Specula, Imagines Mundi*. Every Gothic church symbolized the living Church of Christ; every stone in its walls had its spiritual as well as its structural function to perform. Floor, vault, window, wall, capital, and arch were decorated with figures and designs symbolic of the Catholic Faith, and these symbols were not scattered arbitrarily over the edifice, but were each in their due place in relation to the scheme of the whole. The Middle Ages had the passion for order : Art was organized as carefully and as clearly as dogma, human learning, and society. Therefore the representation of sacred subjects was governed by scientific principles, and was never left to the whim of the individual. Their numerical relation had a symbolic value : three, the Divine number, combines with four, the natural number of the four elements, the four natural virtues, the four Evangelists, to form seven, the human number of the seven ages of man, the seven planets which affect his destiny, the seven days of Creation, the seven Christian virtues, the seven Sacraments which save him from the seven deadly sins; the seven sounds of music and the seven gifts of the Holy Ghost are but further symbols of the harmony that exists between nature and God. Augustine had shown that twelve, formed by the natural number four multiplied by the spiritual number of the Trinity, was the number of the eternal Church : so the twelve patriarchs of the Old Law are balanced by the twelve apostles of the New Testament. Similarly, the four major prophets are the forerunners of the four Evangelists : a window at Chartres shows Isaiah, Ezekiel, Daniel, and Jeremiah each carrying one of the four Evangelists on his shoulders to betoken this. Here is harmony and symphony : there is a certain justice in the saying that Gothic architecture is petrified music.[1] Nor is this numerical symbolism more than a part of the whole. The orientation of the church determines the character of the scenes that adorn it : Old Testament scenes on the north side, where the sun of revelation never shines; New Testament scenes in the glow of the full south ; and the Last Judgement on the west, where the sun will shine as it sets for the last time. The cruciform ground plan of the church is the symbol of the faith that built it. By the great door the image of Christ dominates the figures of which each is a symbol of an age of the world : Kings and Prophets of the Old Law, Saints and Fathers of the New. Beyond are the symbols of the struggle that is life : struggle against sin, expressed by the

[1] At Cluny the capitals of the choir symbolized the notes of the scale, and bore inscriptions based on the work of Honorius of Autun. The sixth had ' Si cupis affectum pietatis respice sextum ' ; the seventh ' Insinuat flatum cum donis septimis almum ' ; the eighth ' Octavus sanctos omnes docet esse beatos '.

XXXIX.   Rheims   Cathedral :   the   Great   Portal

(before the German bombardment)

contrasted images of Faith and Idolatry, Hope and Despair, Charity and Avarice, Prudence and Folly, Humility and Pride; struggle with nature in the figures of the husbandmen at their appropriate toil beneath the zodiacal symbols of the months: and above is the symbol of victory, the angel with a crown. Within the cathedral the scheme is so vast that it can only be apprehended step by step; each scene from the New Testament finds its counter-type in the Old; each series is balanced by another; nothing is misplaced and nothing irrelevant. The great chandelier at Aix la Chapelle, for example, is made in the form of a fortified city defended by towers; it is the City of Light, the New Jerusalem: the beatitudes of the elect are upon its walls, and apostles and prophets stand upon its bastions. An incense burner displays the figures of the three Hebrews in the furnace, for the perfume it gives is like the prayer of martyrs. The immense scale of these symbolic representations can only be compared with the scale of the philosophical arguments of an Aquinas: at Chartres alone there are over six thousand painted and sculptured figures, each with its meaning. Thus the Middle Ages made art embody and teach religion. All that the Christian should know, the history of the world since its creation, the dogmas of his faith, the example of the saints, the hierarchy of the virtues, all the lessons of science, art, and craft, were taught him by the windows and statues of his church. It merited the name given to one of the earliest printed books: the *Biblia Pauperum*, the bible of the *sainte plèbe de Dieu*. It is the house not only of God, but also of his people. From the bishop who officiates, and the clerk who devises the scheme of its imagery down to the carver who executes it [1]; from the feudal lord to the humble craftsman, whose blazon and mark appear side by side in the windows they have offered; from the Doctor of Theology to the peasant woman, ' povrette et ancienne qui riens ne sçait, oncques lettres ne lut ', who can decipher her creed in its sculpture, there is no

---

[1] In 1425 the church of the Madeleine at Troyes had made a set of tapestry with the story of the Saint. Brother Didier studied the story in the books available and wrote out a clear account of the scenes to be represented; Jacquet the painter made a little sketch of them on paper; Poinsète the dressmaker and her apprentice sewed together bed-sheets, on which Jacquet and Simon the illuminator painted the design from which the tapestry weavers worked.

one who is not at home within it.   It is the only edifice within
which France at any one time has been able to shelter all her
thoughts and dreams.   Within its walls speech, music, the
moving drama of the mysteries, the motionless drama of the
statues, and all the arts of their world and time combined to
make something more than art, for though the form is perfect
the spirit is dominant over the form.

Critics have been apt to oppose the symmetry and idealism
of classical art to a supposed naturalism and freedom from the
restraints of symmetry in Gothic art.   This is one of the
fallacies we inherit from the Romantic revival.   To the Romantic,
Gothic art was ruined, incomplete, the work of successive
generations; but if we take the perfected work, governed by
a single controlling mind, abstract what has been added later,
and mentally complete that which remains unfinished, we shall
find that Phidias and Ictinus brought no more to the Acropolis
of Athens than did Suger to St. Denis.

But art, like every personal and national expression, is not
a static thing, but one that inevitably changes with the society
that creates it.   Its religious art is the mirror of the spiritual
history of France.

Of all the countries of Europe France is that in which the
dramatic spirit is most natural and most strong.   Inevitably
it there came into relation with the dramatic mysteries of the
Church; first in metaphor—Hilary of Poitiers wrote a Christmas hymn with the lines

> Totum genus fidelium
> Laudes celebrat dramatum—

and then, by the ninth century, in actual dramatic touches
in the service : gospels read with men taking parts in the
dialogue, and short dramatic interludes in the liturgy itself. The
twelfth century witnessed the development of liturgical art;
soon after 1200 not only is drama liturgical, but also the religious scenes figured in the cathedrals and the illuminated MSS.
are determined by the Gospels of the Feasts.

About 1350 there was a gradual change; certain scenes in
the life of Christ, such as the Baptism and the Miracle at the
Marriage at Cana, were included because of their symbolic importance, and at the same time the authors of the mystery plays

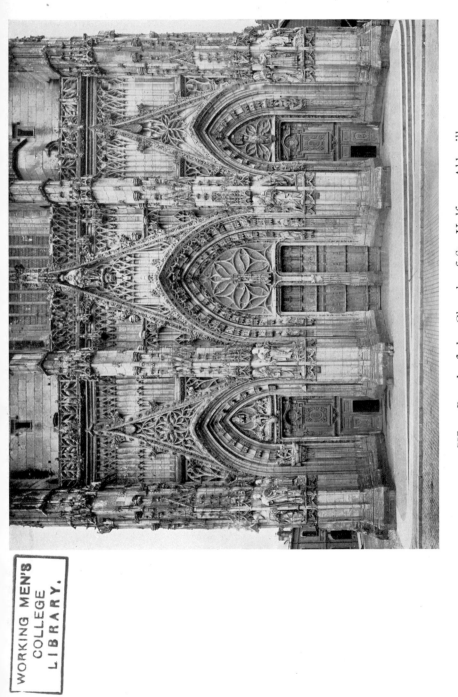

XL. Portal of the Church of St. Vulfran, Abbeville

dealing with the life of Christ drew their material from the canonical and apocryphal gospels, and for the lives of saints from the *Golden Legend*.

In the fifteenth century everything became popular; the wealth of the nation was transferred to the trading cities, the power of the nation to the monarchy and its supporters, the bourgeoisie, and learning passed from the clerk to the layman. Similarly, ecclesiastical influence went to the popular preachers, and religious life was centred in the people. This predominance of a popular lay religion not only modified the subjects represented in religious art and the schemes of its iconography, but also the spirit that informed the whole.

The fifteenth century is the age of mystery plays: in the great towns they attracted audiences of as many as fifteen to twenty thousand people, and demanded a correspondingly large cast: the *Mystère de la Passion* of Arnoul Greban includes 244 characters, as well as innumerable people without speaking parts. Few forms of art can be conceived which would be more essentially popular. They were neither liturgical nor evangelical in inspiration, but turned to a new source: a volume of *Meditations on the Life of Christ* ascribed to the Franciscan Doctor Bonaventura. Gerson's eulogy of his work explains its popular appeal: 'He holds back as far as may be from all curiosity, and knows how to avoid all secular doctrine, dialectic and science disguised as theology; striving to bring light to the soul, his aim is to make pity spring up in the heart.'

The *Meditations on the Life of Christ*—which if not actually written by him are permeated by his influence—were written for a woman, a member of the Franciscan Order of the Poor Clares. They appeal not to the mind but to the imagination and the emotions, and in doing so depart so far from the Scriptural tradition that they may be called the last of the apocryphal gospels. They are full of vivid detail, some pathetic and some puerile. Not only does a feeling for the picturesque pervade both the conception and carrying out of the work, but dialogue is freely used; even God the Father, the Angels, the Virtues, and the souls of the righteous converse. This mixture of imagination and emotion, of scenery and dialogue, is essentially dramatic, and rapidly exercised a profound influence on the mystery plays. Nearly all the plays of the first years of the fifteenth century are lost, but this influence is evident in Mercadé's *Mystère d'Arras* of about 1415, and again in the work of Arnoul Greban, Jean Michel, and the author of the *Mystère de la Nativité* of Rouen. Justice and Mercy, Peace and Truth, who appear in the mystery scenes of the 'procès de Paradis', which is only solved by the Redemption of mankind by Our Lord, step straight from the beginning of the *Meditations*. Thence, too, comes the scene in which the Baptist meets the Holy Family in the Desert on their way back from Egypt, and that scene of the parting between Jesus and His mother before He goes to Jerusalem, when she appeals to Him not to go into danger but to keep the Passover with His own people. From Bonaventura also comes the idea of a Passion of the Virgin parallel to that of Christ,[1] culminating in the taking down from the Cross and her reception of the body—an idea which is also expressed in the *Mystère de la Passion* of Arnoul Greban. Thence, too, comes the scene in heaven after the Ascension and the reception of Christ by God the Father and the Patriarchs, which forms the culmination of Greban's play and ends with the classic line 'Il suffit, le devoir est fait'.

The Mysteries, then, drew inspiration from the *Meditations*, and in its turn the theatre inspired plastic and graphic art. After 1400, for instance, the scheme used in depicting the Nativity completely changes. The Virgin is no longer lying rapt in meditation on a bed within a room, but the scene is shown happening within a thatched hovel open on one side, in which the Child lies on the ground while the Virgin kneels beside Him in adoration and Joseph (and sometimes angels) appear in the background. Even the thatched hovel suggests a part of the *mise-en-scène*. To the same source must be attributed the new scenes which come to be added to the representations of the Passion, such as that of the *Vierge de Pitié* seated at the foot of the Cross. It is, indeed, justifiable to say that all the new scenes which are represented in the religious art of the fifteenth century were acted before they were painted. Sometimes the connexion is direct; the argument between Justice and Mercy, Peace and Truth, for instance, comes from Bonaventura into civic pageantry and into the Mysteries, and from the Mysteries into illuminated manuscripts—and later, printed books—tapestries,

---

[1] Cf. the *Stabat Mater* by the Franciscan, Jacopone de Todi.

XLI.   The Visitation

Rheims Cathedral.   Second half of 13th Century

stained glass, and even sculpture.[1] Similarly, in scenes of the Annunciation the Angel kneels before the Virgin instead of standing upright, a detail followed from the stage directions of the Mysteries which borrow it from Bonaventura.

More often the scene is modified or developed to suit the necessities of dramatic representation, and these modifications or developments are repeated in plastic and pictorial art. Up to 1400, for instance, ecclesiastical art had represented Christ Crucified innumerable times, but had never shown the moment of Crucifixion. The one was the central dogma of the Christian faith, the other an historical fact. But dramatically the moment of Crucifixion is inevitable; it had to form a part of Mysteries of the Passion, and thus—as for instance in manuscripts made for the Duc de Berry—it came to be represented in art. Even more important in artistic history is the reception of the body by the Virgin after the Descent from the Cross, which again appears for the first time in manuscripts made for the Duc de Berry, and which again is taken direct from the religious theatre. Even the iconographic scheme of representing the Trinity is changed. Gothic art up to 1400 had symbolized this by the seated figure of the Father, holding the Son upon the Cross, while the Spirit in the form of a dove was shown hovering overhead. But such a representation was not dramatically possible, and another scheme was sought. In the *Passion d'Arras* the Father says,

> Ça beau fils venez vous asseoir
> Seéz-vous à ma dextre droit-cy,

and the stage direction adds, ' Cy est Jésus assis à la dextre de Dieu le père '. Accordingly after 1400 the early symbolic representation was gradually replaced in art by the dramatic scheme, in which Father and Son sit side by side and the Son shows His wounds.

Scenes from the life of Christ, that were not recorded in the Gospels of the Feasts and which therefore had found no place in the earlier liturgical scheme, entered art. The fourteenth century, for instance, had only represented the angels announcing the birth of Christ to the shepherds, whereas the Mysteries showed the scene of their adoration, and this in the fifteenth

[1] As at Fontaine-sur-Somme.

century appears in art, again for the first time in manuscripts painted for the Duc de Berry. The scene of the Bearing of the Cross is likewise modified; the whole crowd which accompanies Christ in pictures of the fifteenth century comes straight from the Mysteries and shows how its actors were dressed. Similarly the actual Resurrection from the Tomb passes into art. The influence of the theatre is most curious in the representation of the Ascension. Few thirteenth-century windows are more splendid than those which show the figure of Our Lord ascending through a radiant sky. But such a representation could not be given dramatically, and the stage directions for the machinery in the *Mystère de la Résurrection* show that the actor was lifted and carried up by a kind of pulley, 'et le doit-on voir les jambes par dessous l'engin'. Very oddly, this showing of the feet only as the figure ascends became a convention for pictorial art.[1]

Moreover, the mystery play influenced the dress and appearance of their characters when presented pictorially. The angels no longer wear the conventional white robes of the thirteenth century, but appear garbed in church vestments, which we know were borrowed to deck the actors in the mystery plays. Similarly, God the Father wears a heavy cope and an imperial crown; and in certain scenes of the Transfiguration the face of Christ appears golden, as it was actually gilded in the play. From the same source come many minor details—in scenes of the Nativity Joseph carries a candle to show that it is night, and after the Resurrection Christ appears carrying not the usual triumphal cross but a spade, just as the stage directions of Greban's *Mystère de la Passion* describe him, 'en forme d'un jardinier'.

The Mysteries, then, have a triple importance—first as the expression of a popular religion inspired by Franciscan emotion and imagination, second as drama, and third as *tableaux vivants*. Their profoundest influence was to foster *naturalism* in art; God and the saints were no longer magnificently remote, symbols of truths too great to be apprehended by the common man, but approached the human level. In the fifteenth century even Christ lost the nimbus: yet in the thirteenth Aquinas had

[1] It is exemplified, for instance, in the foreign glass that is now in Fairford Church, Gloucestershire.

XLII.   Virgin and Child in Silver Gilt
Given to the Abbey of St. Denis by
Queen Jeanne d'Évreux in 1339

had to include the significance of this purely artistic attribute
in the scheme of his *Summa*.   The symbolism of the Middle
Ages ends in France not in humanism, but in humanity.

This naturalism, this bringing down of the saints to the
level of mankind, is everywhere evident in the art of the fifteenth
century.   They have lost the simple and noble draperies that
invested them with majesty and made them above time; the
soldier saints appear as warriors of the English wars, the doctor
saints—Cosmas and Damian—as doctors of the faculty of
Paris, St. Mark is the prosperous notary, and St. Joseph, in a
statue at Verneuil of the time of Louis XII, appears as a young
carpenter, his bag of tools at his side, his axe in his hand, and
a flower in his cap.   In the fifteenth century the saints cease
to be represented as members of a celestial hierarchy; they are
French and live in France.   The painters of the school of
Bourdichon showed the towers of Tours behind St. Anne's
garden, made St. Martin give his cloak to a beggar on the new
quay of the same city, and depicted the voyage into Egypt
as a journey up the valley of the Indre.   Everywhere the
local type of physiognomy was adopted for the saints; they
are worshipped to this day by men and women made in their
own image.   Since the saints were so near to humanity, men
and saints could be shown together; the figure of the donor
of a window or picture is no longer on a different scale and
clearly on another plane from that of his patron saint.   Thus
at Amiens St. John the Baptist and Jean Bureau, sire de la
Rivière and counsellor of Charles V, appear side by side upon
the buttresses, and at the Chartreuse of Champmol, near Dijon,
Philip the Good and his patron saint appear on an equal scale.
Even the humblest mortal comes to take his place at the bottom
of the celestial hierarchy.   In a window at Beauvais (now
unhappily destroyed) the donor was shown at the feet of
St. Lawrence, saying,

> Saint Laurent patron d'icy prie
> Pour moi, pécheur, Sainte Marie.

St. Lawrence was shown turning towards the Virgin, saying
in his turn,

> Pour celuy-ci, Roine de la sus
> Veuille prier ton fils Jésus.

She turned to Christ with the words,

> Mon fils qu'allaita ma mamelle
> Pour ce pauvre pécheur j'appelle.

Christ from the Cross turned to the Father,

> Mon père ayez compassion
> De ce pécheur pour ma passion.

God the Father replied:

> Par tant de motifs animé
> Me plaît d'avoir pour lui pitié.

The Virgin in the late fifteenth century comes once more to the imperial position she occupied in the Byzantine world [1]; but it is in a new form, as the protectress of humanity, sheltering mankind beneath her outstretched mantle.[2]   The worship of Mary—Villon's *haute Déesse*—is one side of the Franciscan emotional feeling, and is therefore expressed in her representation as the Mother.   She is no longer shown, as in early art, seated upon a throne holding the child as gravely as a priest holds the chalice, but appears simply as the human Mother, smiling and playing with her baby.   The more divine her power, the more human is her image.

Yet another result of the emotional Franciscan teaching, which changed the whole religious atmosphere, is the appreciation of the pathos of death and suffering that is shown in art. Thirteenth-century art had rarely depicted death, and then as a sweet sleep.   Its vision of suffering was poetical and ideal; at Bourges the Cross Christ carries on Calvary is a triumphal one, heavy with jewels.   St. Anselm in his Meditations on the Passion, restrained himself when on the edge of tears; rather should he rejoice, since thence came his salvation.   The Crucifixion had a mystic significance for him; 'Christ bends His head,' he writes, 'since He wishes to kiss us; He stretches out His arms to embrace us, and He seems to say, "Come unto

---

[1] The Act of Canonization of Bonaventura records that he initiated the Angelus.

[2] The type comes from the vision of a Cistercian abbot who saw the monks of his Order thus sheltered.   This version was adopted and changed by the Dominicans, who established the type showing laymen headed by the Emperor on one side, and ecclesiastics headed by the Pope on the other.

XLIII. Saints Jeremiah, Zachariah and Isaiah
from Moses' Well in the Chartreuse of Champmol, nr. Dijon. By Claus Sluter
and Claus de Werve. 1395–1402

me ye who suffer"". But with the fifteenth century a tragic note sounded through the world of art. The triumphant Jesus of the earliest Middle Ages, the teaching Jesus of the thirteenth century, became in the fifteenth century the Man of Sorrows. The gentler emotions grew increasingly strong in the course of the Middle Ages, finding expression first in the *courtoisie* of chivalry and secondly in that religious emotion which with Francis was a kind of *courtoisie* of the soul. The sensibility of men steadily increased; the world, and France in particular, passed in the fourteenth century through horrible sufferings of war, pestilence, and famine, and gained thereby a perception of the pathos of suffering and a sense of communion with the sufferings of others. A strong sense of inevitable death begins to oppress

> Sages et folz, prebstres et laiz,
> Noble et vilain, larges et chiches,
> Petitz et grans, et beaulx, et laids,
> Dames à rebrassez colletz . . .
> Portant attours et bourrelets.

So the sense of the tragedy of suffering became a part of religion, and the mystics began to practise that religious exercise much later recognized by the Church as the 'Stations of the Cross'. The Passion of Christ obsessed the religious mind, and an immense number of hymns and meditations have it for their subject. One of the best known is Bonaventura's:

> Recordare sanctae Crucis
> Qui perfectam vitam ducis
> Delectare jugiter.
> Sanctae Crucis recordare
> Et in ipsa meditare
> Insatiabiliter.

His aim is to suffer with Him,

> Crucifixe, fac me fortem
> Ut libenter tuam mortem
> Plangam donec vixero.
> Tecum volo vulnerari,
> Te libenter amplexari
> In cruce desidero.

In St. Bridget, and even in Gerson, there was a morbid desire for precision in following every detail of the Passion. To take a mental share in it became the principal act of Christian piety. The mass, interpreted by the symbolists of the thirteenth century as an epitome of human history, became in the fifteenth century a commemoration of the drama of Calvary. Nor was this devotion confined to the Church: it spread not only through the populace, but through all classes. Philippe de Maizières, the friend of Charles V, dreamed in his old age of founding a new Order of Knighthood in honour of the Passion.

This preoccupation naturally resulted in an enormous number of representations of the Passion in art. The mystery play introduced the actual scene of the Crucifixion, and from the Mysteries came an absolutely new type of representation of the Passion: the figure of Christ, bound and crowned with thorns, seated waiting while the Cross is set up. From the human, the Franciscan, point of view, it is perhaps the most profound moment, for He still lives. In this figure the pathetic sense of the fifteenth century finds its deepest expression. Consider for a moment how far it is removed from the 'Beau Dieu' of Amiens on the one hand, and on the other from the type created by Michelangelo, beautiful, strong, and serene, that supersedes it in the succeeding century. I do not say compare it with the Greek idea of divinity, for the difference is too great; but compare for a moment the whole course of development of Greek and Mediaeval art. Each naturally falls into three main periods. In Greece the archaic style, borrowing its types and its decoration from Egypt and Assyria, and wrestling with refractory material and in the process evolving a national art, is paralleled in the Middle Ages by the Romanesque style, borrowing its main architectural forms from Byzantium, some of its decoration from Rome, and some of its iconography from the East, and combining them with local elements. Each country in the course of arriving at a solution of practical problems of construction and craftsmanship arrives at a national style. Secondly, there is in Greece the art of the fifth century, the art of Periclean Athens, inspired by philosophic thought, dominated by abstract ideas that make all the decoration a reasonable and integral part of the whole structure. So in the Gothic art of the thirteenth century, the art of the monarchy of the Île de France, there is the crystal-

XLIV.   The Visitation of the Church of St. Jean at Troyes

First quarter of 16th Century

lization of scholasticism, dominated by the abstract scheme of the *summae*, with each of its thousand figures playing its part in the symbolism of the whole. Thirdly, in Greece arose Hellenistic art, the art of the commercial cities of Ionia, with its sense of drama, its sense of pathos, its emphasis on the human element in divinity, and its tendency to naturalism at the expense of symbolism; an art that, however different in its form, has many likenesses of spirit with that of the commercial cities of fifteenth-century France.

IX

THE END OF THE MIDDLE AGES

BEFORE the Hundred Years' War France had enjoyed a state of material prosperity that had not been appreciated until it was lost. Before the Black Death of 1348 when, Froissart tells us, 'la tierce partie du monde mourut', the population of France was more than enough to develop its agricultural wealth. Food was cheap; if the nobles indulged in rich and extravagant dress, even the peasant could afford to furnish his house in a manner not so very different from that of to-day. Just before the war considerable advance had been made in the science of agriculture, and the improved methods had reached even the outlying parts of France. In Artois, for instance, records of 1328 show the yield of corn to have been between seven and eleven measures from land from which the most scientific modern agriculture can only get between eleven and thirteen. In many ways one is reminded of the state of rural England in the happiest years of the eighteenth century; there is the same general prosperity, the same modest comfort among the poor, the same magnificence among the rich, the same gradual decline in spiritual as against temporal things.

All this well-being came to an end with the war. The countryside was pillaged, the towns were sacked and burned, transport and communication were at an end, and prosperity and security vanished. The chronicler [1] tells us that after Poitiers 'the affairs of the realm went from bad to worse, the public weal came to an end and brigands appeared on every side. The nobles hate and despise the villeins; they care no more for the good of the King or of their vassals; they oppress and despoil the peasants of their villages. They no longer trouble to defend the country: to tread their subjects under foot and to pillage them is their only care. From this day the land of France, hitherto glorious and honoured throughout the world, became the laughing-stock of other nations.' The peace of Bretigny left mercenary soldiers all over the country: English,

[1] The Continuator of de Nangis.

XLV.   Statue of Charles V

from the Church of the Célestins, Paris

c. 1370

Walloons, Gascons, Dutch, Spaniards, Bretons, Welshmen, Germans, whose only trade was war, and whose leading passion was to live like the great lords in extravagant luxury.   Neither truce nor peace brought an end to their devastations; no church nor castle was safe from their attack.   Allied English and Navarrese companies surrounded Paris, and were only with great difficulty driven away.   They held sixty fortresses in the Île de France in 1358, and only nine in 1360, but order was not yet restored; King John on his way back to Paris from his captivity had to pay a large sum to a band of brigands to be allowed to pass through his own territory into his own capital city, and in 1363 the Bishop of Paris did not dare to venture outside the city walls to receive the homage of his tenants.   Jean de Venette laments that 'the sweet sound of bells was no longer wakened by the praises of the Lord, but by enemy attacks. "People, take shelter!"' Bertrand du Guesclin was the one man who successfully fought against the depredations of the Compagnies in the three years following the Peace of Bretigny, and thus he earned rank as a national hero.   Deschamps tells us,

> Toute desolacion
> Guerre et tribulation
> Fut ou règne à sa venue
> Mais en consolation
> Mist par sa provision
> Le peuple et la gent menue;
> La guerre leur a tollue
> Et gardé d'oppression
> Dont toute leur oraison
> Estoit pour lui espandue.[1]

But even when du Guesclin had cleared the Companies from the provinces, he had not reconstructed France.   Two powerful elements alone remained: the monarchy, and the newly developed national consciousness.   Charles V, as Voltaire says, 'justement surnommé le Sage, réparait les ruines de son pays par la patience et par les négociations'.   He inherited a poor and dismembered realm, and left a kingdom both stable and prosperous.   Stronger in character than in health, he was

[1] 'There was desolation, war, and tribulation on the whole kingdom when he came, but by his foresight he consoled the nation and the lesser folk ; he saved them from war and kept them from oppression, so that all their prayers were lavished upon him.'

addicted to study rather than to the feudal pursuits of hunting and warfare. He did much to increase the monarchical power, but it was done first by encouraging the study of political theory and secondly by securing the integrity of the royal domain, by entailing it on the King's next heir and enacting that the rest of the royal family should receive not land, but money. He was an organizer, not an innovator; he took up the traditional royal policy, and pursued it with courage. He asserted the royal monopoly of granting communal charters and of conferring nobility, and used these prerogatives to break up the remains of feudal power and to consolidate the alliance between monarchy and bourgeoisie. In innumerable ways the prestige of the feudal nobility was lessened, while every attempt was made by dignified ceremonial and sober magnificence to increase the prestige of the royal court. But much of the progress that he made was brought to nothing after his death. The war between Burgundians and Armagnacs made France a nation divided against itself, and under Henry V England attained to real national consciousness. For the first time an English war with France was an international matter and not an affray between a vassal and his lord. France was beaten at Agincourt, and the Treaty of Troyes left Henry V heir of France; but once Bedford appeared as Regent for his son French national feeling was ready to be fired by any spark of patriotism. Jeanne d'Arc heard the angel's voice:

> Jeune pucelle bien heureuse
> Le Dieu du ciel vers vous m'envoie;
> Ne vous montrez de rien peureuse,
> Prenez en vous parfaite joie.
> Sa volonté et son plaisir
> Est que alliez à Orléans
> En faire les Anglais saillir
> Et lever le siège devant.
> Puis après il vous conviendra
> A Reims mener sacrer le roi . . .
> Et Dieu vous conduira toujours.[1]

Her enthusiasm fired the country; the English were driven from Orléans, and

> L'an mil quatre cent vingt neuf
> Reprint à luire le soleil.

[1] *Mystère du siège d'Orléans.*

XLVI.   St. John the Baptist and Jean Bureau, Sire de la Rivière

Amiens Cathedral, 1373–1375

Gradually the stability of France was restored upon a new basis : the whole policy of Charles VII is a policy of commercial expansion.

The Hundred Years' War had ruined French trade. Brigands on the highways and pirates in the Mediterranean had closed all trade routes. Flanders and Italy were in communication through the valley of the Rhine, and trade and wealth had passed from France to Geneva and Burgundy, which the brilliance of the court of Philippe le Bon, Duke of Burgundy, made a fifteenth-century Versailles. Few foreign merchants remained in the country, and the Fairs of Champagne, Lyons, and St. Denis were no longer held. But as soon as the English and the bands of predatory mercenaries had been driven out of the country the fairs were re-established by the King and dealings with Geneva prohibited. Communication throughout the kingdom was made easier by developing the system of river transport, deepening the channels and removing the tolls. The port of La Rochelle had its harbour improved, and received special privileges. Further, negotiations for the establishment of commercial treaties were entered into with Germany, Switzerland, Denmark, Castille, and Egypt. In all this the King worked hand-in-hand with his minister Jacques Cœur, himself a bourgeois, the son of a tanner of Bourges. His motto was 'À vaillants cœurs rien impossible'; and through commercial enterprise he gained the position of 'Argentier de la couronne' and a place in French politics second only to the King's. Through this position he gained complete control of the commerce of the Midi, and from his chief offices at Montpellier and Marseilles organized a fleet importing Levantine stuffs from Alexandria and Beirut, carpets from Persia, perfumes from Arabia, spices from the Far East, furs from the North, and slaves from Africa, until it was said that there was not a European ship in Eastern seas that did not fly the fleurs-de-lis. His activities were not confined to maritime trade; he owned a silk manufactory at Florence, dye-works and paper mills in France, and began to exploit the French mines.[1] Even when he fell from political power and was banished from the kingdom his activities in the Eastern Mediterranean did not come to an

---

[1] It was an age of metal, of armour and artillery ; clay was even replaced by pewter and latten in making household utensils.

end.   Whether he acted from motives of patriotism or of commercial gain, with his help the trade of France was reorganized and her prosperity re-established.   It is to him as well as to Charles VII that Chastellain's praise should be paid : ' From his realm, laid waste, torn and tattered, like a ship derelict and open to the waves on every side, ruined to its foundations and with all its beauty and magnificence in ruin ; without work, without inhabitants, without trade and without justice, without rule and without order, full of thieves and brigands, full of poverty and discomfort, full of violence and exaction, full of tyranny and inhumanity, with his royal throne lying cast upon the ground— he, with great labour, brought it back to riches and freedom.'

But the France that was re-created after the Hundred Years' War was not the France of the Middle Ages.   Every institution of Capetian France declined after the dynasty of Valois ascended the throne in 1328; feudalism, chivalry, the Church, the university, the cities, the guilds, were all no longer the direct result of the needs of the times.   Roman and hence Canon Law had given the Middle Ages its four dominating political ideas, the Empire, the Papacy, the Monarchy, and the Corporation.   By the fourteenth century these four corner stones of the mediaeval State all showed the two infallible signs of decay : extravagance on the one hand, and weakness on the other.   The theoretical claims of the Emperors were most fully enunciated by their lawyers when Italy had finally slipped from their hands and the nations of Europe had reached full knowledge of their national integrity ; the Papacy, through its inquisitors, was most active [1] at a time when a collection of sermons could bear the title ' Dormi secure '—Sleep in Peace. The monarchy, having absorbed much of the power of its nobles, was most scornful of the unchivalrous people at a time when it was powerless to check popular revolt; and the corporations were increasing the power they claimed over their members at a time when men began to realize that strength lay in individual freedom.   Alain Chartier was justified by fact when in his *Quadriloge invectif* he showed that all four orders of the State were equally responsible for the grievous woes that God had sent upon his country.   Even the focus of the life of

[1] The fourteenth-century Dominican Inquisition in Champagne burned 183 heretics in one day.

France had moved away from Paris; in the fifteenth century French activities were better represented at the courts of Philip the Bold of Burgundy [1] and of Jean Duke of Berri than by the King in his capital. The great artists and sculptors of the fifteenth century did their best work not in Paris but in Burgundy; the historians Georges Chastellain, Olivier de la Marche, and Comines, all belong to the Burgundian court; the *Cent nouvelles nouvelles* is written for the Duke of Burgundy; and Gerson, the greatest theologian of the age, is a Burgundian.

Feudalism had been profoundly modified by the increasing centralization of authority in the monarchy on the one hand and by the rise of the bourgeoisie and the admission of the *tiers état* to political life in the States-General on the other. The nobles had lost the right of striking money in 1346, of levying troops in 1349, of waging private war in 1357; their judicature and their patronage alike were limited. Charles V conferred nobility on many mayors and communal and royal officers, and even sold it for a hundred livres tournois. The bourgeois of Paris were granted the knights' privilege of wearing gold spurs; Jean-sans-Peur had given them the right to hold 'noble fiefs'. Profound misunderstanding existed between all the orders of the nation : nobles, bourgeois, and peasantry were all at daggers drawn, and the old lateral weakness of feudalism was evident in the fact that each class was further divided against itself; province against province, castle against castle, regular against secular, town against town, and each peasant against every one. Chivalry, long divorced from religion, was dying a romantic death; before the war an absurd profusion and extravagance of jousting had been unchecked in France, though ordinances had been passed against tournaments in England. This extravagance had been further intensified by the 'galanterie romanesque' inspired by the Romans de la Table Ronde. Under their influence even the old epic legends were weakened in the fourteenth century by the introduction of enchantments, fairies, quests in search of adventure, monsters, and other irrelevancies. Their effects are seen in the 'Order of the Star' founded by King John in 1351, which both Froissart and its founder declared to be inspired by Arthurian legend. The

[1] The Duke of Burgundy was ruler of a great expanse of territory, including Franche Comté and the Low Countries.

domination of romance over common sense is shown in one of its statutes, 'Et leur convenait jurer que jamais ils ne fuiraient en bataille plus loins que quatre arpents à leur estimation, mais mourraient plutôt ou se laisseraient faire prisonniers'. Six months later Guy de Nesle and a hundred of his knights kept this rule in battle, and were all killed. Moreover, the upholders of this *chevalerie romanesque* were against the employment of the bourgeois militia. Philippe de Valois, Froissart tells us, said in 1347 that he only wished to fight side by side with gentlemen. To take communal forces in battle, he declared, was only loss and encumbrance, for such would melt away in a *mêlée* like snow in sunshine. He allowed the principle first admitted by Philippe le Bel, that while every Frenchman in case of danger should defend France, those who wished should be permitted to defend it with money only, and to buy exemption from active service. From those who were not nobly born, he wished for money to pay the expenses of his gentlemen, but for nothing more. They could stay at home and look after their wives and families, their business and trade. This sole reliance on a feudal chivalry that was already showing signs of decay was disastrous to the military power. The standing mercenary army which du Guesclin had to establish by the *Ordonnance de Vincennes* of 1374 marked the end of military feudalism. By 1445 there was a permanent paid army of fifteen companies of a hundred 'lances', each lance accompanied by three bowmen, a page, and a light-armed soldier, all mounted. Du Guesclin heralded an age of condottieri, using both force and ruse; the last and most martial representative of feudal chivalry, Charles the Bold of Burgundy, died at Nancy in 1477.

The older religious chivalry, too, was gone; in 1307 Philip IV had arrested all the Templars for blasphemy, idolatry, and immorality, and his tool the Pope suppressed the Order because it stood in such bad repute that it could perform no further mission. The suppression of the Order marked not only its own decay but the moral decay of royal justice; the legal process used against them is a monument of the barbarity of French criminal procedure. Torture was freely used; false witnesses were deliberately engaged on the royal side. Fifty-nine Templars were burnt at Paris, and nine at Senlis. The great wealth which the Order had amassed in land, and, through

VII. Georges Chastellain offering his *Instruction d'un Jeune Prince* to
Charles, Duke of Burgundy
15th Cent.

shipping and banking, in money, was nominally transferred by the Pope to the Hospitallers, but much of it stuck to Philip's fingers. Further, the system of seigneurial justice, already weakened by the royal courts, broke down, and all below feudal rank questioned feudal order. The fourteenth century was an age of demagogues and of popular risings in every country of Europe; in France the Vaudois, the Turlupins, the Society of the Poor, the Jacquerie, the Marlottins, were all driven by different currents of the universal flood of restlessness. In Paris in 1358 the citizens wore for the first time the revolutionary cap of red and blue, and for the first time showed that citizenship is not patriotism. As the *tiers état* rose to power the communal institutions of the Middle Ages decayed. The bourgeois oligarchy, no longer content with local power, identified itself with the royal judicature and administration, and civic democracy was dead.

A real middle class gradually arose, of successful merchants and country gentlemen. The line between bourgeois and noble was less definitely drawn; there were *nouveaux riches*, who bought fiefs and patents of nobility, and there were *nouveaux pauvres*, who applied to be enrolled as bourgeois of the trading cities, tried to gain a living by intelligent agriculture, or entered one of the more respectable trades.[1] In Provence we hear of *nobiles mendicantes*, and there is a story of a widowed relative of the Duke of Burgundy who kept an inn.

The country was as much changed as the towns. The immediate consequence of the war was extreme misery in the rural districts; insecurity, famine, and depopulation caused much land to fall out of cultivation: 'Les bois sont venus en France avec les Anglais.' Some districts to the north of Lyons, once fertile, still remain waste as a result of this agricultural decline. To counteract it there was much enfranchisement of serfs; the Abbot of St. Germain des Prés, for instance, at one time enfranchised three villages held by his monastery, 'en considération des guerres, pestes et autres fléaux'. A gradual substitution of contracted service for the servitude of earlier centuries made the shortage of agricultural labour result in the raising of the

---

[1] The new trades of mining and glass-making were considered the most suitable.

labourer's wage under Charles VII to a height never previously attained. In some parts of Provence the proprietor only received an eighth of the produce of his land, and a quarter was deemed a high proportion. Further, since uncultivated lands were often ceded in perpetuity, a class of small proprietors arose and seigneurial rights were still further diminished.

Thus men were no longer bound to the land they tilled, and among those who did not themselves own land there was an increasing tendency to wander further afield in search of better paid work. To these wandering labourers were added bands of wandering journeymen, who were travelling from one city to another in search of a new 'patron'. To these, again, were added the merchants themselves, travelling from their provincial city to the capital, or to one of the great fairs. Besides these legitimate travellers there was a vagabond population, the result of the war—students whose colleges were ruined, priests whose prebends no longer yielded an income, mercenaries of all nationalities thrown out of employment by the peace, gipsies, and beggars. Villon is the King of the Vagabonds, *le roi des gueux*. He has recorded their *argot* in seven of his ballads, and in it all the elements of the vagabond kingdom are represented—foreign words from the mercenaries, archaic French from the peasants, clerical phrases from the vagabond priests, dog-Latin from the students, as well as regular thieves' jargon from the professional criminals. It is true that this floating population gradually became absorbed into the growing prosperity and order of the kingdom, but there can be little doubt that the restlessness, movement, and freedom from local ties which it typified helped further to disorganize the local basis of feudal aristocracy. The social hierarchy was modified by economic fact: a money basis replaced a land basis, and the *Mystère de la Passion* of 1451 declares with justice, 'Il n'est chose qu'argent ne face'.

The Church itself was weakened. The Papacy suffered vitally and permanently from the Avignonese Captivity and the Great Schism. It lost much of its spiritual character and trafficked commercially in spiritual things; it lost its universal character and became sectarian. The falling away of England and Germany from the Avignonese Papacy foreshadowed the Reformation. The older monastic orders were no longer fruitful, and the new had lost the inspiration given by their founders. The secular priesthood had reached its lowest ebb since the Gregorian movement. The tonsure gave them the privileges of the cleric and put them under ecclesiastical law, but everywhere they are found to have married and pursued worldly avocations. In Normandy there are records of rich peasants who were at once clerics and vavassors; at Louviers and Tournai their names are to be found in the list of dyers and dyers' apprentices.

The wars seriously affected the intellectual life of France. Students could not safely attend the universities; the Archbishop of Bordeaux, writing in 1439, declared, 'Those who wish to seek the pearl of knowledge can no longer go to the universities in safety; many have been taken on their way, imprisoned, stript of their books and their goods, held for ransom, and sometimes, alas! slain'. In that very year grass is recorded to have grown in the streets of Paris and wolves to have lurked in the suburbs. Yet academic life went on; and this mere continuance is as remarkable at such a time as fruitful activity shown in a more settled age. But as the century advanced there was a gradual change. Scholastic philosophy had overbalanced itself and tottered on crutches of orthodoxy, and though new life was manifested in the study of science,[1] the logical speculation of the Middle Ages was dead.

The literary *genres* of the Middle Ages each reflect some aspect of mediaeval society : the *Chansons de geste* represent the life of pilgrimage and Crusade, the Romances that of the castle hall; the love song the knight, and the *lais* and the *chansons de toile* the lady. The *fabliau* is the creation of the town; the *Mystère* of the Church, the *Miracles* of the confraternity, the *Summa* of the university. These came to an end with the society that had created them; and the literary influence of France declined with the development of a national literature in Italy and England. Lyric verse and historical prose remained to reflect the life of the fifteenth century. Villon is the first modern poet; Comines the first philosophic

[1] At Montpellier, for instance, dissection began to be practised, and the improved state of medical knowledge led to the separation of the professions of physician and apothecary.

historian. He writes for the generation that inherited the *sagesse* of Charles V, and used it to interpret events and judge character with both subtlety and common sense. The court he knows is that which René of Anjou describes, where a man must

> Tout regarder, et faindre riens ne veoir;
> Tout escouter, monstrant riens ne sçavoir,
> Mot ne sonner des cas qu'on sçait et voit.

He wrote for men whose minds were occupied not with the valiancy of romantic chivalry but with the political calculations of a Machiavellian diplomacy, seeking the relation of cause and effect, viewing all things with curiosity but without enthusiasm, men who find their embodiment in Louis XI. Just as St. Louis is the type of the culminating century of the Middle Ages, so Louis XI is that of the century that marks their close; as the Crusade is the war of the one period, so the struggle between France and Burgundy is that of the other.

None the less, out of decay sprang life. The Emperor had been deprived of any shadowy claim to supremacy; the Pope had been driven from his international position; feudalism, bourgeoisie and monarchy alike had changed; Empire and city were superseded by the nation, and France took her place in the modern world of politics—in a new Europe, a multiplicity of nations believed to be free and equal, governed by a body of doctrine known as International Law. Wars of rights were superseded by wars of interest; the hierarchy was succeeded by the balance of power, and individual experience and opinion overruled the systematic theory of the Middle Ages. Science ceased to be a form of apologetics, and became experiment; scholasticism was gradually eclipsed by the new spirit of classicism. Symbolism in all its functions was superseded by more direct if less beautiful forms of expression. Dante had claimed four meanings for his Divine Comedy: the literal, the allegorical, the moral or philosophical, and the anagogical or mystical significance; Rabelais, in his Preface to the *Gargantua*, wrote, ' Croyez vous en votre foi qu'onques Homère, escripvant l'Iliade, l'Odysée, pensast es allegories . . . Si le croyez, vous n'approchez ni de pieds ni de mains à mon opinion qui décrète icelles aussi peu avoir été songées d'Homère que d'Ovide, en ses Métamor-

XLVIII.   The Duke of Berri at table

phoses, les sacrements de l'Evangile. . . .' Petrarch and
Boccaccio had begun by transferring allegory from theology
to poetry, and it only remained for Renaissance criticism to
justify the existence of purely imaginative literature. An
aesthetic basis for its re-establishment was ready; though the
Poetics of Aristotle had been known in the later Middle Ages
they had been neglected, until the publication in 1498 of Valla's
Latin translation gave them the prestige of fresh discovery.
They gave the rational justification of poetry, as aiming at the
reality of an eternal probability. The difference between the
poetic aims of the Middle Ages and the Renaissance can be
shown by comparing Eustache Deschamps's *Art de dictier* of
1392 with Joachim du Bellay's *Défense et Illustration de la
langue française* of 1549.

The didactic function of symbolism could not be left unful-
filled: moreover, a new devotion to an old teacher, Horace,
justified the didactic aim of art. A definite moralizing tendency
had made itself felt as soon as the duty of preaching had
descended from the scholarly Augustinian to the less learned
mendicant, and the various *Bibles moralisées* of the fourteenth
and fifteenth centuries show the steady destruction of the ancient
parallel interpretation of the Old and New Testaments by this
didactic system. With the Renaissance the duty of moral
teaching was transferred from the cathedral to the printing
press, whence issued an enormous number of little books—such
as Gerson's *Montagne de Contemplation*—which fulfilled the
purpose once achieved by the great windows and the sculptured
façades of the cathedrals. Similarly the representation of the
individual grew more and more exact, as his relation with the
hierarchical scheme of the universe became less defined. Tomb
figures, which had been in the thirteenth century ideal and
impersonal, became more and more strictly portraits: for the
tomb of Charles VI not only the head, but also the hands and
feet, were cast from moulds taken actually upon his corpse.
Gradually, too, the effigy ceased to be at peace, and knelt to
pray; and then—about 1545—began to rest upon cushions
like one who thinks out the solution of the unsolved problem
of life. Art passed gradually from symbolism to history; the
art of the fifteenth century was narrative art, telling stories
of saints, Christ, the Virgin, and martyrs with narrative richness

and naturalism. Finally, by the middle of the sixteenth century, the Christian scheme was applied to human story. In the chapel of Champigny-sur-Vaude (built about 1559) the whole Bourbon family is sculptured, from Robert the son of St. Louis down to Charles, grandfather of Henry IV. The windows show in great detail scenes from the life of St. Louis ; it is the apotheosis of the eponymous hero of the dynasty.

Mediaeval art was inspired by ideals of humility : suffering, sadness, resignation, Passion and Crucifixion. Even in its decline in the fifteenth century it approximated the types of Christ, the Virgin, and the saints to those of the poor and humble folk who represented them in the Mysteries. But the Renaissance found another ideal to express : man, sufficient unto himself, fighting his own battles, shining with strength and beauty, and rising by force of his own power to unknown heights. From representing man's earthly struggles, his ordeal of judgement, and his pardon and redemption in heaven, from expressing before all other things his religious faith, art turned to record his moments of victory and to serve his desire to impress his human personality upon material things. The hidden principle of Renaissance art is pride ; its avowed aim is earthly glory, and its moral teaching is the *danse macabre*.

CHRONOLOGICAL TABLE 800–1483.[1]

Events	Arts and Sciences
800 Coronation of Charlemagne as Roman Emperor. In this century the Northmen begin to invade Western Europe.	
	Palatine Chapel of Aix la Chapelle finished.[2] 804
	Council of Tours orders homilies to be preached in 'lingua Romana rustica aut Teotisca'. 812
817 Monastic reforms of Benedict of Aniane.	
	Death of Einhard. 840
841 The Northmen take Rouen and plunder Seine valley.	
843 Treaty of Verdun: the empire divided, the Western part falling to Charles the Bald. The Northmen take Nantes, raid southward, and winter in Ré.	The Strasburg Oaths. 842
844 The Vikings ascend the Garonne as far as Toulouse.	
845 Paris sacked, and Rouen taken for the second time.	
847 Bordeaux burnt. From now on, constant Northmen raids in valleys of Seine, Loire, and Garonne. Permanent camps set up at river mouths.	
853 Northmen take Orléans and Paris.	Death of Hrabanus Maurus. 856
857 Charles the Bald unites with his nephew Lothair II of Lotharingia against the Vikings in the Île de France.	
858 Charles's brother Lewis of Germany invades France; Viking progress unchecked and widespread.	

[1] For a detailed table (including the other countries of Europe and the East) the reader is referred to A. Hassall, *European History chronologically arranged, 476–1910*, London 1911; M. Morison, *Time Table of Modern History, 400–1870*, London 1908 (second edition).

[2] The buildings indicated are those of which the major part is still in existence.

Events	*Arts and Sciences*
860 Peace with Germany. With help of Robert the Strong, duke 'between Loire and Seine', Charles wars against rebel vassals and the Northmen.	
864 Edict of Pîtres. Cavalry and fortifications to be used against the Vikings.	
866 Death of Robert the Strong at the battle of Brissarthe. Synod of Constantinople makes final breach between Eastern and Western Churches.	
869 Charles crowned King of Lotharingia (Lorraine).	
871 Lotharingia divided by Treaty of Meersen: Burgundy and W. Austrasia to Charles, the rest to Lewis the German.	
875 Emperor Louis I dies without heirs. Contest between Charles the Bald and Lewis the German for succession. Charles invades Italy and is crowned Emperor at Rome.	
876 Death of Lewis the German.	
877 Death of Charles the Bald. Succeeded by Louis II (the Stammerer) who gives up imperial title and Italian ambitions.	Death of Scotus Erigena. **877**
879 Death of Louis II. Louis III and Carloman crowned co-kings. Independent kingdom of Arles (Lower Burgundy) set up for Count Boso.	
	Sequence of Saint Eulalia (circa) 880
881 Louis III defeats Northmen at Saucourt.	
882 Death of Louis III.	
884 Death of Carloman. Union of Frankish kingdom under Emperor Charles the Fat.	
885 Siege of Paris by the Northmen, who are resisted by Count Odo.	

Events	*Arts and Sciences*
888 Death of Charles the Fat. Count Odo of Paris chosen king to exclusion of heir, Charles the Simple. Separation of kingdoms of East and West Franks. Moors settle on coast of Provence.	
890 Duke of Vannes makes himself independent in Brittany.	
893 Charles the Simple claims the throne of France. Civil War.	
898 Death of Odo. His brother and heir Robert makes peace with Charles the Simple, who recognizes him as 'duke of the French'.	
910 Abbey of Cluny founded by William of Aquitaine.	
911 Treaty of St. Clair sur Epte. Viking leader Rollo is baptized, receives lands which form nucleus of later duchy of Normandy, and becomes the vassal of the French king.	
912 Charles becomes King of Lorraine as well as of France.	
922 Revolts and civil wars begin, and continue for rest of reign.	
925 Lorraine finally united with Germany.	
929 Death of Charles the Simple in prison ; his rival Rudolf of Burgundy becomes undisputed king.	
933 Two kingdoms of Upper and Lower Burgundy united.	
936 Hungarian invasion of Aquitaine. Death of Rudolf, Carolingian line restored with Louis IV (d'Outremer), who has constant trouble with his vassal Hugh the Great, Duke of the French.	
946 Louis allies with Otto I, King of Germany, and begins to make progress against Hugh.	
950 Hugh submits.	
954 Death of Louis IV. His son Lothair succeeds.	

Events	Arts and Sciences
956 Death of Hugh the Great. Hugh Capet, his son, succeeds him, and further extends the power of the house.	
967 Hugh Capet marries Adelaide of Poitou, thus extending his claims southward.	
	Gerbert at head of Cathedral School of Rheims. 972
978 Lothair tries to recover Lorraine for France. Otto II in revenge invades France and threatens Paris.	St. Mark's, Venice, rebuilt. 976
980 Peace with Otto II, Lothair renouncing pretensions to Lorraine.	
	Gerbert at Bobbio for a year. 981
986 Death of Lothair, succeeded by his son, Louis V.	
987 On death of Louis V the Carolingian line in France ends, and the Capetian dynasty begins with the election of Hugh Capet as king. This largely due to support of Adalberon, Archbp. of Rheims, and his friend Gerbert.	
	Donjon of Loches built. 991 Gerbert becomes Archbishop of Rheims.
	Donjon of Langeais built. 992
996 Death of Hugh Capet; his son Robert succeeds.	
997 Rising of Norman peasants begins and lasts for two years.	
	Gerbert elected Pope. 998
	Oldest MS. of Beowulf. 1000
1002 Robert II inherits the Duchy of Burgundy.	
1003 Famine for five years.	Death of Gerbert. 1003
	Fulbert Bishop of Chartres. 1006
	Abbey Church of Tournus 1008 begun.
1010 Famine for four years.	
1016 Persecution of the Jews in France.	
1017 Burgundian Crusades against Moors begin.	
1019 Hakem's persecution of Christians in Syria ends.	

Events	*Arts and Sciences*
1022 First persecution of Christian heretics in France (Orléans).	
1024 Revolt of Breton peasants.	
1027 Norman pilgrimage to Jerusalem. Truga Dei proclaimed at Elne.	
1028 Limousin pilgrimage to Jerusalem.	
1031 Death of Robert II, succeeded by his son Henry I. Civil War owing to intrigues of Duke of Burgundy.	Bridge of Tours begun. 1031
1032 End of the kingdom of Arles. After death of Rudolf III Burgundy is incorporated in the Empire.	
1033 Great famine.	
1035 Robert of Normandy dies on pilgrimage to Jerusalem.	
1036 Pax Dei proclaimed in S. and E. France.	
	Death of Avicenna. 1037
1038 Normans established in Apulia.	
1039 Civil War ends.	
	Abbey of Jumièges rebuilt. 1040 *Vie de St. Alexis (circa)*
1041 Truga Dei proclaimed at Nice.	
1043 Plague in France.	
1045 William of Normandy defeats Guy of Burgundy with French aid.	Lund Cathedral consecrated. 1045
1047 William defeats rebellion in Normandy with French aid.	
1049 Leo IX holds Council at Rheims and tries to prevent simony and marriage of the clergy.	
	Bridge of Lyons begun. 1050
1053 Truga Dei extended.	
1054 Henry I forms coalition with Dukes of Aquitaine and Burgundy against William of Normandy, but is defeated at Mortemer.	
1058 William of Normandy wins second victory over coalition at Varaville.	
1060 Death of Henry I, succeeded by young son, Philip I. Baldwin of Flanders Regent. Foundation of Breteuil.	

Events	*Arts and Sciences*
1062 Normans in Sicily under Guiscard.	
	Cathedral of Pisa. 1063 Church of St. Étienne, Caen, 1064 begun.
1066 Norman conquest of England. 1068 Monarchy acquires Gâtinais from Fulk of Anjou.	
	St. Mark's, Venice, rebuilt. 1071 Death of St. Peter Damian. 1072
1073 William the Conqueror attacks and reduces Maine.	
	Canterbury Choir begun. 1074
1075 Seljuks take Jerusalem. Philip I aids Bretons in revolt against William the Conqueror.	Lincoln Cathedral. 1075
1076 Commune at Cambrai. Philip I makes peace with William the Conqueror.	
1077 Death of Baldwin; Philip reigns alone. Commune at St. Quentin.	Bridge of Avignon begun. 1077
	St. Alban's Abbey. 1078 Winchester Cathedral. 1079 Ely Cathedral. Oxford 1080 Cathedral. Mainz Cathedral rebuilt. 1081
1082 Churches of Asia Minor destroyed by Seljuks. Peace Society of Capuchonnés founded. King acquires French Vexin.	
	St. Saturnin, Toulouse, be- 1083 gun.
1084 Carthusian Order founded. 1085 Death of Pope Gregory VII (Hildebrand).	
	Death of Constantinus Afri- 1087 canus.
1090 Norman Conquest of Sicily com- pleted.	
	Durham Cathedral begun. 1093
1095 First Crusade preached at Cler- mont by Pope Urban II, and undertaken.	Council of Clermont recog- 1095 nizes 'Office of the Virgin'. Abbey Church of Vézelay 1096 begun. Norwich Cathe- dral begun.
1097 Cistercian Order founded. Crusade starts under Godfrey of Bouillon.	Donjon of Gisors. 1097

Events	*Arts and Sciences*
1099 Jerusalem taken by Crusaders. Commune at Beauvais. William Rufus takes Maine.	
1100 King buys Bourges and makes his son Louis joint King.	Roman Law studied in 1100[1] France. Moissac Church built. *Roman d'Alexandre* of Albéric de Besançon. Cupola Architecture in Péri- 1101 gord.
1107 Pope Paschal in France : Council of Troyes discusses Investitures.	
1108 Death of Philip I, succeeded by his son Louis VI (the Fat). Commune at Noyon.	Church of St. John, Bey- 1108 rout, built.
1110 Commune at Mantes.	*Chanson de Roland* (? *circa*) 1110
1113 Order of Hospitallers founded. War with Henry I of England.	Abelard turns to study of 1113 theology.
1114 Commune at Valenciennes.	
1116 Commune at Amiens.	
1118 Order of Templars founded.	
1119 Premonstratensian Order founded. French defeated by English at Brenneville.	*Comput* of Philippe de Thaon 1119 Cathedral of Ratisbon built.
1120 Peace with England, through me- diation of the Pope at Council of Rheims.	St. Front de Périgueux. 1120 Barrel vaulting in Île de France.
	Death of William o Cham- 1121 peaux. Abelard's writings condemned by Council of Soissons.
	Suger Abbot of St. Denis. 1122 Benoit's *Vie de St. Brendan* (*circa*).
1123 King establishes commune at Corbie.	
1125 First ville neuve founded at Vau- cresson.	*Chanson de Guillaume.* Philippe 1125 de Thaon's *Lapidaries* (*circa*).
1126 King establishes communes at St Riquier and Soissons.	
1127 Commune at St. Omer. Louis VI avenges murder of Charles the Good, Count of Flanders, by the populace of Bruges.	Death of William of Aqui- 1127 taine.
	Abelard writing hymns. 1129 Adelhard of Bath translates 1130 Euclid from Arabic. Phil- ippe de Thaon's *Bestiaire*.

[1] In this century were also built the Cathedrals of Angoulême, Cahors, Puy, Vaison, St. Paul Trois Châteaux, Autun, and Semur.

Events	Arts and Sciences
	Gormond et Isembard; Couronnement de Louis. 1130
	Noyon Cathedral begun. 1131
	Robert Pulein (Breton) lectures on theology at Oxford. 1133
	(?) Pandects of Justinian rediscovered at Amalfi. *Historia regum Britanniae of* Geoffrey of Monmouth. 1135
1137 Death of Louis VI. Succeeded by his son, Louis VII, who had just married Eleanor, heiress of Aquitaine, which was thus annexed to France.	
	True Gothic style begins. 1140 Doctrine of Immaculate Conception at Lyons. Abbey of St. Denis built. Bernard denounces Abelard's heresies at Council of Sens.
	Death of Hugh of St. Victor and of Abelard. 1141
1142 Commune at Montpellier.	
1144 Fall of Edessa. Charter given to Bourges.	
	Arnold of Brescia at Rome. 1145 *Chansons de Croisade.*
1146 Bernard preaches Crusade at Vézelay.	Château Gaillard des Andelys built. 1146
1147 Louis VII sets out on Crusade, which fails.	Gaimar's *Estorie des Engleis.* 1147
1148 Bernard makes missionary journey in South to repress heresy.	
	Gratian's *Concordantia discordantium canonum.* 1149
	Roman de Thèbes; Pèlerinage de Charlemagne. First French (*circa*) Version of Marbode's *Lapidary. La Chevalerie Vivien; La Prise d'Orange; Audigier.* 1150
1152 Louis leagues with Stephen of England and Henry of Champagne against Henry of Anjou. He divorces Eleanor.	Death of Suger. 1152

Events	Arts and Sciences
	Death of St. Bernard. 1153
1154 Henry of Anjou succeeds to English throne.	Edrisi's *Geography*. Anglo- 1154 Saxon *Chronicle* ends. Wace translates Geoffrey of Monmouth.
1155 Attempt to establish Pax Dei for ten years.	S. Michele, Pavia, finished. 1155 *Les Sept Sages* (*circa*).
1158 Henry II of England secures the succession of Brittany.	University of Bologna found- 1158 ed.
1159 Henry II lays claim to Toulouse and attacks it.	
1160 Peace with England. Henry II established in Toulouse.	Death of Peter Lombard. 1160 Sens Cathedral begun. Laon Cathedral begun. Cathedral of Notre Dame de Paris begun. *Roman du Mont - Saint - Michel*; *Eneas*; *Mystère d'Adam* (*circa*).
1163 Cathari denounced as heretics.	
	Chrétien de Troyes imitates 1165 Ovid. Benoit de St. More's *Troie*. Gautier d'Arras' *Eracle*. Chrétien de Troyes' *Tristan* begun (*circa*).
1166 Brittany does homage to Henry II of England, who holds Normandy, Poitou, Aquitaine, Gascony, Anjou, Maine, Touraine, Quercy, and the Auvergne.	
	Gautier d'Arras: *Ille et* 1167 *Galeron*. Chrétien de Troyes' *Erec* 1168 (*circa*).
1170 Vaudois heresy begins.	School of Paris founded by this 1170 date. *Foulque de Candie*. Thomas's *Tristan*. *Havelok*. Benoit de St. More's *Histoire des Ducs de Normandie*. Chrétien de Troyes' *Cligès*. *Richeut*; *Floire et Blancheflor*.
1171 Etablissements of Rouen drawn up.	Pierre Valdo has certain 1171 books of the Bible translated into French.

Events	*Arts and Sciences*
1172 Eleanor raises Aquitaine against her husband, and Louis attacks Normandy and Anjou. Richard of England enthroned as Duke of Aquitaine.	Chrétien de Troyes' *Lancelot.* 1172
1174 Treaty of Gisors between France and England.	Wace ends *La Geste des Nor-* 1174 *mands. Roman de Rou. Vie de St. Thomas Becket* of Guernes de Pont-Sainte-Maxence.
	Averroes' Commentary stu- 1175 died at Paris. *Lais* of Marie de France (*circa*). *Aiol* ; *Ogier de Dane-marche* ; biblical versions.
	Fierre de Saint-Cloud's 1176 *Roman de Renart* (*circa*).
1178 Saladin attacks Latin Kingdom of Jerusalem.	*Livre des Manières* of Etienne 1178 de Fougères.
1179 Louis's son Philip Augustus is crowned at Rheims.	
1180 Death of Louis VII; succeeded by Philip Augustus.	Death of John of Salisbury. 1180 Lambert li Tort's *Roman d'Alexandre. Chanson d'An-tioche* (*circa*).
1181 Pope sends Cardinal Henri de Clairvaux into Languedoc to convert Albigensians. Henry II of England aids Philip against great vassals.	Marie de France's *Fables.* 1181 Châtelain de Coucy; Conon de Béthune (*circa*).
1182 Banishment of Jews from France decreed.	
1183 Philip wars on Count of Flanders, who cedes Vermandois to him.	
	William of Tyre's *Chronicle* 1184 ends.
1185 First assembly only of bourgeois held. Successful war against Duke of Burgundy.	
1186 Philip attacks Henry II and begins recovery of lands from English.	
1187 Saladin takes Jerusalem. Gregory VII preaches Third Crusade.	Chichester Cathedral begun. 1187
1188 Dîme Saladine imposed. Berri ceded to France. Commune at Toulouse.	Cathedral of Tournai. Ai- 1188 mon de Varenne's *Flori-mont.*
1189 Henry II beaten ; favourable peace concluded.	

Events	*Arts and Sciences*
1190 Crusaders take St. Jean d'Acre. King delegates power in cities to provost and burgesses during his absence on Crusade.	Lincoln Cathedral rebuilt. 1190 Beroul's *Tristan* (*circa*).
1191 Peronne annexed on death of Philip of Flanders at Acre.	
1193 Philip attacks Normandy and takes Evreux ; war with England for five years.	
	Chartres Cathedral rebuilt. 1194 Hélinand's *Vers de la Mort* (*circa*).
1196 Jaffa lost by Crusaders. The Auvergne ceded to France.	Ambroise's *Histoire de la* 1196 *guerre sainte*.
	Death of Averroes. Château 1198 Gaillard rebuilt.
1199 Cathari persecuted in Provence.	Innocent III condemns Metz 1199 translation of sacred books into the vulgar tongue. Death of Adam of St.Victor.
	Roman de Guillaume de Dole. 1200 Raoul de Houdenc's *Meraugis de Portlesguez.* Jean Bodel's *Jeu de St. Nicolas.* André de Coutances' *Le Roman des Français* (*circa*). Death of Peter of Blois (*circa*). Bourges Cathedral begun. Complete Aristotelian philosophy known at Paris (*circa*). Ypres Cloth Hall begun. 1201
1202 Fourth Crusade takes Zara.	Leonard of Pisa publishes 1202 *Liber Abaci* with Arabic numerals and cipher. Jean Bodel's *Congés.*
1203 Saintonge confiscated from John of England.	
1204 Constantinople taken and sacked by Crusaders. Philip conquers and annexes Normandy, Touraine, Anjou, and Poitou from John.	
	Guillaume de Palerne. 1205
1207 Commune at Nîmes.	Villehardouin begins his 1207 *Chronicle* (*circa*).
1208 Albigensian Crusade begins.	Troyes Cathedral begun. 1208

Events	*Arts and Sciences*
1209 Crusade continues.	Cathedral of Nicosia, Cyprus, begun. 1209 University of Valencia founded.
	Rheims Cathedral rebuilt. 1210 Study of Aristotle's works on natural philosophy forbidden at University of Paris. *Aucassin et Nicolete* (*circa*). Translation of *Barlaam and Joasaph*.
1211 Conquest of Southern France begins.	Nevers Cathedral rebuilt. 1211
1212 Christian victory over Moors at Tolosa.	Soissons Cathedral begun. 1212 Death of Villehardouin.
1213 Philip wars with Flanders.	Bayonne Cathedral begun. 1213
1214 Philip defeats English and Emperor at Bouvines with aid of Communes.	Wells Cathedral begun. 1214
1215 Simon de Montfort completes conquest of South and becomes Lord of Languedoc.	University of Paris incorporated. 1215 Béziers Cathedral begun.
1216 Recognition of Franciscan and Dominican Orders by the Church. Philip's eldest son Louis offered crown of England by barons, but renounces it the next year.	Auxerre Cathedral begun. 1216
	Le Mans Cathedral begun. 1217
1218 Crusade in Egypt fails. Death of Simon de Montfort. Albigensian war renewed.	Dominicans at Paris University. 1218
	Franciscans at Paris University. 1219 Amiens Cathedral rebuilt. 1220 Prose versions of Arthurian and Grail legends. *Huon de Bordeaux.* Gautier de Coincy's *Miracles de la Vierge. Vie de Guillaume le Maréchal.*
1221 Damietta lost.	Burgos Cathedral begun. 1221 Death of St. Dominic. *Complainte de Jérusalem.* Dominicans at Oxford. 1222

Events	Arts and Sciences
1223 Death of Philip Augustus; succeeded by his son Louis VIII.	Château de Coucy begun. 1223
1224 Poitou, Saintonge, and all country up to frontier of Gascony occupied by Louis.	University of Naples 1224 founded.
	Rebuilding of Beauvais 1225 Cathedral begun.
	Lisieux Cathedral rebuilt.
1226 Crusade against Languedoc. Perche incorporated in France. Death of Louis VIII; succeeded by infant son, (Saint) Louis IX, under regency of his mother, Blanche of Castille.	Death of St. Francis. 1226
1227 The Great Barons league against Blanche; the citizens of Paris arm to help her.	Toledo Cathedral begun. 1227 Guillaume le Clerc's *Besant de Dieu.*
1228 The officers of the Communes take oath to defend the King.	Treves Cathedral begun. 1228 University of Padua founded.
1229 By the Treaty of Meaux Languedoc is ceded to the French crown. Inquisition established at Toulouse.	Châlons Cathedral rebuilt. 1229
	University of Paris dispersed; 1230 growing importance of provincial Universities. *Li Fait des Romains.* Joffroy of Waterford translates Eutropius and Aristotelian versions (*circa*).
1231 Insurgent barons reconciled to the crown.	Choir of Bayeux begun. 1231
1233 King buys Blois, Chartres, and Sancerre. Ecclesiastical jurisdiction limited.	
1234 Louis marries Margaret of Provence.	Franciscans at Oxford. 1234
	Huon de Méri's *Tournoiement* 1235 *d'Antéchrist.*
1236 Failure of French Crusade. End of Regency of Blanche.	
	Guillaume de Lorris' *Roman* 1237 *de la Rose* (*circa*).
	Bridge of Najac. 1238
1239 Macon bought by King.	
	Sainte Chapelle begun. 1240
1241 Revolt of barons of Poitou assisted by Henry III.	Palace of Provins. 1241

Events	Arts and Sciences
Events	*Arts and Sciences*
1242 Louis IX defeats Henry at Taille-bourg and Saintes.	
1243 Peace with England; only Gascony left in English hands.	*Chronique* of Philippe Mous-ket of Tournai (*circa*). 1243
1244 Sultan of Egypt takes Jerusalem. Louis takes Cross. Albigensian heresy finally extinguished.	
	Image du Monde of Gautier de Metz (*circa*). University of Rome founded. 1245
	Albertus Magnus in Paris. 1246
	Lyons Cathedral begun.
1247 Friars on mission to Persia.	
1248 St. Louis goes on Crusade.	
1249 St. Louis takes Damietta.	
1250 St. Louis defeated at Mansourah; retires to Acre.	Sorbonne founded. University of Salamanca founded. 1250
	Last prose versions of Arthurian legends (*circa*).
1251 Peasant rising of Pastoureaux.	
1252 French Crusaders leave Syria.	
1253 'Peregrinantes propter Christum' founded. Death of Queen Blanche.	Death of Grosseteste and Thibaut de Champagne. 1253
1254 St. Louis returns from Palestine to France.	Cathedral of Clermont begun. 1254
1255 King buys Gévaudan.	Rutebeuf begins to write (*circa*). 1255
1257 King inherits Perche.	University of Cambridge founded. 1257
	Mémoires of Philippe de Novare (*circa*). 1258
1259 Treaty with Henry III of England, who cedes claims on Normandy, Anjou, Maine, Touraine, and Poitou, and receives Périgord and Limousin.	
	Villard de Honnecourt's Album (*circa*). 1260
	Chartres Cathedral consecrated.
1261 Latin Empire of the East destroyed. Charles of Anjou, Louis's brother, accepts crown of Sicily.	
1262 Arles, Forcalquier, Foix, and Cahors united to Crown.	

Events	Arts and Sciences
	Sienna Cathedral finished. 1264 Death of Vincent de Beauvais.
	Livre du Trésor of Brunetto 1265 Latini.
	Merton College, Oxford, 1266 founded.
	Cathedral of Tours rebuilt. 1267
1268 Christians lose Antioch.	Westminster Abbey finished. 1268
	Sens Cathedral finished. 1269
1270 Louis dies on Crusade at Tunis; succeeded by son, Philip III.	*Le Garçon et l'Aveugle*; *Récits* 1270 *d'un Ménestrel de Reims* (*circa*).
1271 All the domains of Toulouse lapse to crown.	
1272 French boundaries advanced to Rhone and Meuse; Archbp. of Lyon takes oath of fealty.	
	Limoges Cathedral begun. 1273 *Etablissements de St. Louis* drawn up.
	Death of St. Bonaventura. 1274 Death of Aquinas.
1275 Commoners permitted to acquire fiefs.	Evreux Cathedral begun. 1275 Marco Polo in Pekin. Adam de la Halle's *Jeu de la Feuillée* (*circa*).
1276 Dominican mission to Bagdad. Unsuccessful war against Castille.	Jean de Meung's *Roman de* 1276 *la Rose* (*circa*). Publication of Albertus Mag- 1277 nus.
1278 Procedure of Parlement of Paris codified.	Cathedral of Rodez begun. 1278 Death of Niccolà Pisano. *Roman de Hem* of Jean Sarrazin. University of Coimbra 1279 founded. *Somme le roi* of the Dominican Laurent.
1280 House of Dauphiné inherits Flanders.	Death of Albertus Magnus 1280 and of Philippe de Beaumanoir. Bruges Cloth Hall begun. 1283 Death of Alfonso the Learned of Castille. Jean de Meung translates 1284 Vegetius.

Events	*Arts and Sciences*
1285 Death of Philip III on campaign in Aragon; succeeded by his son Philip IV (the Fair). Champagne, Navarre, and Brie pass to crown.	Death of Rutebeuf (*circa*). 1285 *Jeu de Robin et Marion* of Adam de la Halle (*circa*). *Tournoi de Chauvency* of Jacques Bretel. R. Lull begins Eastern Travels.
1287 Clergy removed from Parlement and from judicial office.	Upsala Cathedral begun. 1287
	Jeu du pèlerin 1288 Jacquemart Gelée's *Renard le Nouvel*.
1289 Quercy recovered; Edward I does homage for Guienne.	
	Meteorica of Aristotle trans- 1290 lated. *Ysopet de Lyon*. University of Lisbon founded.
1291 St. Jean d'Acre taken by Turks.	Guiart des Moulins' *Bible* 1291 *historial*.
1292 Bigorre falls to the King.	Death of Roger Bacon (*circa*). 1292
1294 War breaks out with England; French troops overrun Gascony, which is declared forfeited.	
1295 Foreigners admitted to Foire du Lendit.	*Testament* of Jean de Meung. 1295
1296 Philip resists the Papacy; exportation of valuables forbidden.	
1297 Quarrel with Pope appeased; he mediates between Philip and Edward I. Philip invades and occupies Flanders.	
	First version of Marco Polo's 1298 *Travels*. Franciscans reach China.
1299 Peace with England.	
1300 Philip again invades Flanders.	Oldest MS. of *Biblia Pauperum*. 1300 *Passion du Palatinus* (*circa*).
1301 Quarrel with Papacy renewed.	
1302 Parlement fixed at Paris. Towns represented at States General. Revolt in Flanders; French defeated by bourgeois at Courtrai.	
1303 Treaty with Edward I, to whom Guienne is ceded.	*Divina Commedia* of Dante. 1303
	Ypres Cloth Hall finished. 1304 Joinville begins his *Memoires*.

Events	Arts and Sciences
1305 Peace with Flanders.	Jean de Meung dead. University of Orleans founded. 1305
	Second version of Marco Polo's *Travels*.
1307 Trial of the Templars and confiscation of their property.	University of Perugia founded. *Chronicle* of Guillaume Guiart of Orleans. 1307
	Death of Duns Scotus.
1308 270 towns represented at States General.	Bridge of Cahors begun. 1308
1309 Pope allowed to settle at Avignon.	
1310 Wholesale execution of Templars.	*Roman de Fauvel.* 1310
	Council of Vienna establishes schools of oriental languages. *Chronicle* of Pierre de Langtoft (*circa*). 1311
1312 Order of Templars formally abolished. Lyons incorporated in France.	
1314 Death of Philip IV ; succeeded by son, Louis X.	
1315 Great famine for two years. Serfs freed on royal domain.	Jacques de Longuyon's *Vœux du Paon* (*circa*). 1315
1316 Death of Louis X ; his brother, Philip of Poitiers, Regent.	Palace of the Popes at Avignon begun. 1316
1317 Regent Philip V becomes King. Salic Law decreed.	*Chronique* of Godefroi de Paris. 1317
1318 Persecution of Mendicants in Languedoc.	
1320 Second rising of Pastoureaux.	*Contes moralisés* of Nicole Bozon (*circa*). 1320
	Death of Pietro de Abano, founder of Paduan School of Medicine.
1321 Persecution of Jews and lepers.	Death of Dante. *Renard le Contrefait.* 1321
1322 Death of Philip V ; succeeded by his brother Charles IV.	
1323 Abolition of Commune at Laon.	
1324 French attack Aquitaine.	*Speculum Humanae Salvationis.* 1324
	Defensor Pacis of Marsiglio of Padua.
1325 Hostilities with English in Guienne.	*Chronique de Morée* (*circa*). 1325
1327 Charles IV relinquishes Guienne to English on accession of Edward III, but retains Agen.	

Events	*Arts and Sciences*
1328 Charles IV dies without male heirs ; nobles choose Philip VI (of Valois).	
1329 Edward III does homage for Guienne and Ponthieu.	
	Guillaume de Machaut be- 1330 gins to write (*circa*). Guillaume de Deguilleville's *Pèlerinage de la vie humaine* (*circa*).
1331 Parliament of England agrees to homage.	
	University of Pisa founded. 1333
1337 Hundred Years War begins.	Death of Giotto. 1337
1338 Flemings under James van Arteveld renounce French allegiance and league with Edward III.	
1339 Edward III invades France from Flanders.	Painter Simone Martini at 1339 Avignon. University of Grenoble founded.
1340 French fleet defeated at Sluys. Truce for two years.	*Miracles de Notre Dame.* 1340– *Roman de Perceforest.* 1400 Petrarch crowned Poet 1341 Laureate at Rome by King Robert of Naples.
1342 War in Brittany.	
1343 Truce for three years.	
1345 Murder of James van Arteveld.	
1346 Nobles lose right of striking money. Edward III invades Normandy, defeats Philip at Crecy. English invade Guienne.	University of Valladolid 1346 founded.
1347 Calais capitulates to English after 11 months' siege. Black Death in Provence.	
1348 Black Death in Northern France.	University of Prague found- 1348 ed.
1349 Humbert, Dauphin of Vienne, sells dominions to King.	Death of William of Oc- 1349 cam (*circa*).
1350 Death of Philip VI ; succeeded by his son John (le Bon).	
	World-Map known as *Lau-* 1351 *rentian Portolano. Bataille des Trente.*
1354 Hostilities with Navarre.	

Events	Arts and Sciences
1355 Black Prince raids Languedoc; Edward III at Calais.	Guillaume de Deguilleville's 1355 *Pèlerinage de l'âme.*
1356 King John defeated and made prisoner at Poitiers.	Berçuire finishes translation 1356 of Livy into French.
1357 Truce for two years. Parisian liberties secured under Etienne Marcel. Nobles lose right of waging private war. Jacquerie in Île de France.	
1358 Revolution in Paris under Etienne Marcel; Jacquerie. Murder of Marcel. Dauphin named Regent.	Guillaume de Deguilleville's 1358 *Pèlerinage de Jésus Christ.*
1359 War between Regent and King of Navarre.	
1360 Treaty of Brétigny between England and France. Calais, Guisnes, Ponthieu, Guienne, Gascony, Poitou, Saintonge, La Rochelle, Limousin, and Angoulême ceded to the English. King John returns.	
1361 Reappearance of Black Death.	
1362 King bestows Duchy of Burgundy on youngest son, Philip the Bold.	University of Cracow found- 1362 ed.
1363 Escape of King's son, Duke of Anjou, who had been left hostage for Treaty in England.	
1364 John voluntarily returns to captivity in England and dies there; succeeded by his son, Charles V.	University of Angers found- 1364 ed.
1365 Breton War continues; Brittany finally ceded to John de Montfort.	University of Orange found- 1365 ed. Froissart's first version of *Méliador.*
1366 War with Castille.	University of Vienna found- 1366 ed.
1367 Du Guesclin invades Spain; defeated at Navarette.	University of Geneva found- 1368 ed.
1369 War renewed with England; Aquitaine revolts to France.	
1370 Massacre of Limoges by Black Prince.	Froissart begins his *Chronicles* 1370 (*circa*). Machaut's *Prise d'Alexandrie.* Nicholas Oresme translates Aristotle's *Ethics* into French.

Events	Arts and Sciences
1372 English driven from South of France.	
1373 Du Guesclin victorious in Brittany. France invaded by Duke of Lancaster.	
1374 Standing mercenary army established.	Death of Petrarch. 1374
1375 English everywhere defeated. Truce for two years.	Death of Boccaccio. 1375
1376 Death of the Black Prince.	Bruges Town Hall begun. 1376
1377 Death of Edward III; Charles conquers all Guienne except Bordeaux.	
1378 Captivity of Popes at Avignon ends; great Schism begins.	
1380 Death of Bertrand du Guesclin. Death of Charles V; succeeded by young son, Charles VI.	University of Siena founded. 1380
1381 Riots against taxation in Paris; revolts in Amiens, Laon, Rouen, and Rheims.	
1382 Burghers of Ghent revolt against Count; defeated by French at Roosebek.	
1384 Philip of Burgundy succeeds to County of Flanders.	Death of Wyclif. Cuvelier's 1384 *Chanson de Bertrand du Guesclin*: end of French epic.
	University of Heidelberg 1386 founded.
	Livre des cent Ballades (*circa*). 1387
1388 Charles assumes the government.	University of Cologne 1388 founded.
	Gerson begins to preach in 1389 Paris.
	Château de Pierrefonds begun. 1390
1392 King becomes insane; Duke of Burgundy acts as Regent. Quarrel between houses of Burgundy and Orleans begins.	Eustache Deschamp's *Art de* 1392 *dictier*. University of Erfurt founded.
	Le Ménagier de Paris. 1393
	University of Palermo 1394 founded.
	Cult of the Passion in 1395 France. *Jeu de Griseldis*.

Events	*Arts and Sciences*
1396 French army defeated by Turks at Nicopolis. Truce with England for 28 years.	Manuel Chrysoloras appointed to Chair of Greek at Florence. 1396
	Christine de Pisan begins to write. 1399
	Death of Chaucer. 1400
	Development of French religious drama.
1401 Attempt to reform finances and judicial procedure fails.	
	Brussels Town Hall begun. 1402
	Confrérie de la Passion incorporated.
	Seville Cathedral begun. 1403
1404 Jean sans Peur succeeds to Duchy of Burgundy.	Death of Froissart (*circa*). 1404
	Death of Eustache Deschamps (*circa*). 1406
	Death of Sculptor Claus Sluter.
1407 Murder of Duke of Orléans by Burgundians.	
1409 Feuds continue for three years between Burgundians and Armagnacs.	University of Leipsic founded. 1409
1411 Civil War.	*Geste des ducs de Bourgogne.* 1411
1412 Peace of Auxerre between Burgundians and Armagnacs.	University of St. Andrews founded. 1412
1413 Cabochian Ordinance regulates government.	
1414 Armagnacs triumph; Treaty of Arras with Burgundy.	Christine de Pisan retires from literature. 1414
1415 Henry V invades France; victorious at Agincourt.	*Mystère d'Arras* of Mercadé. 1415 Charles d'Orléans a prisoner in England.
1417 Henry V invades Normandy and takes Caen.	
1418 Massacre of Armagnacs at Paris. Henry besieges Rouen.	
1419 Henry takes Rouen. John of Burgundy assassinated with Dauphin's connivance on bridge of Montereau.	
1420 Treaty of Troyes; Henry V to be heir of France.	

Events	*Arts and Sciences*
1422 Henry V dies at Vincennes. Death of Charles VI ; infant Henry VI proclaimed King, with Bedford as Regent. Charles VII crowned King at Poitiers.	
1423 English victorious for five years.	University of Dôle founded. 1423
	Dance of Death in Church 1424 of the Innocents, Paris.
	Ghent Cloth Hall built. 1425
	University of Louvain 1426 founded.
	Alain Chartier's *Quadrilogue invectif* (*circa*).
1429 Joan of Arc relieves Orleans. Charles VII crowned at Rheims.	Filelfo's Greek lectures at 1429 Florence.
	Death of Masaccio.
1430 Joan captured by Burgundians and sold to English.	Death of Alain Chartier 1430 (*circa*).
1431 Joan tried for heresy and burnt.	University of Poitiers found- 1431 ed.
	Van Eyck's *Adoration of the* 1432 *Lamb*.
	Cathedral of Nantes begun. 1434
1435 Death of Bedford. Philip of Bur- gundy abandons English and makes treaty with Charles, re- ceiving Somme towns.	Façade of St. Germain 1435 l'Auxerrois, Paris.
1436 Paris opens her gates to Charles VII.	University of Caen found- 1436 ed.
1438 Pragmatic Sanction of Bourges assures liberties of Gallican Church.	University of Florence 1438 founded.
1439 Nobles lose right of levying troops. Standing army established.	
1440 Dauphin joins nobles in conspiracy against his father.	
1441 Ponthieu taken from English.	University of Bordeaux 1441 founded.
	Martin le Franc's *Champion* 1442 *des Dames*.
	Jacques Cœur's house at 1443 Bourges.
1444 Two years' truce with English after French successes in Gascony and Normandy.	Monstrelet's *Chronicle* ends. 1444
1445 Standing army reorganized.	Roger van der Weyden's 1445 *Last Judgement* painted for hospital of Beaune.

Events	*Arts and Sciences*
	Death of Vittorino da Feltre 1446 and of Brunelleschi.
	Louvain Town Hall begun. 1447
1448 Anjou and Maine recovered.	
1449 War with England renewed; Normandy attacked.	*Danse Macabre* acted before 1449 Duke of Burgundy.
1450 English driven out of Normandy.	
1451 Guienne recovered. Arrest of Jacques Cœur.	Arnoul Greban's *Mystère de* 1451 *la Passion.* Jacques Milet's *Mystère de Troie.*
	Alberti's *De re aedificatoria.* 1452 University of Valence founded.
1453 End of Hundred Years War; England only holds Calais and the Channel Islands. Fall of Constantinople and end of Byzantine Empire.	Death of Enguerrand de 1453 Monstrelet.
	First printing done (at 1454 Mayence). Universities of Treves and Copenhagen founded.
	Death of Fra Angelico. 1455
1456 Quarrel between King and Dauphin, who flies to Court of Burgundy.	*Petit Jehan de Saintré* of 1456 Antoine de la Sale. *Cent nouvelles nouvelles.* First dated poem of Villon.
	Death of Lorenzo Valla. 1457 Romance *Pierre de Provence.*
	University of Bâle founded. 1459
	University of Nantes found- 1460 ed. Death of Prince Henry the Navigator.
1461 Death of Charles VII, succeeded by his son, Louis XI. King revokes Pragmatic Sanction.	*Grand Testament* of François 1461 Villon.
1462 Parlement of Bordeaux established. Roussillon acquired.	
1463 Somme towns recovered; Pragmatic Sanction restored.	Château of Plessis lès Tours 1463 built.
1464 Louis assumes Government of Normandy.	University of Bourges found- 1464 ed.
1465 Nobles form League of Public Welfare against the King.	*Pathelin* (*circa*). 1465
1466 Normandy reannexed to Crown.	Birth of Erasmus. Chair of 1466 Greek established at the University of Paris.

Events	Arts and Sciences
1467 Death of Philip the Good, succeeded by Charles the Bold, who wins battle of St. Tron.	
1468 Louis visits Charles at Péronne and is made captive.	Monologue *Franc archer de* 1468 *Bagnolet.*
1469 Louis XI returns to Paris.	First printing press established in the Sorbonne. 1469
	Biblia pauperum engraved 1470 and printed.
	Xenophon's *Cyropedia* translated into French.
1471 Louis attacks Charles the Bold and takes Amiens.	
1472 Louis annexes Guienne.	Death of Leon Battista Alberti. 1472
	Mystère de l'Incarnation of 1473 Rouen.
1474 Franche-Comté occupied.	Marsiglio Ficino's *de Christiana religione.* 1474
	Columbus at Madeira.
	Chastellain's *Chronicle* ends.
1475 Edward IV invades France, but agrees to Treaty of Pequigny. Swiss invade Burgundy.	
1476 Charles defeated at Granson and Morat by Swiss.	University of Upsala founded. 1476
1477 Burgundian power broken at Nancy. Death of Charles the Bold. Louis seizes Burgundy.	First book in French printed at Paris. 1477
	Guillaume Coquillart's *Plaidoyé d'entre la Simple et de la Rusée.*
1478 Treaty between France and Castille.	First French illustrated 1478 book : *Speculum Humanae Salvationis.*
	University of Copenhagen 1479 founded.
1480 Bar occupied. Death of René of Anjou.	
1481 Maine and Anjou revert to the Crown.	
1483 Death of Louis XI. Succeeded by his son Charles VIII under regency of his sister, Anne of Beaujeu.	

INDEX

Persons are indexed under their *Christian* name. Names of Frenchmen are given in their *French* form.

2905   F f

MEDIAEVAL
FRANCE

PRINTED IN ENGLAND
AT THE OXFORD UNIVERSITY PRESS